READING JAPAN COOL

Towasan - cell phone author
add pm to my disc. & Ghost.

READING JAPAN COOL

Patterns of Manga Literacy and Discourse

JOHN E. INGULSRUD AND KATE ALLEN

LEXINGTON BOOKS
A division of
ROWMAN & LITTLEFIELD PUBLISHERS, INC.
Lanham-•-Boulder-•-New York-•-Toronto-•-Plymouth, UK

LEXINGTON BOOKS
A division of Rowman & Littlefield Publishers, Inc.
A wholly owned subsidary of The Rowman & Littlefield Publishing Group, Inc.
4501 Forbes Boulevard, Suite 200
Lanham, MD 20706

Estover Road
Plymouth PL6 7PY
United Kingdom

British Library Cataloguing in Publication Information Available

Library of Congress Cataloging-in-Publication Data

Ingulsrud, John E.
  Reading Japan cool : patterns of manga literacy and discourse / John E. Ingulsrud and Kate Allen.
     p. cm.
  Includes bibliographical references and index.
1. Comic books, strips, etc.—Japan—History and criticism. 2. Literacy—Japan. 3. Popular culture—Japanese influences. 4. Sociolinguistics—Japan. 5. Video games—Japan—History and criticism. 6. Reading—Social aspects—Japan. 7. Popular education—Japan. I. Allen, Kate, 1950– II. Title.
  PN6790.J3I54 2009
  741.5'952—dc22   2008046570

ISBN: 978-0-7391-2753-7 (cloth : alk. paper)
ISBN: 978-0-7391-2754-4 (pbk : alk. paper)
ISBN: 978-0-7391-3507-5 (electronic)

Printed in the United States of America

∞™ The paper used in this publication meets the minimum requirements of American National Standard for Information Sciences—Permanence of Paper for Printed Library Materials, ANSI/ NISO Z39.48–1992.

Contents

Figures

Tables

Preface

Reading Japan Cool: Patterns of Manga Literacy is a culmination of a project that has taken nearly eleven years to complete. It began in response to the findings from a survey to our college students on their reading habits and their reading histories. Manga was repeatedly raised as something they were currently reading and had read since childhood. As teachers of reading and writing, we posed the following question: How does our students' manga literacy relate to other literacies? We also asked: What kind of skills do they possess that we are ignoring? Would a better understanding of these skills help students transfer this knowledge to other areas? Prompted by these questions, we began our project.

As we explain in chapter 1, we only became manga readers ourselves in response to our students' reading patterns. In the course of the project, we have become more knowledgeable and conversant on various manga works, but the world of manga is vast and we are continually amazed at the range of material that is being created and the enormous body of works from past years. We have attempted to link our findings from surveys and interviews with actual manga readers to similar kinds of findings in literacy studies around the world, admittedly in mostly English-speaking countries. We tried to avoid casting manga literacy as particularistic, meaningful only in the context of Japan. We suggest that the manga literacy practices and reading strategies resonate with those in other contexts, and that they inform us on how we understand literacy and media use in general.

In addition, we have provided a description of the study of manga. This was uncharted territory. To date we are not aware of a similar kind of review of the literature. We are well aware that there may be important gaps. Still, we hope the review can serve as a basis for subsequent students to provide more comprehensive descriptions. We have also described manga literacy in terms of the historical development of literacy in Japan. In so doing, we provide an account of the kind of literacy skills taught in school to contrast with manga literacy.

Because our research was conducted in Japan with Japanese-language readers of manga, we use the Japanese titles of the manga works we mention. Consequently, we have paid less attention to the English translations of the works. Where we can, we provide the English translation of the title. However, the medium keeps evolving with new titles translated and new editions with different English titles published. In spite of our efforts, they may not be satisfactory for many English-language manga readers.

When we introduce a Japanese word for the first time, we provide the word in Japanese scripts. The modified Hepburn system has been used for the romanized representation of Japanese. The system involves a macron over the long vowels. For Japanese names, we put the surname first, with the given name following. Exceptions for these conventions are made for names of authors of English-language works, names of companies and brands, and romanized titles of manga, often with the expressed wishes of creators and publishers.

Transcripts from interviews are interspersed throughout the book. If the transcript is in brackets, this indicates that it has been translated from Japanese. If it is simply in quotation marks, then the interview was conducted in English. For these transcripts, we have not "corrected" the English. There are two reasons for this. The first one is a socio-linguistic position regarding world Englishes. Native-speaker norms do not have to apply ubiquitously. The other reason is that these transcripts are actually more expressive and to the point than the translated ones.

Acknowledgments

Reading Japan Cool: Patterns of Manga Literacy has taken us many years to complete. Throughout this time, a large number of people have assisted us and we are deeply indebted to them. This book should be seen as our appreciation for their help. While it is difficult to remember everyone, we would especially like to thank the following: Akiba Yasuhiro, Ehara Tae, Erika Vorland, Fujimoto Naoko, Hara Takuma, Hattori Yukie, Hayakawa Chihiro, Hioki Kenjiro, Hirano Masami, Inada Yoshiko, Inoue Junya, Irie Mitsuhiko, Ishige Hironao, Ishii Yasuo, Ito Eri, Kai Akiko, Kai Kimiko, Kamata Katsuyuki, Kaminaka Hiromi, Kaneko Misato, Kaneko Shogo, Kaneko Takeshi, Kaneko Tomomi, Kato Memi, Kawamata Takanori, Kenji Shimokawa, Kitaguchi Yohei, Kōchi Chieko, Kozaki Kaori, Kuwahara Kazue, Maia Vorland, Manami Sakai, Matsumoto Keishi, Matsumoto Tae, Miyashita Makito, Miyazaki Gentaro, Mori Atsushi, Mori Daiki, Morita Kaori, Murakami Machiko, Nagatani Rumi, Nishi Erisa, Nishibashi Ayako, Noah Vorland, Ogata Mai, Ōi Yūichiro, Ono Yasuhisa, Onoda Sakae, Ota Shinichiro, Otani Sachio, Sadanaga Tatsuaki, Sadanaga Yuko, Sasagawa Kazuma, Sasagawa Makoto, Sato Chihiro, Sesaki Mariko, Shannon Offner, Shimizu Chie, Sutoh Yuki, Takaki Toshirō, Takita Mayuko, Tatsuki Satoshi, Tokita Hitomi, Tsuchiyama Fumiko, Ueno Yuko, Yamaguchi Masafumi, and Yatabe Ayao. For their technical assistance, such as with transcriptions, editing, and statistical advice, we would like to thank Kathy Dix, Nīno Tokie, Sato Naomi, and Siwon Park. For their unstinting support in locating materials, we would like to thank Mizutani Emiko and her staff at Kyushu Lutheran College Library and Tamba Shigeyuki and his staff at Kanda University of International Studies Library. In a book about manga literacy, copyright material is essential, and we thank all the publishers and institutions who have graciously assisted us. We especially thank Tange Yoko of Kodansha, Enomoto Ikuko of Kadokawashoten, and Katagiri Yuko of Shueisha for facilitating the permission process and for their useful suggestions. SHUEISHA Inc. has granted permission for the reprinting of all their illustrations that appear in this book. Finally, any shortcomings with the book rest entirely with the authors.

Manga in the Discourse of Japan Cool   **1**

JAPAN HAS OFTEN BEEN DESCRIBED AS a highly literate nation, boasting literacy rates of nearly 100 percent. While it may be difficult to substantiate such high rates in literacy skills, the perception exists, both in Japan and abroad, that Japanese people are highly literate. In recent years, however, newspaper articles have regularly drawn attention to the decline of literacy skills in Japan. Headlines such as these describe a literacy crisis: "Book-Reading Rate on Decline, Survey Says,"[1] "Diet Group Wants Japan to Get Back to the Books,"[2] and "Ministry Acknowledges Falling School Performance."[3] A drop in rank from eighth to fourteenth position in the 2005 Program for International Student Assessment, followed by a further decline in the 2006 survey by the Organization for Economic Cooperation and Development, acutely intensified this sense of crisis, putting Japan in the company of Britain and the United States, both of whom complain of declining literacy skills.[4]

Apart from a decline in academic skills, the lack of interest in reading among school children is seen to have multiple effects. One concern is that young people have poor language skills, such as difficulty using *kanji* 漢字 (Chinese characters) and properly using honorifics when speaking to elders or people of higher status.[5] The decline in literacy skills is linked to worries about economic success and the preservation of cultural values, as emphasized by this lawmaker's comments: "Widespread concern over the nation's future and a sense of crisis regarding print culture—they're like the two sides of the coin."[6]

In spite of these concerns, the official response by the government to the perceived literacy crisis has been inconsistent. In 2001, the Japanese government passed a bill to increase spending on books for school libraries and to encourage schools to allocate more time for reading.[7] In 2005, another law was passed intended to promote literacy skills. Among the various proposals in the 2005 bill was that the government would encourage the development of school and community libraries. Furthermore, in order to foster public awareness of the importance of reading, a Print Culture Day was to be declared.[8] However, building more libraries, training more teacher-librarians, and having more reading time in school provide only part of the solution. Despite the previous 2001 law promoting reading, few local governments acted. Instead, money allocated for reading promotion was used for purposes other than purchasing books.[9] Even when funds were directed specifically for this purpose, little guidance was given in regard to buying books that were of interest to children. One school principal received the focus of the media because he was seen to have successfully promoted reading in his middle school. As part of his strategy, this businessman-turned-principal stated that "[t]he library has dared to abandon many books unpopular with students."[10] Despite efforts to encourage reading in school, there is limited attention paid to what children read out of school. This divide between literacy practices in school and literacy practices elsewhere has also been identified by literacy studies in Australia, Britain, and the United States.[11]

Although the Japanese media describe young people as *katsujibanare sedai* 活字離れ世代 (the generation withdrawing from print), there is a current upsurge in writing novels to be read on mobile phones.[12] Prize-winning cyber-author Towasan explains that she set the installments of her serialized novel on her website, and she completed her novel based on the response and suggestions from readers.[13] In a television interview, Towasan explained that she had never read novels. Instead, she read lots of manga.[14] What is it about her manga literacy that relates to her ability to write mobile-phone cyber novels?

Becoming Manga-Literate

Our interest in reading manga comes not from being avid readers of manga or even comics. We studied early literacy in China[15] and continued studying the same topic even after we relocated to Japan. However, after surveying our college-age students about their reading habits, we discovered that reading manga not only played a large role in their current literacy practices but that manga existed throughout their development of literacy skills.

Our initial survey on reading practices was administered in 1997. We then developed a survey that specifically focused on the reading of manga and later administered it to junior high school students in 2002, followed by senior high school students in 2005 (see chapter 4). At the same time, our project to study manga literacy compelled us to be manga readers ourselves. John Ingulsrud, although bilingual in Japanese and English, never learned to read manga regularly, in spite of having grown up in Japan. Kate Allen only began to learn Japanese when she came to Japan in 1995. Therefore the two of us, in middle age, embarked on learning to read a new medium. It was not easy; the panels came at us with a cacophony of symbols and images, and the main problems of comprehension were not linguistic ones. We did not get a teacher nor go to classes. Like many of our respondents, we read the manga again and again, concentrating first on works that were easy to understand. Through this experience, we are convinced that manga literacy does not just happen and that reading manga is far from a mindless activity. In 2000, we began reading the weekly *Morning*, published by the large publishing company Kodansha. This is an "adult" manga magazine containing titles of human interest and social critique. Since then, we have purchased, read, and stored each copy. Although it has taken time to become fluent readers, we now enjoy reading *Morning* and look forward to the serialized installments of many of its titles.

By being manga readers, we participate in the manga economy. Manga publishing in Japan is a US$4.5 billion market and accounts for nearly a fourth of the total publishing market.[16] These publications range from manga for children to manga for adults and cover every conceivable topic from sports, romance, drama, science fiction, adventure, and mystery to niche interests such as business enterprises, gambling, fishing, cooking, and childrearing. Japanese manga are classified into a number of categories roughly corresponding to different age and gender groups: *kodomo* 子ども (children); *shōnen* 少年 (boys); *shōjo* 少女 (girls); *seinen* 青年 and *yangu* ヤング (young adult men); *redizu* レディズ and *fujin* 婦人 (women); and *seijin* 成人 and *shakaijin* 社会人 (adult men and, increasingly, women) manga. The market is evenly balanced between manga geared toward children and those targeting adults. In addition, there is a growing market for self-published *dōjinshi* 同人誌, manga "fanzines," parodies, and original works with large *Comiket* (comic market) conventions. Successful manga generate spin-offs such as toys, costumes, and other media products like animation series, light novels, television dramatizations, movies, and video games.

Most manga titles appear first in periodicals published in weekly, biweekly, or monthly intervals. They are readily available in bookshops, convenience stores, and station kiosks, but are generally not available by subscription.[17] *Shōnen* manga, for instance, come in volumes of over four hundred pages published on a weekly basis. These manga volumes may contain up to twenty serialized stories. The stories are printed on recycled newsprint, and except for the cover and a few pages of advertisements, they are set in black and printed on white or light-colored paper. Often groups of stories are printed in different colored text, giving a rainbow effect to thick volumes. These periodicals are inexpensive and read quickly.

Unlike our own manga literacy practice, manga magazines are not intended to be kept and are usually thrown away soon after reading. However, individual titles that are considered successful are later republished as paperback books (*tankōbon* 単行本) called *komikku* コミック (bound comics) or *komikkusu* コミックス, depending on whether it is singular or plural. It is unnecessary to mark the plural for Japanese nouns, but some writers are careful to do so for many English loan words. Once a title has assumed some staying power, it can be published as a *bunkobon* 文庫本. This is still a paperback, but possesses the same paper and binding quality of "proper" novels. These paperbacks are more expensive to buy than manga magazines. After reading the titles in manga magazines, many people collect the bound versions of their favorite series. In our survey of high school students, nearly 75 percent reported that they collected manga *komikkusu*. Some of the well-known titles are available in public libraries, but from our own investigation of local Tokyo public libraries, the selection is limited. There is greater selection at manga Internet cafes where manga *komikkusu* line the walls, and customers can freely choose their favorite titles. In addition, there is a growing business in buying and selling used *komikkusu*. For example, at the used-book chain *Book Off*, manga volumes occupy over half of the shelf space.

Despite the popularity of manga, sales of new manga, both in magazine and *komikku* form, have declined steadily in the past ten years by as much as 20 percent. Sales of books and magazines have also declined. In fact, income from publishing *komikkusu* in 2005 has surpassed that of manga magazines for the first time.[18] Economic commentators suggest that the growth of manga Internet cafes and used bookstores has been the biggest reason for the decline in manga magazine sales.[19] Other reasons include the proliferation of the Internet, particularly the mobile-phone format, and the access to manga stories through these media, together with the continued popularity of manga stories in anime form or as television dramatizations. Nonetheless, it is misleading to judge readership or literacy solely in terms of consumer patterns.

As we describe in chapter 4, the world of the manga reader is complex. Based on our surveys administered to junior high school, senior high school, and college-age students, nearly all of our respondents are readers of manga or have been at various times in their lives. Their reading of manga is inextricably linked with other kinds of reading material, such as magazines and books. Manga reading is also connected with the use of different media like anime and television, as well as video games and the Internet. These forms of literacy can be combined with play, mediated by toys, costumes, and plastic models. These media have inspired new directions in product and industrial design.[20] Indeed, it is difficult, perhaps inappropriate, to consider each kind of literacy practice, media accessing, or entertainment consumption in isolation. Together they form a body of cultural products, practices, and sensibilities that is increasingly called "Japanese cool," "cool Japan," or "Japan cool." In our study of manga literacy, we document the connections to other media where possible, but the reason we focus on manga is that the manga characters, the stories, and indeed the literacy skills serve as a basis for these various media. The poster for the 2007 annual Manga Festival in Akihabara carried the following caption: Japanese Cool の 原点 "Manga"! (Manga, the origin of Japanese Cool).[21]

Reading manga, according to our respondents and interviewees, can be both a communal practice and an individual one. Very few respondents have been taught how to read manga. Instead, they have been introduced or persuaded by friends, family members, television commercials, or simply picked up the manga that were lying around. Once the individual starts reading a manga, comprehending it involves skills at several levels. Manga are written in the comic format, combining the media of graphics and print. In the terminology of systemic-functional linguistics, these media are called modes. Thus the combination of graphics and print results in texts described as multimodal. For Gunther Kress and Theo van Leeuwen, meaning is conveyed at different levels, such as the layout of the pages, illustrations, words, and scripts.[22] A reader must process and interpret the meanings of these layers in order to build an understanding of the text. In addition, the reader acquires expectations of how the manga narrative will be organized. Furthermore, the reader learns to recognize the intertextuality of past narratives and other voices.

Van Leeuwen specifically described how readers comprehend multimodal texts in stages, beginning with the graphics, then the large captions, and on down to the lexico-grammar, the words and sentences.[23] This observation is reminiscent of patterns of text comprehension, such as top-down/bottom-up or macro-/micro-structure that are well established in cognitive linguistics.[24] Although these studies describe the complexity of the reading process, there is no indication how many times a reader is supposed to read a text before comprehending it. We suspect the assumption is only once because the term "comprehension" is most usually associated with testing, and on tests there is only a single encounter. Furthermore, reading comprehension is also associated with speed. Quickly comprehending a text is valued more highly than comprehending at a slow pace.

In the case of manga, we are dealing with a kind of text in which the literacy skills of comprehension are not tested. For our respondents, they learn to read and read by their own volition.[25] Yet one surprising finding is that readers read the same manga over and over again. It is well known that young children repeatedly watch the same video, read the same picture book, and get pleasure out of having the same book read to them. However, our results show that the number of repeat readings does not decrease with age. Readers report that they notice different things each time they read. This discovery of new perspectives, they say, is one way that enhances the pleasure of reading manga.

Structural Features of Manga

Before we describe in detail the nature of manga, it may be useful for those who are not familiar with them to present some of the structural features of manga. To begin with, a manga page, as with any page from a comic, is presented in configurations of panels set in frames. This distinguishes manga from other media. Within the medium, there are different structural genres: the single panel cartoon, the four- to eight-panel gag manga or comic strip, and the story manga or graphic novel. The locus of the information is in the graphics, speech balloons, and occasional commentary, as well as the arrangement of panels itself. Yet not every scene is depicted. The creator has selected scenes to illustrate; therefore, the so-called gutter or border between the panels contains information that requires the reader to infer. At the same time, you cannot read a manga or comic aloud to anyone unless they are reading along with you. The lines in the speech balloons alone are insufficient to understand the text. On the other hand, the graphics alone are insufficient to understand the text. Senko Maynard, for example, included an excerpted text from the manga *Crayon Shin-chan* in the appendix of her book, *Principles of Japanese Discourse*. There are no graphics. The lines of the speech balloons are simply rendered as prose, and as such, they are incomprehensible.[26]

Then how do we process manga? At the simplest level, there are four rectangular panels to a page, and they are read from right to left, top to bottom. The less important information is at the top of the page, while the more important details are in the lower part.[27] However, there is considerable variation in the size, shape, and number of panels to a page employed for pragmatic and literary effect. These techniques affect the comprehension or level of appreciation of the reader. In addition to the panels and graphics, there are symbols to indicate movement, sound volume, tactile qualities, and emotional states. The graphics are usually accompanied by linguistic text in speech balloons. The auditory and tactile information expressed linguistically in onomatopoeia (*onyu* 音喩) and qualities of texture (*gitaigo* 擬態語), as well as the non-linguistic graphic symbols (*keiyu* 形喩) representing movement and intensity, are merged in with the illustrations.[28] Yet manga readers have the additional task of knowing the four kinds of scripts that are employed in manga. These are *kanji*, the two syllabaries of *hiragana* ひらがな and *katakana* カタカナ, and finally *rōmaji* ローマ字 (roman letters). The scripts can vary in how they are presented—that is, horizontally (right to left, left to right) or vertically (top to bottom). Furthermore, the reading of the scripts may be facilitated or hindered by the kinds of fonts used, as well as by the font size. These features provide creators with the resources to make lively and distinctive dialogue for their characters.

Although many manga contain explanatory information to help the reader comprehend the story, the bulk of the linguistic information is dialogic, placed in the speech and thought balloons. The shapes of the balloons also provide pragmatic information, indicating the nature and intensity of the message. Thus even before actually reading the content of the balloons, readers can acquire a sense of what the speaker intends by the way the speech balloons are represented. For instance, balloons with sharp jagged edges may suggest shock or surprise. The size and font of the lettering in relation to the balloon can also indicate the volume of speech or intensity of thought. Curved or jagged lines and the number of lines all depict movement and psychological states.

These techniques to enhance the speech balloons relate to motion lines and other graphic symbols. The symbols and techniques are called "emenata" by many comics creators.[29] To illustrate how a specific kind of emenata can provide a plethora of polysemy, we borrow the example of drops of liquid provided by Takekuma Kentarō, as shown in table 1.1.[30] These drops can represent water, sweat, tears, saliva, and nasal discharge. Drops referring to water, most often, simply denote the physical state of water and being wet. Water drops can indicate the emptiness of a vessel. Drops representing sweat denote feeling hot, but can also represent anxiety, stress, or surprise. Sweat can also mean irritation

Table 1.1: Denotation and Connotation for "Drops of Liquid"

Type of "drops"	Denotation	Connotation
Water	Rain and "wetness"	Emptiness (of a bottle)
Sweat	Feeling hot	Anxiety, stress, or surprise; irritation or anger
Tears	Weeping	Irritation or anger
Saliva	Appetite for food	Consumer or sexual appetite
Nasal discharge	Nasal discharge	Fatigue, sickness, drunkenness, or sexual arousal

Table 1.2:   Binary Feature Analysis of Connotations for "Drops of Liquid"

	Water	Sweat	Tears	Saliva	Nasal discharge
Emptiness	+	-	-	-	-
Anxiety	-	+	-	-	-
Stress	-	+	-	-	-
Surprise	-	+	-	-	-
Irritation	-	+	+	-	-
Anger	-	+	+	-	-
Sadness	-	-	+	-	-
Hunger	-	-	-	+	-
Consumer appetite	-	-	-	+	-
Sexual appetite or arousal	-	-	-	+	+
Fatigue	-	-	-	-	+
Sickness	-	-	-	-	+
Drunkenness	-	-	-	-	+

or anger. Drops representing tears denote crying and connote a heightened emotional state, suggesting anger and irritation. Here the subtleties of meaning overlap with sweat. This overlap raises questions regarding the representation of gender. Drops representing saliva denote an appetite for food, but connote many kinds of appetites, including sexual and consumer appetites. Drops representing nasal discharge, in contrast to the others, hardly ever denote nasal discharge itself—unless the character's cold is part of the story. Takekuma describes nasal discharge as representing a character's loss of self-control. This could mean a state of fatigue, sickness, drunkenness, or sexual arousal.

We have just analyzed the semantics of drops of liquid in terms of denotation and connotation. This kind of binary conceptualization comes out of structural linguistics. Pierre Masson, for instance, has extensively applied structural analysis to comics.[31] No doubt more effort at applying structural categories may produce some results in understanding manga, but few symbols and categories can be organized as neatly as the analysis of drops of liquid. Table 1.2 illustrates this kind of analysis.

Recently, a great deal of information is offered to English language readers through magazines on manga and its kindred media, such as anime, light novels, computer and video games. There is also information in commentaries that accompany translations of manga and on Internet sites. For many years, Frederik Schodt's works, *Manga! Manga! The World of Japanese Comics* and *Dreamland Japan: Writings on Modern Manga*, have served to introduce manga to the English-speaking world and to describe comic-manga connections. More recently, Paul Gravett's *Manga: 60 Years of Japanese Comics* provides a colorful and readable introduction to manga, with informative descriptions of the various genres. We provide a summary of manga genres here because readers interested in manga literacy may not be familiar with the range of material.

Basic Categories of Manga—Age and Gender

Although manga are written for specific age groups and gender, these categories have become increasingly blurred. For instance, aspects that typify *shōjo* manga for girls, such as big eyes and free-form panel arrangements, are found now in *shōnen* manga, which are typically targeted at the male adolescent market. Manga readers have reported (see chapter 6) that girls read both *shōjo* and *shōnen* manga. In spite of these defined markets, manga written for people of differing age groups are sold in the same bookshops, and the traditional classifications are still employed in their placement on the shelves. In presenting these categories, there is a danger of assuming that each one is comparable in readership, numbers of titles, and range of topics. The *shōnen* and the "adult" versions of *shōnen* manga (i.e., *yangu* and *seijin* manga) comprise the largest category and thus are seen as the typical category (unmarked category) of manga, while the other categories are seen as special (marked categories) in contrast to them. Yet at the same time, developments coming out of *shōjo* manga are considered to be more innovative.

In the following sections, we briefly describe the basic age and gender-related categories of manga. The description here begins with manga targeted at young children, then the ones for adolescent boys and girls, followed by those for young adults, and, finally, the wide range of manga available for adult readers. These basic categories of age and gender remain stable, in spite of the continual fluctuations in stylistic representation.

Children's Manga

Manga for children (*kodomo* manga) can be described as entry-level *shōnen* and *shōjo* manga.[32] Two examples of children's manga magazines are *COROCORO*

Figure 1.1.   *COROCORO* and *Ciao* (Covers from *COROCORO* and *Ciao*. © 2007 by Shogakukan. Reprinted with permission of Shogakukan.)

for boys and *Ciao* for girls, both published by Shogakukan. Figure 1.1 presents the covers of the popular manga magazines. Many of the titles that originated in these magazines have been produced as anime, thereby increasing their distribution to a global audience. Indeed, it is these titles that would be most familiar to a non-Japanese reading audience. A number of the popular titles include *Doraemon*, *Asarichan*, *Chibi Marukochan*, and *Pocket Monsters*, a title developed out of a popular video game.[33]

Some commentators claim that there are too few children's manga published and the range of titles available is too limited.[34] For a sales-sensitive industry, the consumer, that is, the young child, is dependent on parental purchasing patterns. When children begin to receive allowances, they are free to purchase manga themselves. Our surveys revealed that while a number of interviewees described beginning with children's manga, far more respondents reported that they began with *shōnen* and *shōjo* manga designed for an older readership. Some publishers, like Shueisha and Kodansha, begin their lines with *shōnen* manga magazines, but also include titles for younger readers, like *DRAGON BALL*.

Shōnen Manga

Shōnen manga, although targeted at adolescent boys, is read by the greatest number of readers and possesses the largest number of titles. Most of the popular periodicals are published weekly and sold in large volumes containing over four hundred pages. These are printed on rough newsprint and cost less than two dollars. Boys, girls, young men, and adult men tend to read *shōnen* manga.

Frederik Schodt has described *shōnen* manga stories as possessing three main features—friendship, perseverance, and winning. These features make for upbeat

Figure 1.2. *Ashita no Joe* and *THE PRINCE OF TENNIS* (Cover from *Ashita no Joe 12* by Takamori Asao and Chiba Tetsuya. © 1993 by Kodansha Comics. Reprinted with permission of Kodansha. Cover from *THE PRINCE OF TENNIS* © 1999 by Takeshi Konomi/SHUEISHA Inc.)

reading and provide inspiring heroes.[35] Topics for titles concern mostly sports, followed by martial arts, action, and adventure. Figure 1.2 presents examples of a vintage *shōnen* manga title and a current popular one. Almost all *shōnen* manga consist of stories based on *Bildungsroman* narrative patterns, where a young man goes through multiple trials and setbacks as he ventures on to a bright and glorious future. In the example shown in figure 1.2 of *Ashita no Joe* (Rocky Joe), Joe, the boxer, goes through rigorous training, deals with his shortcomings, meets much bigger opponents, and achieves victory after victory. In the second title shown in figure 1.2, *THE PRINCE OF TENNIS*, the young scion of a professional tennis player plays for the team of a lackluster middle school. Rather than focusing on individual players or heroes, the school that each team represents assumes character status. As the chapters unfold, the different school characters take stage, illustrating the range of possible school types. Japanese secondary education is thus presented as a diverse, stratified world, in contrast to the stereotype of Japanese schools as being highly uniform.

In spite of the fact that *shōnen* manga titles tend to be limited in theme and are predictable in narrative, they can be creative with subject matter by mixing genres, cultures, and periods. The popular title *ONE PIECE* illustrates this mix. Moreover, some *shōnen* manga titles have adopted features of *shōjo* drawings and examples are presented in figure 1.3. For instance, in the example of *Inuyasha* created by Takahashi Rumiko, many of the characters appear androgynous.[36] Early *shōjo* manga,

Figure 1.3.   *ONE PIECE* and *Inuyasha* (Cover from *ONE PIECE* © 1997 by Eiichiro Oda/SHUEISHA Inc. Cover from *Inuyasha* by Takahashi Rumiko. © 1997 by Shonen Sunday Comics. Reprinted with permission of Shogakukan.)

like *Ribon no Kishi* (Princess knight) and *Berusaiyu no Bara* (Rose of Versailles), have heroines who crossdressed as men.

Shōjo Manga

Unlike *shōnen* manga, *shōjo* manga typically deals with romantic themes and is written mainly for girls. In contrast to the camaraderie-filled narratives, *shōjo* manga has focused more on the subtleties of human relationships, providing readers with psychological vistas from which to gaze on an assortment of characters and personalities. Fujimoto Yukari has written extensively on *shōjo* manga, describing the psychological and ethical themes. She argues that *shōjo* manga characters continually search for their proper place in society. This is most often constructed as a place vis-à-vis the family, and Fujimoto sees this search in the development of romantic relationships.[37]

Figure 1.4 presents two examples of *shōjo* manga. *Garasu no Kamen* (The glass mask) and *D.N.Angel* deal with relationships. In addition, the usual panel structure is broken down for a freer flowing progression. The example from *Garasu no Kamen* represents more traditional *shōjo* manga features, while the more recent one, *D.N.Angel*, contains a variety of panel sizes and character perspectives. These techniques allow for expressing psychological states and emotions.[38]

Figure 1.4.   *Garasu no Kamen* and *D.N.Angel* (Excerpt from *Garasu no Kamen* by Miuchi Suzue. © 1994 by Hakusensha Bunko. Reprinted with permission of Hakusensha. Excerpt from *D.N.Angel* by Sugisaki Yukiru. © 2008 by Asuka. Reprinted with permission of Kadokawashoten Publishing.)

Although the first *shōjo* manga was published in 1902, Yonezawa Yasuhiro contends that since 1945, *shōjo* manga grew in parallel with *shōnen* manga and then experienced increasing popularity somewhat later, from 1975 onward. During that time, he reports, even college men started buying *shōjo* manga. The reason behind the boom was that *shōjo* manga took up themes that were not focused on by other media.[39] One such theme was fantasy (including science fiction). Well-known works like *Tokyo Babylon* and *X* were created by the four-women team, CLAMP.[40] *Shōjo* manga creators have developed new categories of expression and the most important today is the esthetic sense of *moe* 萌.

Sharalyn Orbaugh describes the nature of a typical *shōjo* character in this way: "The overall picture of shojo-ness that emerges . . . is of a slightly confused, dreamy, yet seductive vulnerability—that doe-eyed, 'please don't hurt me' look."[41] Although Orbaugh does not define *moe* specifically, her description accurately captures this quality. The *moe* sensibility in *shōjo* manga has become increasingly popular with the "young" and "lady's" manga, described in detail below. In the examples presented in figure 1.5, the fairy-like girl represents many of the cute and seductive features of *moe*, while the two characters, one smaller than the other, also describe a feature of *moe*. The contrast need not reflect size or strength but also personality and behavior, such as "assertive" as opposed to "passive." The notion that these asymmetries represent a

Figure 1.5. *FAIRIAL GARDEN* and *Little Dog Liar Cat* (excerpt from *FAIRIAL GARDEN*: © 2007 Minene Sakurano/MAG Garden; and *Little Dog Liar Cat* by Kurekoshi Sakuya. © 2005 by Oakla Shuppan. Reprinted with permission of Oakla Shuppan.)

social reality in which many Japanese women find themselves is a point numerous writers have raised.[42] The two boys represent a *shōjo* subgenre called *yaoi* やおい or "boys love." Some observers define *yaoi* as parodies of well-known manga characters produced primarily by amateur creators, whereas "boys love" refers to commercially published original stories of male-male relationships. This distinction has yet to become stable, and both terms are used interchangeably. In their manual on writing "boys love" novels (paralleling the manga), the Hanamaru editorial board insists that writers of these novels assume the implied reader is a woman.[43] Even though the works may be written for women, the readership is expanding to include male readers.

Redizu (Lady's) Manga

Although manga for women do not exactly parallel manga for men, so-called lady's manga for adult women continue the *shōjo* themes of romantic encounters, but tend to be more sexually explicit. In contrast, the *fujin* or "women's" manga, such as *For Mrs.*, tend to focus on childrearing, family-member relations, and other family-centered themes. At the same time, since many manga titles for adults reflect special interests, hobbies, and sports, these *fujin* manga are becoming a part of "adult" manga in general.

Titles of "lady's" manga magazines include *Kiss*, *You*, and *Taboo*. The content of *Kiss* and *You* is less sexually graphic than that of *Taboo* and serves as a transition from *shōjo* manga. In fact, Shueisha published a *Young You* (discontinued in 2006), *You*, and

Figure 1.6.   *Kiss* (Cover from *Kiss* by Ninomiya Tomoko. © 2007 by *Kiss*. Reprinted with permission of Kodansha.)

Office You, marking a gradation of sexual content. Both *Kiss* and *You* are biweekly publications, while *Office You* and *Taboo* are monthlies.[44]

The existence of "lady's" manga presents a conundrum in the context of women being liberated from stereotypical roles and gender victimization. For instance, why would women want to read graphic stories about being raped? Gretchen Jones describes the representation of women and the types of sexual contacts as the same kind of pornography that serves men's fantasies. Although they appear to be serving stereotypical norms for women, Jones argues that these manga have promoted a more assertive sexuality among women. Moreover, she observed that these manga solicit reaction from readers and many of the letters are printed in the margins. This feedback is then used to guide creators as to the kinds of works they produce.[45]

Yangu (Young) Manga

The so-called "young" manga (also called *seinenshi* 青年誌), targeted at young adult men, contains titles that continue *shōnen* manga themes, but often with amplified violence and sex.[46] Many of the covers have photographs of beautiful women, with additional photographs inside. There are fewer titles on organized sports and school and instead, more titles involving gangland violence, consumer items like cars and motorcycles, and stories on extreme sports. These manga appear to serve as an introduction or transition to the special interest "adult" niche manga. For example, *Initial D* is a sports car series about racing, involving a young man who possesses a sports car (see figure 1.7). Another example, *BESHARI GURASHI* (Living by talking), follows the lives of a pair of stand-up comedians who start out as high school students. The story describes the trials of coping with school audiences and contests while dealing with parents and school administrators. A few professionals recognize their talent, and so the story provides information on getting started in the entertainment industry.

Like *shōnen* manga, the "young" manga magazines are published weekly and biweekly, but they are not as thick. They are printed, as are other "adult" manga, on finer newsprint. They are also slightly more expensive than *shōnen* manga magazines. The weekly magazines, listed here in order of increasing sexual explicitness, include *Young Jump*, *Young Magazine*, and the biweekly *Young Champion* and *Young Animal*. Similar in nature to the "lady's" manga *Kiss*, *Young Jump* contains titles such as the soccer story *Captain Tsubasa*, which is virtually *shōnen* in manner of content. In contrast, *Young Animal*, with many sexually explicit stories, contains stories with characters drawn in the *moe* style. It is beyond the scope of our study here to compare the stories in a "young" manga with those of "lady's" manga, such as *Taboo*. Yet it would be interesting to analyze how gender roles are represented. One point in common is a growth in characters depicted in the *moe* style (often called *roricon* ロリコン ["Lolita" comics]) in "young" manga, characters that are drawn to be seductive, while demanding from the reader a small measure of pity. "Lady's" manga contain these images as well. Still the "young" market is greater as it supports weeklies. In contrast, there are no weekly "lady's" manga magazines.

Figure 1.7. *Initial D* and *BESHARI GURASHI* (Cover from *Initial D* by Shigeno Shūichi. © 1995 by Young Magazine Kodansha Comics. Reprinted with permission of Kodansha. Cover from *BESHARI GURASHI* © 2005 by Studio Hitman/SHUEISHA Inc.)

"Adult" Manga

The so-called "adult" manga, also called *seijinshi* 成人誌 or *shakaijinshi* 社会人誌, tend to be the genre with the most serious content. Because *seijinshi* typically refers to pornographic magazines and *shakaijinshi* for those with a broader focus, we refer to these as "adult" manga, for lack of an appropriate superordinate term. There is a large range of content in "adult" manga, but particularly so in *shakaijinshi*, which includes sports, history, current affairs, business, health care, and human relations. Although *Morning*, the weekly magazine discussed previously, has a range of titles, many "adult" manga cater specifically to niche interests by carrying multiple stories on the same theme.[47] Some of these themes include *pachinko* manga, *mahjong* manga, golf manga, and fishing manga. They all tend to be published monthly. Another example of niche manga is cooking manga. The example presented in figure 1.8 features layered sushi for picnics in *Cooking Papa*, carried in *Morning*. The sushi rendered in the manga is a poor representation when compared to a photograph in a glossy Williams-Sonoma cookbook. Despite this media limitation, the long-running title has a loyal readership. The characters travel to different places, encounter new foods, and are put into situations of having to make do with limited or unfamiliar ingredients. The attraction to this kind of manga is the perlocutions (reactions) of the characters to the food. The delights in taste and consistency, as well as the procurement, preparation, and perspectives on food are features that make up the narrative.

In another story, *Kami no Shizuku* (Drops of God), there is a competition between two brothers to find the existence of a list of wines their late father had alluded to in order to benefit from his legacy (see figure 1.9). As the story unfolds, numerous wines are introduced, together with graphic representations of the imagination of the wine taster. Agi Tadashi and Okimoto Shū, a brother and sister team, painstakingly reproduce wine labels in their panels. Internet vendors have used these panels to market the actual wines. Moreover, this manga has been

Figure 1.8.   *Cooking Papa* (Cover from *Morning* by Ueyama Tochi. © 2004 by *Morning*. Reprinted with permission of Kodansha.)

translated into Korean, coinciding with a booming interest among young Koreans in wine.[48] A recent episode presents the perfect red wine to accompany *kimchi*. In another episode, a French red wine is recommended to be drunk with raw red tuna on sushi. Like the illustrations of food, the illustrations of wine labels differ from photographs. They are simulacra, not quite right or real. Yet they are compelling in themselves. Literary and cultural theorists have tried to explain this attraction in terms of perspective, caricature, parody, pastiche, and collage. We will examine these descriptions in more detail in chapter 2.

"Adult" manga not only deal with niche interests but also with stories that come directly out of the workplace. These kinds of stories are popular. One example is the character Shima Kōsaku. Sharon Kinsella describes how this character, created as the model salary man, is successful at work and with women.[49] He has been at the center of several long-running series based on different stages of his life. In recent years, as carried in *Morning*, his exploits in the China market have been chronicled and reflect our own tenure in China. We have been impressed by creator, Hirokane Kenshi, for his descriptions of Chinese society. More recently, the character Shima Kōsaku has begun working in the India market.

Not all workplace titles are success-laden *Bildungsroman*. For example, there is the bittersweet tale of *Hataraki Man* (Working man) (see figure 1.10). The protagonist in this popular series is not a man, but a single woman who is committed to her job. She is competent and hardworking. Unfortunately, not many of her colleagues possess these qualities. She suffers injustices great and small by being put upon, due to incompetence and neglect. She is unlucky in love and, furthermore, her married classmates

Figure 1.9.   *Kami no Shizuku* (Cover of *Kami no Shizuku 10* by Agi Tadashi and Okimoto Shū. © 2007 by Morning Kodansha Comics. Reprinted with permission of Kodansha.)

Figure 1.10.   *Hatakari Man* (Cover from *Morning* by Anno Moyoko. © 2007 by *Morning*. Reprinted with permission of Kodansha.)

with small children have more *savoir-faire.* "Adult" manga is created primarily by men and read mainly by men, yet this is an example of a title written by a woman.

We have described the basic genres of manga, based on gender and age. Yet because of the market-responsive nature of the industry, these genres are not static and continue to evolve. More reference will be made to them chapter 2 where the history of manga and the nature of manga studies are described and in chapter 6 where the respondents' preferences are analyzed.

The Scope of the Book

In order to understand the literacy of manga, we found it essential to take an interdisciplinary approach. Since we both come out of applied linguistics, there is a tendency to look for structural features. There is also a tendency to approach the study of literacy in the social science traditions of education, cognitive psychology, and the ethnography of communication. However, in our study of manga literacy, we have been persuaded to move beyond the confines of literacy studies and borrow the tools and perspectives of history, literary theory, and cultural studies. In chapter 2, we describe how manga has been defined by employing history, linguistics, and literary criticism, as well as the economics of publishing and the sociology of readers. This description is followed by an analysis of manga studies, tracing the epistemologies that have been used to understand manga and the people who promote them and then culminating in a summary of the work that has been done so far on manga literacy. Having described the history of manga in terms of the development of graphic art and popular publishing, in chapter 3 we place the reading of manga in the history of literacy. We then explore what it means to be literate in Japan and situate the study of manga literacy in relation to literacy studies in other contexts and approaches. Chapter 4 focuses on manga readers themselves, their literacy development, their literacy practices, and the connection with other kinds of literacies. In chapter 5, we look more closely at the strategies readers employ when reading manga. These include strategies to cope with problems of comprehension and strategies used to enhance the pleasure of reading manga. In chapter 6, we explore reasons why readers read manga and analyze their preferences. In chapter 7, we revisit the "literacy crisis" discourse in terms of our findings and then address the opposite concern over the capacity of popular reading material to influence readers. We employ these polarities to summarize our findings.

Looking at the chapter titles, it is evident that literacy, especially in terms of practices, behaviors, and values is the focal interest of the book. In attending to this focus, it has become clear to us that the discourses surrounding the literacies must also be described. We therefore attend to the discourse of manga. The term "discourse" is used here in the widest sense, from attributes of media features and genres described above to controversies and representations of taste, ideology, and epistemology. Our understanding of discourse is similar to Jacqueline Berndt's explanation: "Manga discourse is not limited to manga criticism; it also includes the ways in which social institutions—the mass media and the educational system, among others—define manga and its social relevance."[50] In the following chapter, we direct our focus to the definitions of manga, the history of manga's development and the ways it has been understood.

Notes

1. "Book-Reading Rate on Decline, Survey Says," *Daily Yomiuri*, November 1, 2003, 3.

2. "Diet Group Wants Japan to Get Back to the Books," *Daily Yomiuri*, March 1, 2005, 4.

3. "Ministry Acknowledges Falling School Performance," *Daily Yomiuri*, March 12, 2005, 4.

4. Kato Risa, "Lawmakers Tell Govt That Print Matters," *Daily Yomiuri*, April 4, 2005, 3; "Japanese Students Slip Further in OECD Tests," *Daily Yomiuri*, December 5, 2007, 1.

5. "Govt to Check Citizens' Japanese-Language Ability," *Daily Yomiuri*, January 7, 2005, 2; "Survey: Students Still Lacking Basic Skills," *Daily Yomiuri*, July 19, 2006, 4.

6. Kato, "Lawmakers Tell Govt," 3.

7. "Education Ministry Urges Children to Spend More Time Reading Books," *Daily Yomiuri*, July 22, 2002, 7.

8. "Reading, Writing Key to Education, Culture," *Daily Yomiuri*, July 18, 2005, 4.

9. "Book-Buying Fund to Miss Targets," *Daily Yomiuri*, June 11, 2002, 2; "Local Govts to Cut Funds for School Library Books," *Daily Yomiuri*, May 10, 2004, 2.

10. "Businessman-Turned-Principal Shakes Up Library," *Daily Yomiuri*, March 22, 2005, 14.

11. Donna E. Alvermann, Kathleen A. Hinchman, David W. Moore, Stephen F. Phelps, and Diane R. Waff, eds., *Reconceptualizing the Literacies in Adolescents Lives* (Mahwah, NJ: Lawrence Erlbaum Associates, 1998); Jenny Cook-Gumperz, "Introduction: The Social Construction of Literacy," in *The Social Construction of Literacy*, ed. Jenny Cook-Gumperz (Cambridge: Cambridge University Press, 1986), 1–15; Glynda A. Hull and Katherine Schultz, "Connecting Schools with Out-of-School Worlds: Insights from Recent Research on Literacy in Non-School Settings," in *School's Out: Bridging Out-of-School Literacies with Classroom Practice*, ed. Glynda A. Hull and Katherine Schultz (New York: Teachers College Press, 2002), 32–57; and Sandy Muspratt, Allan Luke, and Peter Freebody, eds., *Constructing Critical Literacies: Teaching and Learning Textual Practice* (Cresskill, NJ: Hampton Press, 1997).

12. "Futsū no Wakamono ga Keitai Shōsetsu Besutosera mo Zokuzoku" (A string of bestselling cell-phone novels by regular young people), *asahi.com*, 2007, www.asahi.com/culture/update/0211/008.html (accessed March 9, 2007).

13. "Daiichi Nihon Keitai Shōsetsu Taishō no Hyōkishiki ga Kaisai" (The first mobile-phone novel award ceremony was held), *ASCII.jp*, 2006, ascii24.com/news/i/topi/article/11/28/print/666144.html (accessed March 9, 2007).

14. NHK News, *Ohayō Nippon* (Good Morning Japan), March 8, 2007, 7:45.

15. John E. Ingulsrud and Kate Allen, *Learning to Read in China: Sociolinguistic Perspectives on the Acquisition of Literacy* (Lewiston, NY: The Edward Mellen Press, 1999).

16. "Japan Economic Report, October–November, 2006. Japanese Publishing Industry," *JETRO*, 2006, www.jetro.go.jp/en/market/trend/industrial/pdf/jer0611-2e.pdf (accessed September 12, 2007).

17. Anne Cooper-Chen and Miiko Kodama, *Mass Communication in Japan* (Ames: Iowa State University Press, 1997).

18. *JETRO*, "Japan Economic Report."

19. *JETRO*, "Japan Economic Report."

20. Ōba Tokiko, "Design Books Showcase Japanese Cool," *Daily Yomiuri*, June 30, 2007, 22.

21. "Akihabara Enta Matsuri! (2007, October 20–28)," www.entama.com/ (accessed September 3, 2007).

22. Gunther Kress and Theo van Leeuwen, *Multimodal Discourse: The Modes and Media of Contemporary Communication* (London: Arnold, 2001).

23. Theo van Leeuwen, "Multimodality, Genre and Design," in *Discourse in Action: Introducing Mediated Discourse Analysis*, ed. Sigrid Norris and Rodney H. Jones (London: Routledge, 2005), 73–93.

24. For example, David E. Rumelhart, "Schemata: The Building Blocks of Cognition," in *Theoretical Issues in Reading Comprehension: Perspectives from Cognitive Psychology, Linguistics, Artificial Intelligence, and Education*, ed. Rand J. Spiro, Bertram C. Bruce, and William F. Brewer (Hillsdale, NJ: Lawrence Erlbaum Associates, 1980), 33–58; Roger C. Schank and Robert P. Abelson, *Scripts, Plans, Goals, and Understanding: An Inquiry into Human Knowledge Structures* (Hillsdale, NJ: Lawrence Earlbaum, 1977); and Teun A. van Dijk and Walter Kintsch, *Strategies of Discourse Comprehension* (New York: Academic Press, 1983).

25. Kate Allen and John E. Ingulsrud, "*Manga* Literacy: Popular Culture and the Reading Habits of Japanese College Students," *Journal of Adolescent & Adult Literacy* 46, no. 8 (2003): 674–83.

26. Senko Maynard, *Principles of Japanese Discourse* (Cambridge: Cambridge University Press, 1998); Usui Yoshito, *Crayon Shin-chan* (Tokyo: Futabasha, 1990).

27. Natsume Fusanosuke, "Manga Bumpō Niokeru Koma no Hōsoku" (Rules for frames in manga syntax: Categories and relationships between frame to frame and frame to page), in *Manga no Yomikata* (How to read manga), ed. Inoue Manabu (Tokyo: Takarajimasha, 1995), 196–205.

28. Natsume, "Manga Bumpō."

29. Jessica Abel and Matt Madden, *Drawing Words and Writing Pictures: Making Comics: Manga, Graphic Novels, and Beyond* (New York: First Second, 2008), 8; Mort Walker, *The Lexicon of Comicana* (Port Chester, NY: Museum of Cartoon Art, 1980).

30. Takekuma Kentarō, "Hitome de Wakaru 'Keiyu' Zukan" (Easy guide to "graphic symbols"), in *Manga no Yomikata* (How to read manga), ed. Inoue Manabu (Tokyo: Takarajimasha, 1995), 78–105.

31. Pierre Masson, *Lire La Bande Dessinée* (Reading comics) (Lyon: Presses Universitaires de Lyon, 1985).

32. Frederik L. Schodt, *Dreamland Japan: Writings on Modern Manga* (Berkeley, CA: Stone Bridge Press, 1996).

33. The children's manga titles: *COROCORO* (magazine) (Tokyo: Shogakukan, 1977); *Ciao* (magazine) (Tokyo: Shogakukan, 1977); Fujio F. Fujiko, *Doraemon* (Tokyo: Shogakukan, 1969); Muroyama Mayumi, *Asarichan* (Tokyo: Shogakukan, 1978); Sakura Momoko, *Chibi Maruko-Chan* (Tokyo: Shueisha, 1989); and Anakubo Kōsaku, *Poketto Monsutā* (Pocket monsters) (Tokyo: Shogakukan, 1996).

34. Ishida Kanta, "It's Time for Adults to Give *Manga* Back to Children," *Daily Yomiuri*, May 20, 1998, 7.

35. Schodt, *Dreamland Japan*.

36. The shōnen manga titles: Toriyama Akira, *DRAGON BALL* © 1984 by Bird Studio/ SHUEISHA Inc.; Chiba Tetsuya and Takamori Asao, *Ashita no Joe* (Rocky Joe) (Tokyo: Kodansha, 1968); Konomi Takeshi, *THE PRINCE OF TENNIS* © 1999 by Takeshi Konomi/ SHUEISHA Inc.; *ONE PIECE* © 1997 by Eiichiro Oda/SHUEISHA Inc.; and Takahashi Rumiko, *Inuyasha* (Tokyo: Shogakukan, 1996).

37. For example, Fujimoto Yukari, *Watakushi no Ibasho wa Dokoniaruno? Shōjo Manga ga Utsusu Kokorono Katachi* (Where is my place to be? The human psyche through *shōjo* manga) (Tokyo: Gakuyōshobō, 1989); *Shōjo Manga Damashii* (The soul of *shōjo* manga) (Tokyo: Hakusensha, 2000); and *Aijyō Hyōron: "Kazoku" wo Meguru Monogatari* (A critique of love: Narratives about "the family") (Tokyo: Bungei Shunshū, 2004).

38. The *shōjo* manga titles: Tezuka Osamu, *Ribon no Kishi* (Princess knight) (Tokyo: Kodansha, 1953); Ikeda Riyoko, *Berusaiyu no Bara* (Rose of Versailles) (Tokyo: Shueisha, 1972); Miuchi Suzue, *Garasu no Kamen 1* (The glass mask 1) (Tokyo: Hakusensha, 1994), 45; Sugisaki Yukiru, *D.N.Angel*, Asuka 6 (Tokyo: Kadokawashoten, 2008), 15; Sakurano Minene, *Fairial Garden, Comic Blade* (Tokyo: Mag-Garden, 2007); and Kurekoshi Sakuya, *Little Dog Liar Cat* (Tokyo: Oakla Shuppan, 2005).

39. Yonezawa Yasuhiro, "Shōjo Manga no Keifu" (The roots of *shōjo* manga), in *Bessatsu Taiyō: Shōjo Manga no Sekai*, vol. 1 (Taiyō special edition: The world of *shōjo* manga, vol. 1), ed. Yonezawa Yasuhiro (Tokyo: Heibonsha, 1991), 4–8.

40. CLAMP, *Tokyo Babylon* (Tokyo: Shinshokan, 1990); *X* (Tokyo: Kadokawashoten, 1992)

41. Sharalyn Orbaugh, "Busty Battlin' Babes: The Evolution of the *Shōjo* in 1990s Visual Culture," in *Gender and Power in the Japanese Visual Field*, ed. Joshua S. Mostow, Norman Bryson, and Maribeth Graybill (Honolulu: University of Hawai'i Press, 2003), 204.

42. For example, Fujimoto Yukari, *Shōjo Manga Damashii* (The soul of *shōjo* manga) (Tokyo: Hakusensha, 2000); Orbaugh, "Busty Battlin' Babes"; and Schodt, *Dreamland Japan*.

43. Hanamaru Henshūbu, *Boizurabu Shōsetsu no Kakikata* (How to write boys love novels) (Tokyo: Hakusensha, 2004).

44. The manga magazines for women: *For Mrs.* (Tokyo: Akita Shoten, 1993); *Kiss* (Tokyo: Kodansha, 1992); *Office You* (Tokyo: Shueisha, 1985); *Taboo* (Tokyo: Sanwa Shuppan, 1992); *You* (Tokyo: Shueisha, 1982); and *Young You* (Tokyo: Shueisha, 1986).

45. Gretchen I. Jones, "Bad Girls Like to Watch: Writing and Reading Ladies' Comics," in *Bad Girls of Japan*, ed. Laura Miller and Jan Bardsley (New York: Palgrave Macmillan, 2005), 97–109; see also Setsu Shigematsu, "Dimensions of Desire: Sex, Fantasy, and Fetish in Japanese Comics," in *Themes and Issues in Asian Cartooning: Cute, Cheap, Mad, and Sexy*, ed. John A. Lent (Bowling Green, OH: Bowling Green University Popular Press, 1999), 127–63.

46. "Young" manga magazines: *Young Animal* (Tokyo: Hakusensha, 1992); *Young Champion* (Tokyo: Akita Shoten, 1988); *Young Jump* (Tokyo: Shueisha, 1979); and *Young Magazine* (Tokyo: Kodansha, 1980). "Young" manga titles: Morita Masanori, *BESHARI GURASHI* © 2005 by Studio Hitman/SHUEISHA Inc.; Shigeno Shūichi, *Initial D 1* (Tokyo: Kodansha, 1995); and Takahashi Yōichi, *Captain Tsubasa* (Tokyo: Shueisha, 1981).

47. "Adult" manga magazine: *Morning* (Tokyo: Kodansha, 1982). "Adult" manga titles: Ueyama Tochi, *Cooking Papa, Morning 20* (Tokyo: Kodansha, 2004), cover; Agi Tadashi and Okimoto Shū, *Kami no Shizuku 10* (Drops of God), *Morning Kodansha Comics* (Tokyo: Kodansha, 2007), cover; and Anno Moyoko, *Hataraki Man* (Working man), *Morning 26* (Tokyo: Kodansha, 2006), cover.

48. "Taste of Heaven: Manga Spreads 'Drops of God' in Asia," *Daily Yomiuri*, June 29, 2007, 12.

49. Sharon Kinsella, *Adult Manga: Culture and Power in Contemporary Japanese Culture* (Richmond, UK: Curzon, 2000), 179–80.

50. Jaqueline Berndt, "Considering Manga Discourse: Location, Ambiguity, Historicity," in *Japanese Visual Culture: Explorations in the World of Manga and Anime*, ed. Mark W. MacWilliams (Armonk, NY: M. E. Sharpe, 2008), 295.

The Nature of Manga Discourse   **2**

OR MOST ENGLISH-LANGUAGE READERS, comics are more familiar than manga. We begin this chapter by comparing the two so as to describe what is distinctive about manga. The distinctiveness of manga, we argue, arises out of its history. At the same time, not all scholars agree on what is salient in the historical development of what we know today as manga. In presenting the views on manga history, we revisit in more detail many of the genres presented in chapter 1. In addition, we describe the landscape of manga studies, reviewing the vast and varied body of works that describe manga. We analyze the works in terms of their epistemological methods, with the intention of providing an account of what we do know about manga and what there is yet to learn.

Manga is most often defined in English as simply "Japanese comics," an accurate label from a media point of view, since there is little or no difference between manga and comics. Essentially they are made up of panels containing graphics and print. Both refer to "comic strips," as well as longer narrative works, which are sometimes categorized by the more specific terms of "graphic novels" or *gekiga* 劇画. Single paneled cartoons have also been called manga. Similarly, television cartoons were referred to as manga up until the 1970s, when the term *anime* gained currency.

From a structural perspective, there are more similarities between manga and comics in North America and Europe than there are differences. In Jessica Abel and Matt Madden's *Drawing Words and Writing Pictures*, an extensive coursebook on creating comics, manga is presented together with comics in a seamless manner.[1] Both are drawn in panels, requiring the reader to infer information between the panels to a greater or lesser degree. Both employ graphics, as well as numerous symbols and icons, to signify mood and qualities of sensations. Both place the core of their linguistic content in speech and thought balloons. Both suffer from being trivialized because, prototypically, they are supposed to be funny and are often referred to as "the funnies" or "funny papers."[2] This view of triviality is emphasized, according to Thierry Groensteen, by the historical connection of comics with caricature.[3] Caricatures function as expressions of parody, pastiche, and burlesque. Moreover, caricatures and, by extension, comics tend to trivialize. The cliché about aging "we become caricatures of ourselves" does not have a positive meaning, evoking a sense of dehumanization. It refers not only to our bodies getting old but the sense of becoming worthless when withdrawing from a job-centered career. This is possibly why comics, seen as parodic, trivial caricatures, can arouse such intense emotional reactions. One such reaction, which was anything but trivial, occurred as a response to the September 2005 cartoon rendition of the prophet Mohammed appearing in a Danish newspaper, and resulted in worldwide demonstrations and numerous deaths.[4]

Association with caricature is not the only source of the trivialization of comics. Groensteen points out that because of the graphic nature of comics, they are often associated with children's picture books, thus providing the impression that comics are juvenile and not to be taken seriously.[5] Many travelers to Japan express surprise at seeing adults in public places reading manga because such behavior in their own countries is considered juvenile. Frederik Schodt, both in his writing and public speaking, has repeatedly made this observation.[6] Most of our students who write papers on manga mention this stereotype, arguing that the view of reading manga as juvenile smacks of condescension, and at best, the practice of reading manga as adults is misunderstood. While the practice of adults reading manga in public is accepted in Japan, it is not considered a preferred reading practice. The following examples illustrate this tension between accepted reading practices and preferred ones. The first one is actually from a manga (see figure 2.1). The second one is from a newspaper article. One woman complained in a newspaper advice column that her husband read manga in front of her four-year-old son and wished he would be a less childish model, reflecting attitudes similar to those found outside Japan.[7]

Comics creators also think comics are misunderstood. Creators like Will Eisner have long argued that comics should be considered art and, in Eisner's case, he promoted the term "sequential art" as a substitute for the less-serious sounding "comics."[8] Comics and manga creators, as well as commentators, are acutely aware that their subject is not taken seriously by the literary world, the creative arts, and, until recently, by academia.[9] In the case of academic inquiry, the motivation to study

Figure 2.1.   Reading Manga as a Contested Practice (Excerpt from *NANA* © 1999 by Yazawa Manga Seisakusho/SHUEISHA Inc.)

comics has been prompted less by the drive to reinterpret the medium as fine art, but more to examine them with a postmodern imperative, viewing them as cultural products where attitudes, ideology, and taste intersect. On the other hand, comics and manga have been taken seriously by the publishing world as commercial reading material that can sell. Indeed, marketing decisions have shaped the development of manga's format and content. In contrast, comics in the United States have been influenced not only by business decisions but also by social critics.

The publishing industry is not the only group that takes comics seriously. Psychiatrists, education organizations, and parent groups regard comics seriously, as possessing a strong external influence on children. Comics, particularly in the United States, have suffered from disrepute and even persecution as a result of the fear of negative influence. The fear is based not only on the sex and violence depicted in comics but also because they are merely a part of "pop culture" and nothing more. Compared with products of high culture, popular culture, especially comics, is exemplified as being inferior, impermanent (lacking in institutionalization), and mediocre.[10] This cultural perception rendered comics defenseless in the face of social and psychological critique. In 1948, psychiatrist Fredric Wertham published a paper suggesting that the juvenile delinquents he treated all had one thing in common: they read comics. This observation led to some self-censorship on the part of the publishers. But even more restrictive was the self-censorship and official censorship that came after Wertham published *Seduction of the Innocent: The Influence of Comic Books on Today's Youth* in 1954. His contention was that deviance came not from internal psychological distress, but from external issues relating to an individual's social environment.[11] The publication of Wertham's book and the resulting congressional investigation led to the industry adopting more self-regulation through a restrictive and strictly enforced Comics Code.[12] Some local governments went even further by establishing their own censorship regulations. The criticism also accused comics of promoting ideologies that were incompatible with prevailing assumptions on how American society should be constructed. For instance, Wertham felt superheroes evoked fascism and thus posed a potential threat to democracy.[13] More basically, the mere fact that comics were mass-produced suggested to Wertham that they were mediocre and of no aesthetic value.[14] We consider Wertham's work again in chapter 7.

In the Philippines, Taiwan, and South Korea, John Lent described similar restrictions on publishing comics.[15] Each of these countries was strongly influenced by the United States in the 1950s, and in the cases of Taiwan and South Korea, the restrictions served nationalistic interests in their postcolonial efforts at resisting Japanese cultural influences. The cultural and social defamation of comics had a long-term effect, as revealed in the attitudes of two prominent comic creators and commentators. Both Will Eisner, in *Comics and Sequential Art*, and Scott McCloud, in *Reinventing Comics*, plead with their readers to recognize the inherent value of comics. McCloud implores: "Comics offers a medium of enormous breadth and control for the author—a unique intimate relationship with its audience—a potential so great, so inspiring, yet so brutally squandered, it could bring a tear to the eye."[16]

In contrast to the United States, there is no sense of loss in Japan that manga as a medium has not fulfilled its potential. Moves toward censorship and self-censorship have not affected manga's creative development. Attempts at censorship in Japan have been less drastic, leaving the industry to self-regulate. Only occasionally does work get banned.[17] Although parent groups have attempted to be vigilant, it was only after several murders were committed by young men who were insular, read manga, and played video games that an outcry was heard more widely. These *otaku* オタク, or niche-obsessed people, were considered to be influenced by violent manga content, which led them to commit the crimes. The thinking here is similar to Wertham's, that is, the social environment is the main determinant of behavior. Manga apologists, such as Frederik Schodt and Natsume Fusanosuke, are quick to point out, however, that in spite of the proliferation of sex and violence represented in manga, the crime rates in Japan, particularly violent crime, are still relatively low.[18]

One result of self-censorship, according to Lent, is that shops do not carry certain kinds of manga.[19] In addition, we have observed in a number of bookstores, the practice of wrapping manga in plastic or binding them with rubber bands. The reason for these efforts is to stop *tachiyomi* 立ち読み (the practice of browsing and reading in a shop while standing). However, we suspect the aim of this practice is less to protect minors from browsing inappropriate material, but more to encourage potential readers to buy. In contrast, convenience stores allow for *tachiyomi*. In the case of *Book Off*, the largest chain retailer of used *komikku* (bound single titles of manga), we have noticed that there is little control over the kind of manga offered for sale. The highly pornographic titles tend to be more expensive, as are current popular ones. The variation in observed censorship practices indicates that the efforts are local and perhaps temporary.

Although Japanese society provided a conducive environment for manga to develop in its myriad ways, there exists a sense among many Japanese that manga still possesses little cultural capital. Manga researcher Kure Tomofusa attributes manga's low social status to it being cheap, disposable and widely read, thus echoing the attitudes of American critics of comics.[20] Indeed, some of our seminar students express embarrassment about studying manga. Others doubt whether manga are worthy enough to be a subject of a university-level research project. At a university manga club, members complain that the student government pesters them about their activities, that they do not really study or draw manga, but "just do video games," revealing that playing video games has even lower status than reading manga. Unlike most Japanese creators of anime, Miyazaki Hayao (creator of *Nausicaä of the Valley of the Wind*) went directly into animation without a career in drawing manga, after being unsuccessful in getting his manga published. Miyazaki attended Gakushūin University, originally founded for the aristocracy and affluent families. Although university students are free to set up their own clubs, no manga club existed at *Gakushūin*, at least when Miyazaki was there.[21] However, attitudes are changing, largely due to the growing international acclaim for manga, especially for certain works and creators. An adult manga reader, during an interview, remarked that "Tezuka Osamu's work is not really manga," implying works cease to be considered as manga once they are seen to be products of high culture.

Distinctiveness of Manga

Comics and manga share the structural features of the comic medium. They are also viewed as trivial, but most Japanese people do not consider reading manga to be juvenile. Both are targets of censorship, but in general, comics have been more effectively censored than manga. While many similarities exist between the two, manga are distinctive in four realms: a) graphics and language; b) the manner in which manga are presented and published; c) the special relationship of manga with other media; and d) its history. These four distinctions are considered here in further detail.

Graphics and Language

We have already described in the previous chapter some of the underlying meanings of the symbols or emenata, for example, the shapes of the speech balloons and drops of liquid employed to represent the nature of the characters' communication. While sweat as nervousness might be shared with comics, nasal discharge as loss of self-control may be distinctive to manga. Many manuals on drawing manga begin with a description of the tools. Natsume and Takekuma, for instance, have described in detail the pens that have been developed, showing how different psychological states can be depicted through line thickness and quality.[22] These techniques allow for a great deal of inventiveness. They also provide the basis of techniques for characters to be drawn in varying degrees of "caricaturization."[23]

Scott McCloud developed a "picture plane" to show that where comic characters can be situated depends on the degree of iconicity (photograph-like-ness), in contrast to more symbolic (simple) representation. The diagram is based on the semiotics of Charles S. Pierce, who proposed a tripartite scheme to illustrate the relationship between symbol and reality.[24] This approach stands in contrast to the dualistic approach, between sign and signified, of Ferdinand de Saussure. McCloud's picture plane, shown in figure 2.2, graphically illustrates the tripartite scheme. The complex drawing of *Spider-Man*, for instance, would fall toward the left. This is contrasted with the simple lines of *Peanuts*, by Charles Schulz which would fall toward the right. Most of the characters in comics are stable; they do not change. However, in many manga, the characters themselves can be drawn in degrees of iconicity or caricaturization, representing differing psychological states and positional identities. An example is provided in figure 2.3, where there are multiple degrees of caricaturization.[25]

Notice that the most iconic depictions are in the panels at the bottom of the page. These are then followed by the panel at the top of the page. The next level of abstraction would be the middle panel on the right. Finally, the panel to the left depicts the crowd extremely simply, almost as symbols. We count four levels and each one could be plotted on McCloud's picture plane. Presumably there is a function for each, requiring hermeneutic analysis to reveal.

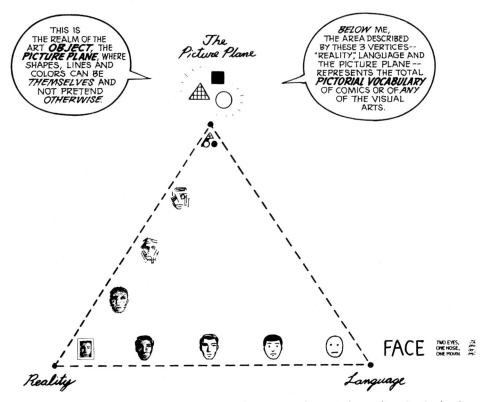

Figure 2.2.   McCloud's Picture Plane (Selection from p. 51, from *Understanding Comics* by Scott McCloud. © 1993, 1994 by Scott McCloud. Reprinted by permission of HarperCollins Publishers.

Figure 2.3.   Degrees of Caricaturization (Excerpt from *Little Dog Liar Cat* by Kurekoshi Sakuya. © 2005 by Oakla Shuppan. Reprinted with permission of Oakla Shuppan.)

Often in English-language newspapers and magazines, manga is described as having a unique style for drawing characters. Christopher Hart, in his book *Manga Mania: How to Draw Japanese Comics*, explains that manga characters tend to be drawn in rounder shapes, as opposed to the more angular American-comic style. At the same time, we observe that many *shōjo* manga characters are also drawn in an angular style. Hart goes on to describe in detail the drawing of eyes, in particular, how eye shape and quality can indicate roles and personalities of characters. Aihara Kōji and Takekuma Kentarō, in their book *Even a Monkey Can Draw Manga*, provide step-by-step details on how manga characters are drawn, exaggerating the simplicity of actually a difficult task. For those who are more advanced, *Japanese Comickers* and *Japanese Comickers 2* present the work and explain the techniques of many young Japanese creators.[26] The diversity we see in manga, however, seems to confound these efforts at prototypifying manga character representations. Manga style is not limited to character drawings but also includes panel shapes and arrangement, as well as content and narrative structure. Comparing the drawings of American children and Japanese children, Masami Toku observes that Japanese children have been clearly influenced by manga. This influence is seen not only in the way they draw characters but the manner in which they manipulate perspective and exaggerate certain body features.[27]

More examination of work in graphics design and art education might provide productive tools for analysis. Practitioners of multimodal discourse analysis have yet to develop tools that account for line qualities, shading, degrees of iconicity, and the qualities of facial shape and features. As far as we know, no studies to date have applied McCloud's picture plane, assigning characters a code and using the analysis for a range of comparative studies.[28] Analysts of multimodal discourse, including us, have come out of applied linguistics and thus carry a bias in favor of language.

The Japanese language itself has shaped manga. The onomatopoeia written in Japanese, for example, become part of the graphics. Yet recent translations have demonstrated that these onomatopoetic expressions do carry across languages, though not with all of the semantic content. This is because each of the scripts in Japanese has a functional role.[29] The four scripts—*kanji*, *hiragana*, *katakana*, and *rōmaji*—provide creators with enormous pragmatic resources for manga discourse. Although each script serves specific functions in Japanese texts, breaking these functional rules is a common technique used to particularize a character's speech. Moreover, while roman letters require a left-to-right arrangement, *kanji*, *hiragana*, and *katakana* are not constrained in this way. They can be written right to left or up and down. However, most Japanese text in speech balloons is written vertically.

The nature of the script itself is an essential dimension. The *hiragana* and *katakana* scripts, as well as *kanji*, do not represent individual sounds, but syllables. From a developmental perspective, it is easier to teach children symbols representing syllables rather than sounds. This is because the teacher can accurately model a syllable and the child can easily reproduce the syllable, in contrast to a single sound, which demands the child to make a conceptual leap.[30] Some have argued that the use of syllabaries, like *hiragana* and *katakana*, with their consistent phoneme-grapheme relationships, has provided the foundation for high rates of literacy in Japan.[31] The *kanji* script possesses not only phonological features but also semantic features, and learning the vast numbers of *kanji* is no easy task. However, in a great deal of reading material, including manga, *furigana* 振り仮名 (rubies of *hiragana*) are added to instances of *kanji*, allowing young readers to decode *kanji* and thus providing access to sophisticated text early on. This is why Japanese children learn to read more quickly than their English-speaking counterparts, who have to develop a large reading vocabulary before they can access texts with engaging content.

Moreover, the practice of reading to young children in Japan is not as widespread as in many English-speaking countries. Kato-Otani Eiko conducted a comparative study of middle-class mothers in the United States and Japan. The Japanese mothers who read to their children did so for bonding and aesthetic reasons and not for literacy development, which was a priority for the American mothers.[32] Furthermore, in Takano Ryōko's survey to parents in Chiba Prefecture, those parents who reported reading to their children were only slightly more than half of the whole group.[33] The ease of acquiring Japanese scripts allows children access to texts at an earlier age, and so they are less dependent on adults to mediate through reading aloud. Yet learning to read the graphic parts of manga may involve additional skills.

Tezuka Osamu has demonstrated that manga drawings, particularly manga characters, are made up of symbols. These symbols, resembling strokes in *hiragana* or *kanji*, plus basic shapes prompted Natsume to observe that Tezuka's characters were seen to be constructed like *kanji*: a configuration of symbols.[34] The symbols individually are arbitrary, like phonological sounds, but in their configurations, selected symbols together take on meaning. In manga, while the linguistic representation constitutes symbols, much of the graphics involve symbols as well.

Another source of distinctiveness of manga has been argued in terms of syntax. Kure attempts to describe a manga as being similar to sentences in Japanese text: the panels represent words in *kanji* and the *kana* represent the linear elements in the gutter between the panels that hold them together. Indeed, among the four scripts, the *kanji* does represent content words (*katakana* also is used to represent content words, most often for loan words), while *hiragana* represents the function (grammatical) words.[35] Although a Chinese text of solid Chinese characters does not appear, at first glance, to have the same sense of chunking that a multiscript Japanese text does, any reader of Chinese would assert that the text is made up of chunks of content words linked together with function words. Similarly, a text in English, in spite of the single script, has detectable content and function words. The distinctiveness of the Japanese language in relation to manga is not due to syntactic features. It is due to semantic features. The multiscript resource in Japanese simply offers more possibilities for nuance that any single-script language can provide.

Our discussion has centered on graphics and language. We have argued that the two are interrelated, and thus you cannot read a manga aloud because the language component alone is insufficient to understand the text. In the same way, looking at the graphics and not being able to read the language renders the literacy event as less than satisfactory. Saitō Nobuhiko suggests a three-part structure in which graphics (lines), language, and panels work together in an elastic manner to provide a cohesive significance to the manga medium.[36] There are times when one part assumes more prominence, such as a two-page spread of a single panel with no language. Yet when one part consistently assumes too much prominence, the work ceases to be manga, as in the case of an illustrated book, where language is prominent over the graphics. In the following section, we describe the role of panels in manga.

Presentation and Publication

The second realm of manga distinctiveness from comics is its presentation and patterns of publication. First, there is variation in the kinds of panel arrangements. Some manga have six to eight same-sized boxes or panels on the page, but most have a huge range of sizes reflecting the influence of the cinema.[37] In a newspaper article, Schodt has observed that manga, particularly Tezuka's manga, tends to be more expansive than American comics, as a single scene may take two to three times as many panels.[38] Some pages show close-ups and detailed movements. Other times, a whole two-page spread would comprise one panel. While this freedom depends on the work or genre, the deliberate manipulation of panel size, shape, and arrangement for expressive effect has been developed most extensively by manga creators. An example of this kind of presentation is shown in figure 2.4.[39]

Figure 2.4.   Cinematic Effect of Panel Arrangement (Excerpt from *X* by CLAMP (2000). © 2000 CLAMP. Reprinted with permission of Pyrotechnist Co. Ltd. and Kadokawashoten Publishing.)

Figure 2.5.   Six Types of Panel Transitions (Selection from p. 74 in *Understanding Comics* by Scott McCloud. © 1993, 1994 by Scott McCloud. Reprinted by permission of HarperCollins Publishers.)

The arrangement of panels is basic to the analysis of manga. Kure's analysis described earlier is a linear one assuming the progression of time, an essential element of narrative. McCloud presents a more complex analysis of panel progression, suggesting six types, including moment-to-moment, action-to-action, subject-to-subject, scene-to-scene, aspect-to-aspect, and transitions with no relationship, which he calls non-sequitur.[40] Abel and Madden add an additional type which they call a "symbolic transition" to describe the use of visual metaphors.[41] They use these panel transition types as a heuristic for comics' creators. Unlike McCloud, they do not use them as a method of analysis.

McCloud demonstrates how these panel transitions could be used to typify and thus categorize comics. The majority of comics, he contends, have mostly the second type, action to action. In contrast, he points out that manga more frequently contain aspect-to-aspect transitions, the number five category in figure 2.5.

McCloud does not elaborate on how he reached his findings and we struggled to replicate them. Together with our students, we spent three months studying and practicing this analysis. We then conducted an analysis of several manga titles across genres, calculating our inter-rater reliability. In only two cases we achieved a reliability coefficient of over 0.70. The main problem we found with McCloud's analysis was distinguishing moment-to-moment (category 1) from action-to-action (category 2). This is because both kinds of panel transitions involved time, thus making it difficult to distinguish between the two types. A similar replication was conducted at Keio University, with results analogous to our own findings.[42] Perhaps these panel transition types, in their current state, are more useful in the creating process. Still these transition types provide a compelling approach to the analysis of manga. Additional effort would be needed to refine the types, but if it could be done and the analysis carried out more easily, this would function as a useful tool for genre analysis and ultimately critical analysis.

So far we have discussed panel shapes and arrangement, arguing that they serve as integral techniques of manga expression. In our second point, we describe the rhetorical structure of manga and how this relates to publishing. Although four-panel strip manga called gag manga exist, the vast majority of manga is written as narrative and the most popular ones are serialized. This is because they appear in magazines. While color pages are beginning to be inserted, manga is still over-whelmingly published on newsprint in monochrome. Magazines carry multiple stories, often printing each story or sets of stories in a different color. These maga-zines are published as weekly, biweekly, or monthly periodicals and are comprised of three-hundred- to five-hundred-page volumes. That means there is a huge output, with hundreds of manga creators working for the industry. Some observers have commented that the pressure to produce large quantities of manga for magazines has resulted in low-quality graphics and stories.[43] Others have raised the issues of low pay and inadequate protection of copyrights.[44]

However, success in manga publishing can result in better income and working conditions. To be successful, feedback from fans is essential. In the magazines, there are self-addressed stamped postcards where readers are asked to provide feedback as to which stories they like. If the title is successful, then it will continue as a serial and the earlier installments are compiled into *komikkusu* to be sold as books. As long as the title generates fans, the publication of *komikkusu* will follow, and the fortunate few enjoy the popularity and income. Successful creators such as Hirokane Kenshi (of the *Shima Kōsaku* series) and Inoue Takehiko (of the *Slam Dunk* series) have multiple stories produced at the same time with the help of a staff. Large diversified companies publish the bestselling manga. These companies not only publish manga but other books and magazines as well.[45] This situation stands in contrast with pub-lishers of comics in the United States, where the companies are associated directly with their comics' lines.

Relationship with Other Media

The third realm of manga distinctiveness is that manga survives in spite of the growth in other media such as anime, light novels, television dramas, video games, and the In-ternet. Although manga sales have begun to decline, they continue to hold their share in the publishing world. One reason for this is that the media forms, while competing, serve to complement each other. Internet cafés, for example, are called *manga kissa* マ ンガ喫茶 (manga cafés), even though manga are only one of several media forms that can be accessed. Many stories originate in manga. For instance, the *Berusaiyu no Bara* (Rose of Versailles), a well-known *shōjo* manga by Ikeda Riyoko, was rendered into a staged musical by the all-women Takarazuka Revue.[46] Miyazaki Hayao is a creator of anime. However, after success with several animations, he embarked on writing an epic science fiction manga, *Nausicaä of the Valley of the Wind*. Although the manga series was produced over thirteen years, midway through this period, the story

Figure 2.6.   Ishihara Satomi and Misora Aoi (Cover from *Morning* by Koshino Ryō. © 2006 by *Morning*. Reprinted with permission of Kodansha.)

Figure 2.7.   Caricatured Actor Introduces Herself (Excerpt from *N's Aoi* by Koshino Ryō. © 2006 by *Morning*. Reprinted with permission of Kodansha.)

was produced as an anime. Consequently, sales of the manga version went up sharply, even though the ending differed from the anime version.[47]

In the promotion of the television dramatization of the "adult" manga *N's Aoi*, a serialized narrative taking up issues of Japan's healthcare system, the front cover of *Morning* carried the manga character, Misora Aoi, with photographs of the actor, Ishihara Satomi. Inside the manga magazine, there was a caricaturization of Ms. Ishihara introducing herself to Misora Aoi. The manga character is thrilled to meet the caricatured actor and thus the actor received permission to perform her television role. This interchange recognizes the manga rendition as the urtext, and the caricaturization of the actor highlights the fact that she is not the same as the character. In figure 2.6, the photo of the actor is shown with the manga character. In figure 2.7, the caricatured actor meets the manga character.[48]

Three realms of manga have been raised in this section: the graphics and language, the presentation and manner of publication, and relationship with other media. These realms appear to set manga apart from comics in other countries. Yet perhaps the most important distinctiveness of manga is its history. In the next section, we describe two approaches to the origins of manga.

Origins of Manga

The origins of manga are not as apparent as some commentators would like us to believe. Some say there is a long history of drawing manga, dating back to the temple scrolls of the twelfth century, where drawing caricatures served as a form of entertainment and social critique. With the development of woodblock printing technology, many people have identified, from among a broad range of publications, traces of what could plausibly develop into manga. These traces, in addition to the nineteenth-century influence of comic creation in Europe and North America, served to provide the origins for manga as we know it today.

Others say manga in their present format developed in the 1950s, as a result of social conditions and the availability of quality works by creators like Tezuka Osamu, the writer of children's manga such as *Janguru Taitei* (Jungle emperor) and *Tetsuwan Atomu* (Mighty atom). The English animated versions were named *Kimba, the White Lion* and *Astro Boy*, respectively. Today there is a wide range of manga titles catering for all kinds of readers, from children to adults. Yet the explosion of manga in publishing volume, beginning in the late 1950s and continuing with minor abatement, has been unprecedented. So the question is posed, what was the basis for this rise in readership and publication? Was it the ancient traditions of caricature drawing? Was it the socioeconomic conditions of the post–World War II period?

These two approaches to the history of manga roughly correlate with the first two realms of manga distinctiveness described earlier—namely, the language and graphics on the one hand and the manner in which manga is published on the other. Writers on manga who focus on language and graphics, particularly graphics, tend to emphasize the connection to traditional Japan's pictorial arts. On the other hand, writers who focus on manga format, rhetoric, and publishing, pay little attention, if any, to the traditional arts.

The first approach takes a cultural-historical view, arguing that the phenomenon of manga naturally arose in the cultural context of Japan. Modern manga is the descendent of the painting and woodblock print traditions of medieval and early modern Japan. Added to the indigenous tradition is the nineteenth and early twentieth centuries' influence of comics from the West, both in format and caricature drawing. This historical approach has proved attractive to English-language writers like Frederik L. Schodt, Paul Varley, and Kinko Ito, as well as Japanese writers such as Shimizu Isao and Okada Toshio. Paul Gravett and Natsume Fusanosuke have also written about these earlier forms.

The second approach takes a socioeconomic perspective. Proponents of this approach include Takeuchi Osamu, Kure Tomofusa, Sharon Kinsella, Azuma Hiroki, Nakano Haruyuki, and Jacqueline Berndt. These writers do not see manga as a natural development of indigenous traditions aided by a little stimulus from the outside. Rather, they view manga today as a unique result of specific historical events, social conditions, and economic practices, together with the good fortune of gifted creators.

Based on this socioeconomic approach, there is general consensus that the end of World War II in 1945 is regarded as the beginning of modern manga. The proponents of this approach contend that it is out of both the conditions imposed and the cultural influences provided by the United States Occupation, together with the impoverished circumstances of most Japanese people, which led to the rise of a flourishing manga industry from the late 1950s onward. While both approaches, the one valuing traditional pictorial arts and the one valuing social and economic factors, recognize the importance of post–World War II developments, particularly the emergence of Tezuka, the difference between them lies in whether the earlier influences possess any relevance. Moreover, among those who emphasize the cultural roots of manga, there is no agreement over what constitutes the main source. In the following sections, we first summarize the material on the early roots of manga, followed by a summary of the post-1945 developments.

Cultural-Historical Approach

Perhaps one of the most comprehensive treatments of the history of manga in English has been provided in Schodt's *Manga Manga: The World of Japanese Comics*. The manga commentators Natsume and Okada both applaud Schodt on his analysis.[49] According to Schodt, the historical threads that led to the development of late twentieth-century manga are threefold. The first is the indigenous drawing tradition; the second is the woodblock print tradition; and the third is the influence of comics from the west.

The history of manga goes back to the seventh-century caricatures drawn on temple walls and ceilings. Many were caricaturized depictions of demons and ghosts, yet some of the most famous of these pictures were drawn on temple scrolls in the twelfth century. Unlike earlier pictures, these were funny—for instance, the *Chōjū Giga* (Humorous animal pictures), which satirized the rich and the powerful of the day as animals, particularly the Buddhist clergy (see figure 2.8). There were other examples of caricature drawing, like the simple-lined Zen pictures used as illustrated metaphors and parables. These pictures mostly were in the possession of the upper classes.

While these caricature drawings have received a great deal of attention, there is a more basic point of format that may have just as much relation to the development of modern manga. This is the format of drawings and paintings on scrolls. The style of scroll drawing and painting was not indigenous to Japan, but was borrowed from China. The scrolls contain both graphics and writing, providing an established tradition for combining these two modes in a single visual field. One could then

Figure 2.8.   *Chōjū Giga* as Rendered in the Manga *Hyougemono* (Excerpt from *Hyougemono* by Yamada Yoshihiro. © 2007 by *Morning*. Reprinted with permission of Kodansha.)

ask, which mode on the scrolls was dominant? Was the writing serving the graphics or were the graphics illustrating the writing? These are relevant questions because in both traditional China and Japan, the painter and the calligrapher were equally regarded for their skills. The greatest artists could do both, evoking a coherent register in the cohesion of the graphic and textual modes.

The *Chōjū Giga* and *Tale of Genji* scrolls were part of an exhibition in 2006 at the Kyoto National Museum, where the promoters explicitly described the *Chōjū Giga* scrolls as the "origin of manga." In a television program based on the exhibition, program guests, including the exhibition curator and manga commentator Natsume, discussed the expressive detail and the playfulness in the lines. The contributors commented that these techniques were quite unprecedented for the period. Natsume pointed out that, unlike China, Japanese art and literature were not limited by religion, philosophy, or even literary conventions. Japanese cultural products had, at an early stage, taken on fictional material. The *Tale of Genji* and the *Chōjū Giga* are good examples of this. Following the discussion, a short video clip was shown of a 1982 interview with Tezuka, who stated that the drawing techniques in *Chōjū Giga* and other works had much in common with the drawings of modern manga.[50]

Although the figures in these early scrolls resemble those in modern manga, they were not products of popular culture. In figure 2.9, the same manga rendition of the *Chōjū Giga* accurately depicts high-ranking people looking at the pictures. One character is amused while the other is bored.[51]

Reading material for a wide audience only came with improvements in publishing technology. Publishing in Japan has a long history dating back to the eighth century. Initially for religious texts, publishing then slowly expanded to other types of texts.[52] The large expansion of publishing came during the Edo Period (1603–1868), a time marked by peace and stability. Although moveable type technology existed, a great deal of publishing in this period was done by woodblock printing technology. This was because, according to Mary Elizabeth Berry, carving the text allowed for carving the graphics on a single page.[53] Therefore the technology

Figure 2.9.   Viewing the *Chōjū Giga* in the Manga *Hyougemono* (Excerpt from *Hyougemono* by Yamada Yoshihiro. © 2007 by *Morning*. Reprinted with permission of Kodansha.)

already reflected textual preferences. Peter Kornicki reports that woodblocks were made of cherry wood, and each block could be used to print eight thousand copies.[54] The graphic woodblock prints usually depicted secular themes, and they often functioned as advertisements. A large number of these advertisements took on narrative form to promote products such as medicines.[55] Moreover, a lot of woodblock print artists employed the format of multiple panels on one sheet of paper, setting the stage for sequential panels in manga. Many of these artists borrowed a number of the *Chōjū Giga* techniques in their drawings on which they based their prints.[56] Indeed, the term *manga* 漫画 is attributed to the master woodblock print artist Katsushika Hokusai, even though there is evidence of earlier artists using the term.[57] The following example of Hokusai's "manga" illustrates a variety of reading postures (see figure 2.10). The humor in this work is reflected in the contrasts to how reading postures at the time were strictly prescribed.

Yet perhaps the most influential tradition on the development of manga was not the single-page woodblock prints, but the *kibyōshi* 黄表紙 (yellow-covered booklets).[58] The *kibyōshi* tradition, dating back to the eighteenth century, came out of an earlier kind of picturebook publishing technique called *kurobon* 黒本 (black books) and *akabon* 赤本 (red books), reflecting the colors of their covers. *Kibyōshi* were published for adults and dealt with a range of subjects. The narrative presentation in these books, with both graphics and text, draws similarities to factors that relate

Figure 2.10. Hokusai Manga (Excerpt from *Denshin Kaishu Hokusai Manga*, vol. 8. Reprinted with permission of Tokyo Metropolitan Foundation for History and Culture Image Archives.)

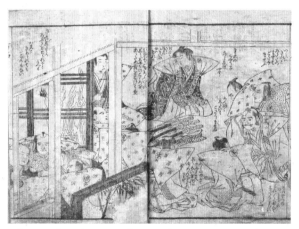

Figure 2.11. *Bunbunidō Mangokutōshi* (Excerpt from *Bunbunidō Mangokutōshi* (Twin arts threshing device). Reprinted with permission of Tokyo Metropolitan Foundation for History and Culture Image Archives.)

to manga. According to Natsume, there were no speech balloons, although there were thought bubbles, and this technique allowed for plural scenes on one frame, harkening the advent of panels. Furthermore, the use of lines and smoke foreshadowed manga graphic symbols, though they signified different meanings from today. However, Natsume insists that *kibyōshi* were not manga, as they did not distinguish between narration and speech, and most examples employed full-page panels. The example in figure 2.11 is a double-page spread from a 1788 work by Hōseidō Kisanji. Another example of woodblock publishing was the pornographic *shunga* 春画 (spring pictures), often compiled in volumes called *enbon* 艶本. These books contained stories with colorful graphics, depicting sexual encounters of various kinds.[59] Many of these books were published in the *kibyōshi* format.

Adam Kern's colorful and extensively researched history of the *kibyōshi* is titled *Manga from the Floating World: Comicbook Culture and the Kibyōshi of Edo Japan.* From the title, one could gain the impression that *kibyōshi* are equivalent to manga or at least manga's forerunner. However, in the book, Kern is more tentative about the connection. He offers this explanation:

> Thus, contrary to the intimations of the proponents of *manga* culture, the modern *manga* was *not* the inevitable culmination of the *kibyōshi*. Nor did the *kibyōshi* entail the manga. The modern *manga* would have come into existence even without the *kibyōshi*. Furthermore, even if it could be demonstrated that the modern *manga* borrowed this or that convention or style or trope from the *kibyōshi*, the *kibyōshi* cannot be meaningfully described as a major influence, let alone as the direct progenitor.[60]

If for these reasons, *kibyōshi*'s link to modern manga is tenuous, Kern's classification of *kibyōshi* as "comic-book culture" may also be seen as tenuous. Yet Kern makes the point that *kibyōshi* were, like manga and comics, mass-produced and consumed as products of popular culture. And as such, *kibyōshi* works were often created with content that was aesthetically, socially, and politically on the edge. Unfortunately, the reforming authorities perceived them to have overstepped the edge, and *kibyōshi* publishing in its popular form was stamped out by 1806. The format, however, survived with acceptable material.

The first Western influence on comic art came in the second half of the nineteenth century and was expressed as caricature drawing in single-paneled cartoons. Publications like *The Japan Punch* had foreign cartoonists and Japanese ones who were primarily drawn from the *ukiyoe* 浮世絵 tradition of woodblock print pictures. Later, *Tokyo Puck,* modeled after an American magazine, carried cartoons and articles of social interest. From the late nineteenth century and into the twentieth century, a number of Western comics were translated into Japanese, including titles like *Bringing up Father, Mutt and Jeff,* and *Felix the Cat.*[61] These translations were important in that they introduced many of the conventions of comics. Manga creators quickly assimilated the techniques, and soon magazines were carrying comics based on specific characters with episodes. The Yomiuri newspaper, in the late 1920s, started including four-page spreads of comics in Sunday papers. During this period, manga tended to consist of the so-called funnies, focusing on humor and satire.[62]

By the outbreak of World War II, manga in Japan had developed to a technical level that rivaled that of the United States and Europe. The levels of readership also increased. There was even a monthly magazine of over hundred pages called *Shōnen Club,* published in the 1930s, that provided an early version of the thick manga magazines, which have become familiar today.[63] At the same time, the development of manga was not simply a linear progression. There were influences from other media, notably the practice of *kamishibai* 紙芝居, translated as "paper plays," "paper theatre" and "picture cards."[64] In pre-television Japan, *kamishibai* performers provided a low-cost form of entertainment. *Kamishibai* is a narrated set of cardboard pictures, often with the script on the back. It is this rendition of narrative and the various effects of the narrators that were influential on manga creators. The choice of scene from the story for graphic display, in addition to the oral sound effects and body movements used for dialogue and narration, provided stimulation to many manga creators. Another influence on manga was the cinema, furnishing ideas for new designs in panel construction with experimentation in focus and perspective.[65] Many of Tezuka Osamu's early work, such as *Shintakarajima*, surprised readers with its cinematic use of panels. In addition, Fuse Hideto observes that Tezuka's work drew on the use of lighting and perspective found in Western painting.[66]

Socioeconomic Approach

We have presented some of the well-known origins of manga. Most commentators will agree that each of these sources does indicate features of manga, for instance, the use of caricatures with text, the use of panels in narratives, as well as the beginnings of mass production in publishing and popular literacy. In this section, we present the other approach that emphasizes modern manga as a post–World War II phenomenon. We first describe the position of this approach and then chronicle the socioeconomic currents and manga genres, together with specific manga magazines and titles that have shaped manga as we know it today. Both the cultural-historical approach and the socioeconomic approach serve the interests of *nihonjinron* 日本人論 (the discourse of Japanese uniqueness). The connection is obvious for the former approach: manga developed out of a long, particular history of cultural development. The latter approach parallels manga's development with Japan's phenomenal economic growth, an episode that is seen by many as being unique.

Manga researcher Kure takes the position that historical-cultural sources have little to do with present-day manga and are trotted out by promoters to display manga's high culture credentials. Kure holds the view that modern manga has arisen out of specific historical and economic conditions. He argues that among those publications in the first half of the twentieth century, only works like *Tokyo Puck*, *Shōnen Club*, and the newspaper manga have a direct connection to manga after 1945.[67] In these examples, the format, the creative process, the paper, and the manner of distribution are similar to what came later in the century.

Japan's defeat in 1945 resulted in a dramatic change in political discourse. Kure explains that the defeat offered a sense of liberation, and although the U.S. occupation did censor the media, access to American popular culture provided a huge stimulus in the development of Japanese media.[68] Many American servicemen read comics.[69] At the same time, the economic conditions of the Japanese people were closely connected to the literacy practices that they engaged in. Moreover, the kind of manga that was published was linked to readers of almost all age groups. At the same time, the manner of publication and distribution also affected the demands on the manga creator.

There are a number of manga histories in chart form that describe the socioeconomic development of manga from 1945 onward. The most comprehensive and accessible chart in English is the timeline provided by Paul Gravett.[70] This two-page spread lists the major milestones in manga publishing, together with the events of the day and movements in the kindred media of anime and television. Okada Toshio provides another chart in Japanese in his book *Introduction to Otakuology*.[71] Beginning his timeline at 1959, Okada focuses on magazine titles and publishing houses, showing the rise and fall of popular manga titles and themes. Similarly, Kure's chart, *Gendai Manga no Rekishi* (History of modern manga), focuses on the development of manga genres.[72] What is helpful about this chart is that it shows the rise and fall of genres, as well as the relative degrees of popularity at different points in time. The attraction of this chart is that it indicates popularity by the width of the bars. However, the timeline only extends to 1990. We have adapted his chart by estimating the scope of developments, based on data provided by Nakano Haruyuki, and by doing so we have succeeded in extending the chart into the twenty-first century.[73] Our adaptation of Kure's *Manga no Rekishi* has taken shape in the chart below, "The Development of Manga from 1945."

Moving from left to right (see figure 2.12), the monthly manga magazines for boys (also including *shōjo* for girls) are a descendant from the earlier *Shōnen Club*, which was resumed in 1946, together with a magazine *Shōjo Club*. These are mostly serialized story manga. As Nakano points out, the monthly magazines in this period

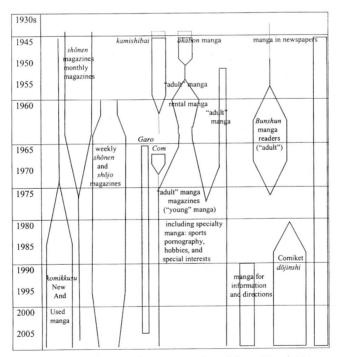

Figure 2.12. The Development of Manga from 1945 (Adapted from "Gendai Manga no Rekishi (The history of modern manga)" in *Gendai Manga no Zentaizō* by Kure Tomofusa. Used with the permission of the author.)

were not exclusively devoted to manga as they included print articles and stories. In 1950, Tezuka Osamu begins publishing his serialized work *Jungle Taitei* in *Manga Shōnen*.[74] As is indicated in the chart (figure 2.12), the monthlies begin to be eclipsed in the 1960s, yet continue to this day, especially among *shōjo* and "lady's" magazines like *Cookie* and *Taboo*.

By the 1960s, the economic growth of Japan is flourishing. Nakano produces statistics showing how children's allowances grew exponentially in this period. As a consequence of this increased spending power, children themselves started buying manga, whereas traditionally, parents bought the monthlies for their children.[75] As mentioned in chapter 1, children's manga has not experienced the growth that manga for other age groups have. This is because they are dependent on parents to do the purchasing. The success of manga has been linked to the agency of the readers themselves, either by purchasing or renting.

During the 1960s, weekly manga magazines (entirely manga) begin to appear and in five years dominate the market. Schodt describes the difficult transition experienced by the manga creators, with a shift from monthly deadlines to weekly ones for the same production output.[76] Yet it would appear that the transition process was not detrimental for the industry. One of our adult informants describes, in English, her feelings during the period:

> When I was a first year junior high school student, the first *Margaret* appeared. They are monthly magazine, but *Margaret* is weekly. At that time, weekly magazines so fresh. Most magazines monthly, so weekly magazines so fresh.

Margaret was first published in 1963 as a biweekly manga magazine. It continues to be published. This memory slip does not lessen the impact of the increased frequency of publication. The reader went on to say that with weeklies, one did not have to wait so long for the next installment in the serialized stories.

These *shōnen* and *shōjo* magazines grew into big volumes of five hundred or more pages, and consequently the large volumes became the prototypical manga. "Manga" continues to be the superordinate term for the medium, but because the manga magazine has become the prototype, the bound volumes of specific titles are not called manga, but instead are called *komikku* or *komikkusu*. Kure has not included them in his *Gendai Manga no Rekishi*. In response to the situation today, we feel they are worth putting in the chart because, as printed matter, these possess more value over time than the magazines. They are the format in which manga is collected, lent, borrowed, and sold. Moreover, by 2005, they have overtaken manga magazines in terms of income for publishers.[77]

From the latter half of the 1990s, a slow decrease in the sales of the *shōnen* manga magazines has occurred. Many people blame the proliferation of new and used *komikkusu*.[78] This proliferation has been facilitated through commercial outlets that buy used *komikkusu* and sell them at a reasonable price. They also encourage *tachiyomi*. Figure 2.13 shows a sign for one of the largest outlet chains, *Book Off*. Similarly, the availability of *komikkusu* in manga Internet cafes provides another option for readers. Competi-

Figure 2.13.   Used-Book Outlet *Book Off*.

tion from other media, such as television and video games, is also raised as a factor for the decline. However, Nakano complains that there are no quantitative methods to measure the literacy practices surrounding the use of used bookshops and manga Internet cafes. Indeed, it is these kinds of unquantifiable literacy practices that we have documented and present in chapter 4.[79] Yet what we provide is only a glimpse into this enormous market of neighborhood retail and entertainment outlets.

In the middle of the chart, shown in figure 2.12, there are two thin bars. These refer to *Garo* and *COM*, two monthlies dealing with the experimental and the avant-garde, respectively. They attracted manga artists from the *akabon* 赤本 (red book manga) and book rental industry, that is, artists who were writing *gekiga* or graphic novels. *Akabon* was cheaply printed on rough newsprint and often had covers in red ink, hence its name.[80] These manga should not be confused with the *akabon* published in the Edo period (1603–1868). The manga creators were allowed a great deal of artistic latitude, and later many became contributors to *Garo* and *COM*. They were, perhaps, more "graphic" than the story manga in the *shōnen* and *shōjo* series. *Garo*, which began publication in 1964, offered an outlet for artistic innovation and became the platform for artists such as Tsuge Yoshiharu and Mizuki Shigeru.[81] *COM*, on the other hand, was established by Tezuka Osamu and became an outlet for some of his innovative work such as *Hi no Tori* (Phoenix) (1967), together with the works of his associates. *COM* was short-lived, but served to reinvigorate the graphic novel in the young and adult sectors.

We mentioned that Tezuka Osamu had created story manga for the monthly *Manga Shōnen* in 1950. In fact, Tezuka was working out of his native Kansai (Osaka area) and the invitation to publish in the Tokyo-based monthly was based his work in the *akabon* "red book" comics. Nakano calls this *akabon* period the "incubator" for modern manga.[82] The *akabon* market soon declined and was replaced by the book rental market that published *gekiga* on slightly better paper and initially with hard covers.[83] Many of these works were created for adult consumption. Naiki Toshio points out that the book-rental manga catered not only to adult men but women as well, by offering romantic titles. The book rental shops also provided novels.

The proliferation of book rental shops reflected the lack of disposable income in the 1950s. Hasegawa Yutaka recounts his boyhood growing up in a home where his parents ran a book rental shop. His father returned from internment in Siberia during the mid-1950s and, with a loan from a relative, opened a book rental shop in a residential neighborhood in southwest Tokyo. There were several shops like it in the area, but not all succeeded. The success of his parents' venture lay in the constant stocking of new material. Initially this strategy required his father to hold down two jobs.[84]

Like *kamishibai*, the book rental shops served a relatively impoverished population. From a literacy standpoint, it is noteworthy that literacy practices of the people allowed the book rental shops to be a commercial success. However, the book rental shops began to decline, not necessarily from a lack of interest in reading, but from affluence. People gradually could afford to buy their own manga and television sets. Because many of the book rental creators dealt with adult themes, the creators slowly switched over to working for the "adult" manga magazines. By 1972, publication for the book rental market ceased.[85]

Another trend in manga publication, shown in figure 2.12 at the top of the chart, is the *kamishibai*. We have already introduced these professional one-person players that provided entertainment in the impoverished years after World War II. The English-language sources, however, do not describe how *kamishibai* is presented. Let us briefly explain. A *kamishibai* work consists of twenty to forty thin cardboard panels. In a forty-panel story, for example, the lines for panel one are written on the back of panel forty. When panel one is completed, the panel is placed at the back of the stack, revealing the lines for panel two and so on. The skillful presenter will also make great efforts at embellishing the stories while providing a range of facial and sound effects. *Kamishibai*, as a medium, was widely used in educational settings and was enthusiastically appropriated by Christian missionaries. *Kamishibai*, as entertainment, was replaced by television, which became widespread by 1960.

According to the chart in figure 2.12, the adult manga stream has two origins, the book-rental publishing industry and a burgeoning adult manga magazine industry, which began in the late 1950s as monthly publications. The magazine industry grew as people became affluent and began buying the magazines. Large publishers attracted successful *gekiga* artists working for the book-rental markets, thus drawing on a broad fan base.[86] These *seinenshi* 青年誌 (youth magazine) or *seijinshi* 成人誌 (also known as *shakaijinshi* 社会人誌 ["adult" magazines]) included, in addition to the serious *gekiga* or graphic novels, works that contained pornography. To distinguish themselves from the light and childish manga, the manga initially adopted the term "comics" コミック. The weekly *Magazine Big Comics* マガジーンビッグコミッ

ク continues to this day. However, this genre tends to have the prefix *yangu-* ヤング, as in *Young Jump*. Those without the prefix usually have more serious stories.

In the 1950s, there were short-lived "adult" manga titles such as *Bunshun Manga Dokuhon* 文春漫画読本 (Bunshun manga readers). In the chart, "adult" manga make up the "island" near the top of the chart and Kure describes this kind of manga as being read by so-called up-market adult readers. They contained a variety of manga types from cartoons to four-panel manga to graphic novels. By the 1970s, this genre could not compete with the expanding *shōnen*, "young," and *shōjo* publications. The surviving "adult" manga adopted the *shōnen* format. The "adult" manga today, such as Kodansha's *Morning* and *Evening* and all the niche manga, are published in monochrome on newsprint with multiple stories, mostly serialized and interspersed with articles providing extra information on a topic treated in a story.

At the far right of the chart in figure 2.12 is a long but constant bar, which represents the category of funnies in the newspapers and magazines. They are not the colorful inserts that come with Sunday papers in the United States, but instead tend to be in the four-paneled gag manga format. Furthermore, to the right of the chart (see figure 2.12), there is a short bar. Kure categorizes this as representing anything in the manga format that appears in a non-manga publication. Examples could include a public service manga illustrating disaster response procedures, a manga illustrating the process of conducting a bureaucratic procedure, or a manga in a manual illustrating how to operate a mechanical device. Yet this seemingly utilitarian genre has spawned characters that have become various kinds of mascots. Matt Alt and Hiroko Yoda, for instance, have documented many of these mascots in their book *Hello, Please*.[87]

Finally, at the bottom right of the chart in figure 2.12, we have an expanding bar labeled *Comiket* and *dōjinshi*. The venue for *dōjinshi* (fanzines, parodies, and original works) is the biannual *Comiket* (comic market) conventions where the full range of manga types, created by amateurs, are exhibited, given away, or sold. The conventions have been held since 1975 and have swelled to huge attractions of over thirty-five thousand participants, not counting the customers and browsers. These conventions require the venue of Big Site located on the shores of Tokyo Bay. According to Yonezawa Yasuhiro, the participants who present their work do so individually or as part of a manga club. Participants from clubs make up about 96 percent and among these, 71 percent are women. Most participants offer their work for free, but roughly one-third charge a range of prices. Some participants are actively looking for commercial recognition, while others prefer to keep their work within the confines of *Comiket*. For all participants, it is important to be promoted in the convention catalogue that is included with the price of admission.[88] Yonezawa, who spearheaded the *Comiket* movement since 1975, died of cancer at the age of fifty-three in late 2006. Many feared that his passing would negatively affect the conventions. According to commentator Ishida Kanta, the 2007 summer convention had even more participants, suggesting that *Comiket* was becoming more of a venue for consumers to buy fanzine work than for amateur creators to simply exhibit their work. This change, according to Ishida, is a sign that the niche manga markets for *otaku* are becoming more mainstream.[89] In addition, *dōjinshi* creators need not wait for the conventions, but can sell their work through manga outlets such as *Mandarake* or on the Internet.

For many years now, the mainly amateur creators of *shōjo* manga have forged the vanguard of the *dōjinshi* world. One of their achievements is the proliferation of *moe*. We have described *moe* as an aesthetic sensibility coming out of *shōjo* manga, connoting cuteness, vulnerability, and pubescence, as well as "little sister (brother)-ness." *Moe* also stands for the reader/consumer response to a *moe* character: an acute sense of feeling both sorry for and feeling seduced, followed by an excessive interest in the character.[90] Morinaga Takurō goes further saying that *moe* involves a reader falling in love with a character, filling a void for *otaku*, the niche-obsessed consumers, who find it difficult to make and maintain personal relationships. Morinaga, who studies the economics of *moe*, observed that the stock of *moe*-related companies in 2005 rose almost 14 percent in just three months. The industry includes the *dōjinshi*, but also the kindred media of anime, video games, toys, and costumes.[91]

The term *otaku* generally refers to men and boys, although it is possible to refer to women and girls as also *otaku*. There is another related term for women and girls called *fujoshi* 腐女子. These are the reader-consumers of the *shōjo* manga subgenre of *yaoi* やおい, another achievement of the amateur female creators. Beginning in the late 1970s, manga with themes of male-male relationships have been written by women for women. These manga started out with stories of young schoolboys (*shōnenai* 少年愛). Then they were expanded with parodies of well-known manga called *yaoi*. This acronym for *yamanashi-ochinashi-iminashi* (no climax—no resolution—no significance) was initially used as a euphemism for the content. It is also written as 801 because the numerals can be pronounced as *yaoi*. Another source contends that *yamanashi-ochinashi-iminashi* was a favorite expression of Tezuka when encountering badly composed manga, and thus the creators gleefully adopted the acronym.[92] Yet later, Kubota Mitsuyoshi suggests many creators of the genre came to realize that their stories, depicting subtle human relationships in a timeless, existential manner in narratives with minimal development, accurately reflected the rhetorical patterns intrinsic to the name *yaoi*. In a *yaoi* story, the romantic/sexual encounters happen without fanfare and fade away in the conclusion. Many of the commercial *yaoi* stories were published in the monthly manga magazine *June*. Recently, however, the commercial versions are called "Boys Love" or BL.[93]

A similar kind of genre exists in the English-language fanzine circles called slash fiction. Here, well-known characters from literature or the media are reassembled in a same-sex encounter. These stories focusing on the encounter are also called "Plot? What Plot?" or PWP for short.[94] Slash fiction, however, requires the urtext narratives. They make sense in these contexts. Many *yaoi* stories also are parodies on well-known narratives, but Kaneda Junko points out that *yaoi* is more diverse, including stories not dependent on well-known urtexts.[95] For instance, character types can possess their own contexts.

Suzuki Kazuko observes that there are two types of character dyads. One is a dyad of equal statured characters. She makes reference to slash fiction-type fanzines in the English-speaking world, for example, Captain Kirk and Mr. Spock from the television series *Star Trek*. In this dyad, stature is roughly equal, but the characters possess different strengths. The other dyad is described as unequal with one partner larger and more macho, while the other is smaller, more slender, and feminine. Suzuki argues that Japanese women are attracted to both kinds. The first kind of dyad represents an ideal type of relationship, often with the tension of having the slightly more outgoing partner being the passive one in sexual contact.[96] The second kind represents unequal relationships, with the smaller partner evoking that pubescent seductive vulnerability described as *moe*.

The graphic expression of the characters in a dyad is not the only method used to describe the "tension" in a relationship of which the assertive-receptive dichotomy is one kind. While roughly equal in physical appearance, the partners may represent different age groups or socioeconomic rank. Confucian sensibilities are evident in the complex variety of speech patterns used to address each partner. Yet in spite of this kind of stratification, it is often the younger and lower ranked partner who takes on the assertive role in sexual contact. The frictions of inequality, difference, and spontaneity provide the building blocks of a *yaoi*/BL narrative. Kaneda observed that many *yaoi*/BL manga stories have not been serialized. With more becoming serialized, the stories achieve more complexity. Many of the earlier works depicted tall, handsome characters with only occasional flaws. In this sense, the stories were the stuff of fantasy.[97] Typically, while *yaoi*/BL catered to women readers, there was a small line of manga catering to gay men. Recently the boundaries have blurred as the *fujoshi* have expanded their taste to stories of working people and more depictions of muscles, body hair, and skin lines.[98] The inclusion of skin lines and other bodily features, called *oyajibyōsha* オヤジ描写 (depictions of dad), does not mean that warts and all are drawn. The manga medium allows for these features to be selected. The characters might be still handsome and tall, but now they might have hairy legs.

Amateur manga creators have pioneered the *yaoi*/BL genre. In their *dōjinshi*, amateur creators have experimented with this kind of narrative, most commonly by using parody. Characters from popular manga titles will be chosen for a tryst that has no climax, no resolution, and no significance. However, the content and discourse patterns attributed to *yaoi*/BL have begun to be found in mainstream manga. In 2005, *Shūkan Shonen Jump* carried a new title called *TAIZO MOTE KING SAGA*. This story contained numerous parodies of previous manga characters and scenes, but particularly draws on *JOJO'S BIZARRE ADVENTURE*, including boys love allusions and outright appropriations of graphics and text, as shown in figure 2.14. *JOJO* had also been carried in the same magazine, *Shūkan Shonen Jump*. Together with *dōjinshi* of the same urtext, this body of manga works has come to be called *jojoparo* ジョジョパロ (parodies of *JOJO'S BIZARRE ADVENTURE*).[99] What is significant here is that a large manga publisher has realized that parody can sell. On the blogosphere, similar genres have been identified:

Figure 2.14. Contrast of Scene from *JOJO'S BIZARRE ADVENTURE* and *TAIZO MOTE KING SAGA* (Excerpt from *JOJO'S BIZARRE ADVENTURE* © 1986 by Hirohiko Araki/SHUEISHA Inc. Excerpt from *TAIZO MOTE KING SAGA* © 2005 by Dai Amon/SHUEISHA Inc.)

teniparo テニパロ (parodies of *THE PRINCE OF TENNIS*), and *wanpīsuparo* ワンピースパロ (parodies of *ONE PIECE*).

With many works devoted to parody of well-known manga at *Comiket*, issues with copyright cannot be escaped. Yonezawa Yasuhiro convened a symposium on copyright issues on the heels of a 1999 court case, involving a *dōjinshi* creator who wrote a parody of *Pokémon* and sold copies of it. The parody rendered the character in suggestive acts of pedophilia and the company, Nintendo, who held the rights, pressed charges against the creator. The news media at the time cast the story as evidence of mass pirating, even though the court acquitted the creator.[100] Yonezawa maintains that, strictly speaking, parodying is illegal. But given that most of *Comiket* is composed of amateur creators simply offering their work to any willing audience for free, there should be no issue.[101] Still it depends on the work that is being parodied. Kubota Mitsuyoshi explains that this seems to be a loosely defined area with some companies strictly forbidding parodying and others allowing it, just as long as it is not pornographic.[102] In the *yaoi dōjinshi* of well-known characters we have read, the sexual content tends not to be explicit but suggestive. Possibly, the reason it is allowed to continue is that these *dōjinshi* generate interest in the characters, thus providing publishing companies with free advertising.

Yet tensions with copyright continue. While *Comiket* is generally regarded as a carnival where most kinds of infringements might be overlooked, some *dōjinshi* creators have actively sold their work on the Internet. One such creator published a *komikku* that claimed to be the final installment of *Doraemon*. Manga creator Fujio F. Fujiko died in 1996 after completing forty-four volumes of *Doraemon*, but did not create a final work to the series. The graphics in this *dōjinshi* possessed a nearly identical resemblance to the original. After complaints from the publisher, the creator stopped selling the work, but then the value for the work soared on Internet auction sites.[103]

Comiket is only one venue for fan activity. The blogosphere involves many more people as only a fraction of manga readers are engaged in creating. The results of our own surveys of high school students indicate that less that 29 percent of girls and 9 percent of boys have ever created a manga. The blogs involve discussions around favorite titles and characters, but also information on events, such as opportunities for *cosplay*. Other blogs provide background information. Some of these bloggers engage in kinds of discourse analysis. One such blogger called MoruB is an avid fan of *Jojo's Bizzare Adventure*. He has inventoried many of the intertextualities to Western popular culture, particularly music from the 1960s through to the 1980s. Many of MoruB's identified allusions could be contested, but as far as we know, author Hirohiko Araki has not intervened, leaving fans free to speculate about his intent.[104]

We have described the history of the various streams of manga that have developed since 1945. The description was based on the historical analysis provided by Kure Tomofusa, who takes the position that the developments in this period are most influential on the nature of manga today. Still, the cultural origins are compelling to many people. The fascination with the connection of medieval and early modern pictorial art to manga today conceivably remains strongest amongst those people who are themselves manga creators—the ones most receptive to drawing. That is why Tezuka Osamu, engaged in creating, identified with the older forms. Others, such as Frederik Schodt and Natsume Fusanosuke, also come out of experience in creating. In contrast, those who minimize the connections to the older forms, such as Kure Tomofusa and Nakano Haruyuki, have never been manga creators.

Perhaps this is one sign that the study of manga is coming of age. In the study of literature, for example, a student is not judged by his or her ability to write literature. Nor does a student of the visual arts have to produce paintings. However, regarding manga as well as comics, the people who have had authority have been the creators and not the students. The landscape may be changing as more people attempt to understand the world of manga. In the following section, we review some of the sources about manga.

The Study of Manga

Because manga falls into the category of popular culture, informative sources on manga have tended to reflect the popular tone of manga themselves. Mila Bongco, writing about the status of comic research, makes the following observation:

> The problems confronting the reassessment of comics reflect the dilemmas which attend the study of other forms of popular culture: the attempts to smooth the friction between refined aesthetics and mass popularity and the struggle to legitimize its status through critical academic approval—in short, preoccupations with acceptance and hierarchies which have long plagued the field.[105]

Although manga are widely accepted as reading material for all ages, they are not considered products of high culture. Consequently, much of the commentary on manga tends not to be critical but descriptive and sentimental, prompting Sharon Kinsella to observe that many manga commentaries are "celebratory" of manga.[106]

In this section, we analyze the sources that inform us about manga. Our initial categories are the same as the two approaches to the history of manga. The sources that emphasized the cultural roots are also the same sources that tend to be celebratory of manga. These are the manga commentaries. We review these materials first, not only because they are more widely read but also because they provide valuable resources for the analysis of manga. The other approach, for lack of an appropriate title, is termed the "research" approach. These sources are not necessarily academically rigorous, but are sources in which the implied readers are students of manga studies as opposed to manga enthusiasts. These include literary criticism, social analysis, economic analysis, discourse analysis, and literacy studies. Authors of materials we cite may resist these kinds of identities, as their works may possess more functions than we acknowledge. Indeed, for example, Natsume Fusanosuke, perhaps the most prolific writer on manga, would most naturally find company with the manga commentators. Yet in recent years, he has engaged in critical analysis. For example, in 2002, he was invited as a plenary speaker to the first conference of the Japan Society for Studies in Cartoon and Comics, where he and Kure Tomofusa set the stage for manga research. He has also written *Mangagaku eno Chosen* (Challenge to manga studies), in which he plots the landscape of criticism.[107] Where we can, we would like to distinguish the work and not typify the author.

A helpful start to the study of manga is the bilingual, *A Guide to Books on Japanese Manga* written by Hosogaya Atsushi and Jaqueline Berndt.[108] As an annotated bibliography of works written in Japanese, the *Guide* provides a full-paged description of each work with helpful cross-referencing. Not all of Hosogaya and Berndt's sources are in print, and this reflects a frustrating reality of procuring valuable resources on manga.

Manga Commentary

The sources of manga commentary are written by people who are or have been closely associated with manga creation, including the development of kindred media products such as anime and video games. We have already mentioned Frederik Schodt's *Manga! Manga! The World of Japanese Comics* and *Dreamland Japan: Writings on Modern Manga,* and Paul Gravett's *Manga: 60 Years of Japanese Comics* as accessible sources of manga commentary in English. Natsume Fusanosuke, Takekuma Kentarō, Ishinomori Shōtarō, and Okada Toshio have all produced works explaining the nature of manga, the artists, how manga is created and how it is published, as well as providing numerous manga examples of the process. Ishinomori Shōtarō and John Hart also take the perspective of the manga artist, describing the layers of meaning that go into a panel.[109]

Although Natsume has published nearly thirty books on manga, arguably one of the most valuable books on understanding manga is *Manga no Yomikata* (How to read manga) where he and Takekuma Kentarō have contributed numerous chapters. The book presents manga in detail, by beginning with qualities of lines, symbols, metaphors, onomatopoeia, and the features that distinguish manga genres. Similar books on manga and comics in English often begin with drawing faces.[110] In contrast, the books by Japanese authors begin with drawing lines and descriptions of pens.[111]

Figure 2.15. Cover of *Manga no Yomikata* (Cover of *Manga no Yomikata*, edited by Inoue Manabu. © 1995 by Takarajimasha. Reprinted with permission of Takarajimasha.)

Unfortunately, *Manga no Yomikata* is out of print. Furthermore, it is not included in Hosogaya and Berndt's *Guide*, although they make reference to it. They claim that some of the content can be found in Natsume's *Manga wa Naze Omoshiroi Noka* and in Aihara Koji and Takekuma Kentarō's *Even a Monkey Can Draw Manga*. We feel that these books fall short of replacing the analytical breadth of *Manga no Yomikata*. The cover is shown in figure 2.15.

Not all commentators focus on manga alone. Instead, they present manga in the context of anime, television dramas, video games, and toys. For example, Okada Toshio in his representative work *Introduction to Otakuology* puts manga and these kindred media under the category of *otaku*. Although the term refers to people who are preoccupied with aspects of popular culture and certain products, it also refers to the popular media as well. While Okada and others are proud to identify themselves as *otaku*, many people are uncomfortable with it. This is because the name carries negative connotations of isolated individuals prone to be antisocial. As the "king of *otaku*," Okada was instrumental in shifting attitudes toward *otaku*, arguing that they are knowledgeable and smart, although awkward in social settings.[112] Perhaps he has been too successful. Recently he published a book called *Otaku wa Sude ni Shindeiru* (The *otaku* have already died) lamenting the loss of *otaku* culture's edge with its homogenization into the mainstream. Unlike many *otaku* who keep to themselves, who read and consume media products alone, Okada engages in gregarious group discussions on television.

A great deal of manga commentary is not written in expository prose, but made up of transcripts of lectures and discussions that are later edited and published as books. These transcripts represent what Norman Fairclough calls "interdiscursivity." This is a discourse phenomenon in which genres reflecting diverse purposes are mixed.[113] These transcripts in play-script format are widely used in Japan and may not be necessarily actual transcripts of speech. Instead, they function as expository text, providing information. Most likely they are heavily edited, especially by the speakers. Yet because each part is labeled with a speaker, the prose approximates the illocutionary force of spoken text. Each speaker tends to "speak" in a paragraph, and there are few instances of one-line interactions that are customary in natural discussions. It is not only the structural aspects that are problematic. The reason for the selection of participants is often opaque, prompting the question: Whose casual views are to be noted?

One example of this kind of transcript is Okada Toshio's *Tōdai Otaku Kōza* (University of Tokyo lectures on *otaku* studies). These lectures provide much information on manga and its relationship to kindred media. Moreover, they include a great deal of insight into attitudes. For example, Okada assumes his student audience is made up of *otaku*, who are considered "us," and non-*otaku*, who are considered "them." The lectures include the transcript of guest speaker, Frederik Schodt, who, in Japanese, assists Okada with his unit on manga. Another source in transcript format is the annual *Nippon Otaku Award*. This takes the form of a panel discussion with Okada Toshio, Karasawa Shuichi, Minda Nao, Kiridoshi Risaku, and Hikawa Ryusuke, plus other guests for that year. This lively discussion of the new creations in the *otaku* media takes place on commercial satellite television. The transcripts are then edited and published as a yearbook. In the two volumes that we possess, Okada is the dominant voice.[114]

An additional source in transcript format is the books on the public sponsored NHK late-night satellite television talk show, *Manga Yawa* マンガ夜話 (Manga night talk). Close to twenty volumes have been published. On the program, a theme or artist is chosen and three or four experts, many of whom are cited here, appear and exchange views, memories, and background information. The nature of information can range from technical details to sentimental reminiscences. Natsume, who regularly appears on the program, calls it *hihyōteki goraku* 批評的娯楽 (criticism with amusement). The high level of manga literacy in the viewers' responses impresses him. He finds the program a more satisfying venue for manga study than the emergent academic associations and considers it a more appropriate one, given manga's place in popular culture.[115]

The works of the commentators have provided information about manga and for many years, their works have been the only sources. The limitation of many of these materials, especially those written to introduce the world of manga, is the assumed authority. Frequently, judgments and selections of works are made without clarifying the criteria. For instance, commentators have produced catalogues of selected manga, often using a single page to show its cover, and given a synopsis and short review, without explaining the criteria for the selection.[116] In another example, the bilingual *Little Boy: The Arts of Japan's Exploding Subculture*, based on an exhibition in New York, provides an introduction to Japanese popular culture, including manga.[117] It carries a "transcript" of an interview with Okada, providing English-language readers with an example of his conversations. Many interesting works were included in the collection, but the selection begs the question, why these particular ones? The reader is asked to trust the tastes and the sensibilities of the commentators and artists.

Manga Research

Perhaps the biggest event for manga research was the establishment, in 2001, of The Japan Society for the Study of Cartoon and Comics, the first academic association for the study of manga in Japan. The society began at Kyoto Seika University, the home of the first university department for manga studies. The society is now based at the International Manga Museum, also in Kyoto. It publishes a biannual journal called *Manga Studies*. So far the journal has published a wide range of articles including literary criticism, media studies, education, and even literacy. The society could represent for the researchers what the television program *Manga Yawa* represents for the commentators, even though not all researchers and commentators associate with these venues. Curiously, while academia tends to be criticized for its ivory-tower exclusivity, the society, in the case of manga studies, is more open, allowing people with limited knowledge and experience to participate. In contrast, participation in *Manga Yawa* or a related venue is more exclusive, requiring extensive knowledge of works and contact with creators, and more importantly, name recognition through media exposure. The process of becoming a manga commentator is less transparent, like getting started in show business.

In an attempt to further manga studies based on the work of the commentators, Makino Keiichi, professor at Kyoto Seika University, has co-authored a book with Ueshima Yutaka on perspective and manga expression.[118] This is not an academic treatise on art and perspective, but a collaboration between a manga creator and physicist specializing in optics. The significance of the work is not the findings in visual behavior, but the meeting of two different epistemological traditions, exploring the kinds of knowledge that should and can be valued.

The manga researchers are beginning to clarify their epistemologies. Many works have employed linguistic analysis and literary criticism. Some of the notable ones have already been mentioned such as Kure Tomofusa's *Gendai Manga no Zentaizō* (The portrait of modern manga), Natsume Fusanosuke's *Mangagaku eno Chōsen* (The challenge of manga studies), and Yomota Inuhiko's *Manga Genron* (The principles of manga). Other works include Fuse Hideto's *Manga wo Kaibo Suru* (Dissecting manga) and Ōtsuka Eiji's *Monogatari Shōmetsuron* (The destruction of narrative). One of the difficulties with these works is that the methods are not clearly explained. Single examples from different texts are selected to illustrate an approach, without attention paid to the context of the work. Of the sources mentioned above, Yomota and Ōtsuka attempt to apply some of the critical methods associated with postmodernism. Yomota argues that choices for symbols and variations of symbols represent assumed ideologies. Yet the critical tools here do not seem to serve specific social or political positions, but instead, they are meant to serve the creators and readers. The purpose behind Yomota's critical approach is to encourage readers to break free from powerful intertextualities that inhibit the telling of new stories. On the other hand, Ōtsuka Eiji argues that symbols and narratives in manga, anime, and light novels serve specific ideological positions by which unsuspecting people are exploited.

The notion that manga is stuck in the past is eloquently described by Itō Gō in his book, *Tezuka is Dead: Postmodernist and Modernist Approaches to Japanese Manga* (author-supplied English title).[119] He shares with Yomota a resistance to the notion that, since Tezuka Osamu's work, manga is not interesting. Itō refutes this by demonstrating the complexity in the manga medium. He does so by resisting Tezuka's claim that manga graphics can be reduced to arbitrary symbols. He uses the analytical tools presented in *Manga no Yomikata*, specifically the chapter by Saitō Nobuhiko, where he lays out the structure of manga in a tripartite fashion: language, panels, and graphics.[120] Itō took the graphics portion and redefined it as *kyara*. A *kyara* is distinct from the "character." A character has a context and is firmly grounded in a narrative. A *kyara* is independent of any particular context or narrative. *Hello Kitty*, for instance, is a *kyara*. We are not reminded of a narrative when we encounter it, nor do we for many Disney characters. Itō argues that characters in narratives can achieve *kyara* status, thereby becoming available for use beyond their context. Azuma Hiroki and later Ōtsuka Eiji refer to this essential portion of characterization as the "database."[121]

Azuma's conceptual understanding of the "database" in his book *Dobutsuka no Posutomodān* (Postmodernism with animal instincts) comes out of Jean Baudrillard's notion of reality as simply simulacra or simulations. He also applies Baudrillard's work on "consumption" to the *otaku* patterns of media use. Azuma argues that narratives containing *moe* and violence are simply consumed by the individual, without reference to an "other." Yokota-Murakami Takayuki in his *Manga wa Yokubōsuru* (Manga do desire) also takes up the notion of "consumption." He provides examples from manga, including ones from American comics, illustrating how issues and methods of gender, sexuality, identity, and parody represent plural meanings. Although others have raised the question of taste and high culture regarding manga, Yokota-Murakami addresses the question by employing Pierre Bourdieu's metaphor of cultural capital. In doing so, he raises questions like: What does it mean for a work to be too manga-like? Has anyone been complimented on reading only manga?[122]

From a less critical stance, Natsume Fusanosuke begins with the aesthetic theories of his novelist grandfather, Natsume Sōseki, and mentions several approaches but provides little application.[123] This contrasts with his earlier work that offered specific ideas for analyzing manga. For Natsume, however, there seems to be other more pressing issues. The economics of manga creation, publishing, and copyright take up over half the book, and he insists these are integral to any theory of manga.[124] The reason is that the format, pace of creation, and narrative planning are all constrained by the economics of readership, so criticism must take this in mind. Yet in spite of his reference to ancient origins, like the *Chōjū Giga* and the *kibyōshi*,[125] his insistence on including the economics of manga in any theory would seem to put him together with those who emphasize the post–World War II development of manga.

The strongest work on the economics of manga is Nakano Haruyuki's *Theory of Manga Industry*.[126] Already mentioned as an advocate of the position of manga as a post–World War II phenomenon, the volume not only describes the current economic situation of manga but also provides historical background and the economics of manga's kindred media, that is, anime, video games, and television. In English, Sharon Kinsella also provides an overview of the manga industry and, furthermore, offers an intimate view of the industry based on her tenure working at a large publishing firm in Tokyo.[127]

Yonezawa Yasuhiro presents a retrospective of thirty years of the comic market industry. Although Yonezawa's ideas are in transcript format, there is a great deal of statistical analysis and historical information regarding *Comiket*'s development. Despite the wealth of data, there is little critical analysis of the *dōjinshi* movement in terms of what it represents in society or history. Building on this information and her own surveys and interviews, Kaneda Junko attempts to describe the nature of the participants in *Comiket*. More references will be made to her work below. Morinaga Takurō, whom we referred to earlier, focuses on the *moe* phenomenon and describes it in its sociological context, illustrating in detail the nature of *otaku* and how they consume media products. For example, Morinaga explains that many young and middle-aged people have difficulty making and maintaining personal relationships. Thus the *moe* character, as a receptacle for their obsession, functions as a surrogate.[128]

A further attempt to examine the social significance of manga is a book of essays entitled *Manga no Shakaigaku* (The sociology of manga). The chapters represent a broad range of scholarly quality, from informal descriptions of seminar lessons and student projects to critical applications of sociological and literary methods, such as the chapters by Ishida Saeko and Yokota-Murakami Takayuki.[129] This book has been received with mixed reviews, including a scathing rebuke of its shallowness by Natsume Fusanosuke, who accuses academics of dabbling in areas they know nothing about. He further points out that basic sources had not been consulted.[130] What then are the basic sources? If we look at Itō Gō's *Tezuka is Dead*, the analytical approach was based on *Manga no Yomikata*. Natsume, in a later article, lavishes praise on Itō for consulting basic sources and pushing manga analysis to another level.[131] We can only induce that basic sources include *Manga no Yomikata*, as Itō refers to it extensively. This book, as already mentioned, has been out of print since the mid-1990s, shortly after it was published.

Yokota-Murakami Takayuki responds to Natsume in his book *Manga wo Yokubōsuru* (Manga do desire) by likening the controversy to the debate between John Searle and Jacques Derrida. In speech act theory, promoted by Searle, illocutions, or sincerely intended speech, are central to language and, in contrast, writing, drama, and humor are "parasitic" or secondary. Derrida countered that such distinctions could not be maintained, that writing or humor are as central as speech in expressing sincere intentionality. Yokota-Murakami, by citing this example, tries to explain that manga can be approached by various epistemologies, and that these approaches need not be limited to "systemized" ones.[132]

The use of epistemologies, however, especially critical ones, can be problematic. Morikawa Keichiro cautions that they need to be applied flexibly.[133] For example, he raises a situation of applying feminism. There is a line occasionally spoken by *yaoi*/BL manga characters: "I'm not gay, but I love you." This and similar kinds of expressions have been branded as homophobic, and as a result *yaoi*/BL works have been widely criticized. Morikawa suggests that feminist researchers would be forced to distance themselves or even dismiss the *fujoshi*, the mostly women creators and readers of this genre, for such an attitude because they would need to maintain the syntagmatic link between feminist discourse and the discourse of gay/lesbian liberation, and, in the process, shirk their task of empowering a subaltern group of women.

Who are the *fujoshi*? Why do they read *yaoi*/BL manga and novels? Why is there not a corresponding GL genre, at least of *shōnen/shōjo* proportions? These are questions in the forefront of manga research today. Since *otaku*, as Okada Toshio lamented, has gone mainstream (especially for men), the category that still has an edge is *fujoshi*. Literally *fujoshi* means "corrupted woman." Yet "corrupted" is too strong. The *fu* morpheme is the same *fu* for *tofu* 豆腐. It refers to the process of transforming soybeans into curd. *Fujoshi* refers to a woman with a dirty mind, continually imagining possibilities of trysts and enjoying the combinations of unlikely couples. A male with similar practices is called *fudanshi* 腐男子 (corrupted man) or *fukei* 腐兄 (corrupted elder brother). *Fukei* 父兄 is the traditional term used for referring to parents as a group such as the PTA. Since it means, in this case, "fathers and elder brothers," it was seen as feudal and inappropriate when most of the parents coming to gatherings would be mothers. The more neutral term *hogosha* 保護者 (guardian) is preferred. The double entendre for *fukei* is irresistible.

The venue for debating *fujoshi* practices and the related cultural products is not in the academic journals, but the literary magazine *Eureka: Poetry and Criticism*. Two special issues of over two hundred pages have been published on these issues in 2007 alone. The first one featured the *fujoshi* phenomenon and within six months, there was an issue heralding "Boys Love Studies."[134] Both manga commentators and researchers participate, with academic articles and essays appearing side-by-side, interspersed with transcripts of discussions and even selections of recommended manga written in the one-page format. All the text genres of the study of manga are contained in this magazine.

Indeed, Morikawa's cautionary article reflects a frustration with the explanations offered so far for the *yaoi*/BL phenomenon. Kaneda Junko provides an extensive review of the literature and comes up with six explanations for the phenomenon.[135] They are all of a social and psychological nature, but none of them has considered the historical connections, that is, before the 1970s. In contrast, some observers such as Mark McHarry and Mark McLelland describe the connection of *yaoi* manga with *nanshoku* 男色, the representation in fiction and graphic arts of male relationships, including the traditional graphic representations of men as *bishonen* 美少年 (beautiful boys).[136] Mark McLelland further describes historical *nanshoku* patterns and the nature of homosexual relationships and queer representation in Japan today.[137] Yet in the discourse of *yaoi*/BL, these connections are not raised.

Fujimoto Yukari painfully admits that the idea she popularized in the 1990s, of women being attracted to *yaoi*/BL works because the situation of the characters reflected their own position in society, may no longer be the only reason. She argues that women's social oppression was the initial attraction, but now while oppression issues continue, women are more confident and enjoy "playing" with gender.[138] Kaneda Junko agrees that Fujimoto's ideas were instrumental in mitigating the alarmists' perplexity over these works, but unlike Fujimoto, she describes the *fujoshi* as having a "stigmatized identity" through their literacy practices of creating and reading *yaoi*/BL manga. Even the term *fujoshi*, created by the women themselves, is self-deprecating. Through her interviews and surveys, Kaneda has found that women did not want their *yaoi*/BL literacy practices be known. They were afraid people would see them as *otaku* and thus socially inept and incapable of securing a partner.[139]

We refrain from drawing conclusions about the questions surrounding the *fujoshi* and the *yaoi*/BL works. Like Kaneda's respondents, ours too were reluctant to reveal their practices. The works are evolving rapidly and so are the social attitudes and the self-assessment of the readers. The labels we use for the movement reflect this rapid evolution. What is central here are literacy practices and literacy preferences. Moreover, these practices and preferences are not neutral and carry with them issues of gender, identity, and social positionality. But before we address these issues in the next four chapters, we describe the studies specifically focused on manga literacy, studies conducted in the traditions of the social sciences.

First, there is market research by commercial publishers. The economics of manga production are sensitive to the literacy practices of manga readers. While most manga magazines rely on feedback from their own readers, there are surveys on reader preferences, for example, the annual readers' survey conducted by the *Mainichi Shimbun* (newspaper) since 1954.[140] While the survey data contain a great deal of information about the frequencies of reading books, magazines, and newspapers, as well as other media use, it is difficult to estimate actual manga reading levels as they span the categories of books and magazines.

Next, there are school-based studies. We have found an article in English written by Hatano Kanji about a 1955 survey conducted on manga reading practices in elementary school. He chose two schools, one in a working-class neighborhood of

Tokyo and the other in rural Fukushima in northeastern Japan. The rural schoolchildren had very limited access to manga compared with the city children. Although neither set of children had money to buy manga, the rural children relied on the limited resources of the school library, while the city children borrowed, lent, and used rental bookshops.[141] Like our own respondents, the practices of borrowing and lending tended to increase with age.

In the early 1990s, a group of researchers in Chiba Prefecture began to study manga literacy employing surveys and tests. Ōnishi Jun developed an instrument that measured the reading attitudes and practices of 1,256 children in grades 4 and 6, as well as the second year of junior high school.[142] Recognizing that parents might shape attitudes and practices, Takano Ryōko then surveyed 633 parents, mostly mothers, by employing an instrument that complemented Ōnishi's. The surveys produced some interesting findings. For example, those children who identified themselves as avid readers of manga also exhibited self-confidence in reading skills and drawing. Self-confidence was moreover found among the fewer children who deliberately did not read manga and, in their case, the confidence was in math and composition. The largest group, consisting of casual manga readers, tended to lack self-confidence in schoolwork, suggesting that simply being exposed to manga did not relate in either way to academic achievement.[143]

In addition to the surveys, Nakazawa Jun and Nakazawa Sayuri developed an instrument called the Chiba University Comic Comprehension Test. The test focuses on the knowledge of symbols, character expressions, and sequence of panels, as well as the ability to recall manga previously read. They developed one for young children and one for older children, up to the second year of junior high school. They found, not surprisingly, that high grades in Japanese language correlated with high scores on the test. However, other results raised more questions than they answered. For example, most of their respondents said they enjoyed reading manga, particularly the younger children. Yet many children scored low on the test. In spite of low scores, children still responded that they enjoy reading manga.[144] These seemingly contradictory results indicate the complex nature of manga literacy. As a medium to be read for pleasure, readers found aspects that interested them which were not identified or valued on the test.

In the following chapters we describe the nature of manga literacy. We begin by describing the history of literacy in Japan and the practices that people engaged in.

Summary

When compared to comics in Europe and the English-speaking world, manga is distinctive in four areas: first, the particular kinds of graphics and the multiple scripts in Japanese; second, the manner of presentation and the economics of publication; third, the complementary relationship with the kindred media of anime, light novels, mobile-phone novels, television, video games, and the cinema; and fourth, the history. The second point is of particular importance because the manner of publication actually affects the creative process and the nature of the narratives. Popular manga genres carry stories that are serialized, often with weekly installments. Less popular genres tend to have one-off stories because readers may not buy the periodicals regularly. When a periodical receives a reliable readership, the stories become serialized.

The greatest distinctiveness of manga in contrast to comics elsewhere is its history. This point relates to the particular economic patterns of publication because many believe it was the impoverished state of readers in the post–World War II period, together with American cultural influence and the presence of hard-working and talented creators, that served to shape what manga is today. Others argue that manga has a long history reaching back to the caricature drawings of the twelfth century, progressing in a relatively steady manner through the woodblock printing culture and on into the nineteenth century, when modern printing technology and Western comic drawing made an impact. Critics who emphasize the historical roots tend to be those who are interested in promoting manga as art, fighting the continual battle for its recognition as high culture. Critics who emphasize the view that manga is primarily a post–World War II phenomenon are interested in social, economic, and cultural analysis.

Among those who study the nature of manga, the more established group consists of the manga commentators. These people come out of creating manga themselves or are working in the kindred media of anime and video games. Their publications and television programs are consumed by manga enthusiasts. In contrast to the manga commentators, manga researchers are primarily academics who study manga through the epistemologies of the humanities and social sciences. Their publications are consumed by students of academic disciplines. A closer look at the works by both groups indicates a range of empirical quality, including some scholarly analyses by the commentators.

At the same time, there are those in both groups who say it is possible to analyze manga by focusing on its expressive features, without making reference to assumed ideologies or patterns of power. Others, mainly in manga research, take a critical view not only of manga's future but also of how ideologies are expressed through the medium. Using various versions of critical theory, they attempt to uncover issues of class, gender, sexuality, politics, and faith, and in doing so, elucidate social and cultural patterns. Critics who focus on manga expression tend to be optimistic of manga's future, but in the process, they are reacting against the notion that the manga produced after Tezuka Osamu and others in his generation lack creativity. They try to demonstrate that the manga created today are genuinely creative and new.

The vanguard of new manga is seen to come out of *shōjo* manga, initiated by amateur women creators and supported by mainly women readers. The fact that these *yaoi* and "Boys Love" manga deal with male-male relationships and are written for women readers continues to bewilder both commentators and researchers. To try to provide plausible explanations for the phenomenon, observers in both groups are grasping at a range of epistemological straws while the genre itself evolves, merges with other subgenres, and hurtles toward the mainstream.

As manga becomes more popular around the world, there are some people who are already imagining what a manga canon would be like. There are a number of works that might have broad agreement for inclusion. Yet it is still unclear who would be most influential—the commentator, the researcher, or the reader—in deciding which works become manga classics.

Notes

1. Jessica Abel and Matt Madden, *Drawing Words and Writing Pictures: Making Comics: Manga, Graphic Novels, and Beyond* (New York: First Second, 2008).

2. Arthur Berger, "Comics and Culture," *Journal of Popular Culture* 5, no. 1 (1971): 164–78; Elaine Millard and Jackie Marsh, "Sending Minnie the Minx Home: Comics and Reading Choices," *Cambridge Journal of Education* 31, no. 1 (2001): 25–38.

3. Thierry Groensteen, "Why Comics are Still in Search of Cultural Legitimization," in *Comics Culture: Analytical and Theoretical Approaches to Comics*, ed. Anne Magnussen and Hans-Christian Christiansen (Copenhagen: Museum Tusculanum Press, 2000), 29–41.

4. "The Muhammad Cartoons Row," February 7, 2006, news.bbc.co.uk/2/hi/4677976 .stm (accessed August 1, 2007).

5. Groensteen, "Why Comics are Still in Search," 35.

6. Frederik L. Schodt, *Manga! Manga! The World of Japanese Comics* (Tokyo: Kodansha International, 1986), 13–26; Frederik L. Schodt, *Dreamland Japan: Writings on Modern Manga* (Berkeley, CA: Stone Bridge Press, 1996), 19–32; and Okada Toshio, *Tōdai Otaku Kōza* (University of Tokyo lectures on *otaku* studies) (Tokyo: Kodansha, 1997), 124–35.

7. Yazawa Ai, *NANA 1* (San Francisco: Viz MEDIA, LLC (Shojo Beat), 2005), 149; "My Nice Husband Is a Manga Maniac," *Daily Yomiuri*, November 30, 2007, 16.

8. Will Eisner, *Comics and Sequential Art: Principles and Practice of the World's Most Popular Art Form* (Tamarac, FL: Poorhouse Press, 1985).

9. Groensteen, "Why Comics Are Still in Search," 29–41; Kure Tomofusa, *Gendai Manga no Zentaizō* (The portrait of modern manga) (Tokyo: Futaba Bunko, 1997), 17–26; Scott McCloud, *Reinventing Comics: How Imagination and Technology Are Revolutionizing an Art Form* (New York: HarperCollins, 2000), 2–3.

10. Mila Bongco, *Reading Comics: Language, Culture, and the Concept of the Superhero in Comic Books* (New York: Garland Publishing, 2000), 14–16.

11. Amy Kiste Nyberg, "Comic-book Censorship in the United States," in *Pulp Demons: International Dimensions of the Postwar Anti-Comics Campaign*, ed. John A. Lent (Madison, NJ/London: Fairleigh Dickinson University Press and Associated University Presses, 1999), 42–68; Fredric Wertham, *Seduction of the Innocent: The Influence of Comic Books on Today's Youth* (New York: Rinehart, 1954); and Bradford W. Wright, *Comic Book Nation: The Transformation of Youth Culture in America* (Baltimore: Johns Hopkins University Press, 2003), 92–98.

12. Reprinted in Reinhold Reitberger and Wolfgang J. Fuchs, *Comics: Anatomy of a Mass Medium* (Boston: Little, Brown, 1971), 248. Descriptions of the enforcement can be found in David Hajdu, *The Ten-Cent Plague: The Great Comic-Book Scare and How it Changed America* (New York: Farrar, Straus and Giroux, 2008), 305–18.

13. The following sources analyze Wertham's positions: Martin Barker, *A Haunt of Fears: The Strange History of the British Horror Comics Campaign* (Jackson: University Press of Mississippi, 1984), 56–70; Martin Barker, "Fredric Wertham: The Sad Case of the Unhappy Humanist," in *Pulp Demons: International Dimensions of the Postwar Anti-Comics Campaign*, ed.

John A. Lent (Madison, NJ/London: Fairleigh Dickinson University Press and Associated University Presses, 1999), 215–33; Wright, *Comic Book Nation*, 154–72; and Hadju, *The Ten-Cent Plague*, 97–111, 228–44.

14. Wertham, *Seduction*, 251–70.

15. John A. Lent, "Comics Controversies and Codes: Reverberations in Asia," in *Pulp Demons: International Dimensions of the Postwar Anti-Comics Campaign*, ed. John A. Lent (Madison, NJ/London: Fairleigh Dickinson University Press and Associated University Presses, 1999), 179–214.

16. Eisner, *Comics and Sequential Art*; McCloud, *Reinventing Comics*, 3.

17. Joshua S. Mostow, "Introduction," in *Gender and Power in the Japanese Visual Field*, ed. Joshua S. Mostow, Norman Bryson, and Maribeth Graybill (Honolulu: University of Hawai'i Press, 2003a), 5–10. A more detailed analysis of censorship practices can be found in Anne Allison, *Permitted and Prohibited Desires: Mothers, Comics, and Censorship in Japan* (Berkeley: University of California Press, 2000).

18. Schodt, *Dreamland Japan*, 49–53; Natsume Fusanosuke, *Manga Sekai Senryaku* (Manga world strategy) (Tokyo: Shogakukan, 2001), 86–91.

19. Lent, "Comics Controversies and Codes," 179–214.

20. Kure Tomofusa, *Gendai Manga no Zentaizō* (The portrait of modern manga) (Tokyo: Futaba Bunkō, 1997), 17–26.

21. Shimizu Masashi, *Miyazaki Hayao wo Yomu* (Reading Miyazaki Hayao) (Tokyo: Tokeisha, 2001).

22. Natsume Fusanosuke, "Manga Byōsen Genron" (The theory of drawn lines), in *Manga no Yomikata* (How to read manga), ed. Inoue Manabu (Tokyo: Takarajimasha, 1995), 52–59; Takekuma Kentarō, "Dōgu to Tacchi no Hyōgen Hensen Shi" (The history of changes in expression in terms of drawing tools and techniques), in *Manga no Yomikata* (How to read manga), ed. Inoue Manabu (Tokyo: Takarajimasha, 1995), 38–51; and Saitō Nobuhiko, "Hajime ni 'Sen' Ariki" (In the beginning there is a "line"), in *Manga no Yomikata* (How to read manga), ed. Inoue Manabu (Tokyo: Takarajimasha, 1995), 26–37.

23. Natsume, *Manga Sekai*, 15–18.

24. Scott McCloud, *Understanding Comics: The Invisible Art* (New York: HarperPerennial, 1994), 51; Rosemary Huisman, "Narrative Concepts," in *Narrative and Media*, ed. Helen Fulton, Rosemary Huisman, Julian Murphet, and Anne Dunn (New York: Cambridge University Press, 2005), 11–27.

25. Kurekoshi Sakuya, *Little Dog Liar Cat* (Tokyo: Oakla Shuppan, 2005), 159.

26. Christopher Hart, *Manga Mania: How to Draw Japanese Comics* (New York: Watson-Guptill, 2001); Kōji Aihara and Kentarō Takekuma, *Even a Monkey Can Draw Manga* (San Francisco: Viz Media LLC, 2002); Comickers Magazine, ed., *Japanese Comickers: Draw Manga and Anime like Japan's Hottest Artists* (New York: Collins Design, 2003); and Comickers Magazine, ed., *Japanese Comickers 2: Draw Manga and Anime like Japan's Hottest Artists* (New York: Collins Design, 2006).

27. Masami Toku, "Cross-cultural Analysis of Artistic Development: Drawing by Japanese and U.S. Children," *Visual Arts Research* 27, no. 1, 2001, www.csuchico.edu/~mtoku/vc/Articles/toku/Toku_Cross-cultural_VAR01.html (accessed June 29, 2008); Brent Wilson, "Becoming Japanese: Manga, Children's Drawings and the Construction of National Character," in *The Arts in Children's Lives: Context, Culture, and Curriculum*, ed. Liora Bresler and Christine M. Thompson (Dordrect, The Netherlands: Kluwer Academic Publishers, 2002), 43–55.

28. Even elaborate schemes like Matthiessen's domain model do not appear to account for these aspects. Christian M. I. M. Matthiessen, "The Multimodal Page: A Systemic Functional Exploration," in *New Directions in the Analysis of Multimodal Discourse*, ed. Terry D. Royce and Wendy L. Bowcher (Mahwah, NJ: Lawrence Earlbaum Associates, 2007), 40–43.

29. Hart, *Manga Mania*, 139–43.

30. John E. Ingulsrud and Kate Allen, *Learning to Read in China: Sociolinguistic Perspectives on the Acquisition of Literacy* (Lewiston, NY: The Edward Mellen Press, 1999), 90–96.

31. For example, John Downing, *Comparative Reading: Cross-national Comparisons of Reading Achievement* (New York: Macmillan, 1973); Makita Kiyoshi, "The Rarity of Reading Disability in Japanese Children," *American Journal of Orthopsychiatry* 38, no. 4 (1968): 599–614.

32. Kato-Otani Eiko, "Story Time: Mothers' Reading Practices in Japan and the U.S.," Harvard Family Research Project, 2004, www.gse.harvard.edu/hfrp/projects/fine/resources/digest/reading.html (accessed April 11, 2008).

33. Takano Ryōko, "Hahaoya to Manga: Hahaoya Eno Ankēto Chōsa Kara" (Mothers and manga: A survey to mothers), in *Kodomo to Manga: Manga Dokkairyoku wa Dō Hattatsu Suruka* (Children and manga: How manga comprehension develops), ed. Akashi Yōichi and Nakazawa Jun (Tokyo: Gendaijidōbunka Kenkyūkai, 1993), 55–84.

34. Tezuka Osamu, *Manga no Kokoro: Hassō to Tekunikku* (The mind of manga: The inspiration and techniques) (Tokyo: Kobunsha, 1994), 73–77; Natsume Fusanosuke, *Manga no Chikara: Seijuku Suru Sengo Manga* (The power of manga: The maturing of postwar manga) (Tokyo: Shōbunsha, 1999), 196–203.

35. Kure, *Gendai Manga*, 105–11.

36. Saitō Nobuhiko, "Manga no Kōzo Moderu" (A model of manga structure), in *Manga no Yomikata* (How to read manga), ed. Inoue Manabu (Tokyo: Takarajimasha, 1995), 220–23.

37. Yomota Inuhiko, *Manga Genron* (The principles of manga) (Tokyo: Chikuma Shobo, 1994), 14–19.

38. John Jerney, "Tezuka's Manga Faces Tough Transition to New Media," *Daily Yomiuri*, August 21, 2007, 18.

39. CLAMP, *X 15* (Tokyo: Asuka Comics, Kadokawashoten, 2000), 62–63.

40. McCloud, *Understanding Comics*, 74.

41. Abel and Madden, *Drawing Words*, 44.

42. Our findings are analyzed in Nagai Ryō, "An Essay on Panel Transitions: Panel-to-panel no Kanōsei" (bachelor's thesis, Meisei University, 2007), 15–23. The Keio University study is analyzed in Kurata Keiko, "Manga no Yomi ni Okeru Shinteki Kikō: Moji to Gazō no Yugōteki Chikaku to Monogatari Seisei" (The central structure of reading manga: The integration of script with graphics, and the generating of narratives), www.cirm.keio.ac.jp/media/contents/2002kurata.pdf (accessed June 5, 2006).

43. Sharon Kinsella, *Adult Manga: Culture and Power in Contemporary Japanese Culture* (Richmond, UK: Curzon, 2000), 180–88; Schodt, *Dreamland Japan*, 68–72.

44. Natsume, *Manga Sekai*, 69–73.

45. Aso Tarō and Hirokane Kenshi, "Orijinaru Kakuryō Kaigi" (Original cabinet meeting), *Big Comic Original* 34, no. 26 (Tokyo: Shogakukan, 2007), 1–3.

46. Ikeda Riyoko, *Berusaiyu no Bara* (Rose of Versailles) (Tokyo: Shueisha, 1972).

47. Schodt, *Dreamland Japan*, 275–82; Shimizu Masashi, *Miyazaki Hayao wo Yomu* (Reading Miyazaki Hayao) (Tokyo: Tokeisha, 2001), 133–212.

48. Koshino Ryō, "N's Aoi," *Morning* 7 (Tokyo: Kodansha, January 31, 2006), cover and 8.

49. Natsume, *Manga Sekai*, 52–54; Okada, *Tōdai Otaku*, 124.

50. "Art Unfurled, Meters at a Time: Glamorous Genji Frolicking Frogs Featured on Ancient Scrolls," *Daily Yomiuri*, May 4, 2006, 13; Shinnichiyō Bijutsukan (New Sunday at the museum), April 23, 2006.

51. The two figures depicting the *Chōjū Giga* are renditions in Yamada Yoshihiro, "Hyougemono," in *Morning* 43 (October 11, 2007), 395–96.

52. Peter F. Kornicki, *The Book in Japan: A Cultural History From the Beginnings to the Nineteenth Century* (Leiden, The Netherlands: Koninklijke Brill NV, 1998), 78–168.

53. Mary Elizabeth Berry, *Japan in Print: Information and Nation in the Early Modern Period* (Berkeley: University of California Press, 2006), 31.

54. Kornicki, *The Book in Japan*, 137.

55. David Pollack, "Marketing Desire: Advertising and Sexuality in Edo Literature, Drama and Art," in *Gender and Power in the Japanese Visual Field*, ed. Joshua S. Mostow, Norman Bryson, and Maribeth Graybill (Honolulu: University of Hawai'i Press, 2003), 71–88.

56. Shimizu Isao, *Nempyō Nihon Mangashi* (Chronological history of Japanese manga) (Kyoto: Rinkawa Shoten, 2007), 6–8.

57. Adam L. Kern, *Manga from the Floating World: Comicbook Culture and the Kibyōshi of Edo Japan* (Cambridge, MA: Harvard University Asia Center, 2006), 141.

58. Natsume Fusanosuke, *Manga no Fuka-Yomi, Otona-Yomi* (Deep reading and adult reading of manga) (Tokyo: Īsuto Puresu, 2004b), 93–97; Schodt, *Dreamland Japan*, 136–39.

59. Joshua S. Mostow, "The Gender of *Wakashu* and the Grammar of Desire," in *Gender and Power in the Japanese Visual Field*, ed. Joshua S. Mostow, Norman Bryson, and Maribeth Graybill (Honolulu: University of Hawai'i Press, 2003b), 49–70.

60. Kern, *Manga, Floating World*, 152.

61. Schodt, *Manga! Manga!*, 38–49.

62. Kure, *Gendai Manga*, 120–22.

63. Paul Gravett, *Manga: 60 Years of Japanese Comics* (London: Laurence King Publishing, 2004), 23.

64. "Paper plays" in Schodt, *Manga! Manga!*, 62; "paper theatre" in Gravett, *Manga: 60 Years*, 38; and "picture cards" in Kinsella, *Adult Manga*, 24.

65. Yomota, *Manga Genron*, 14–19.

66. Tezuka Osamu, *Shintakarajima* (New treasure island) (Tokyo: Shintakarajimasha, 1947); Fuse Hideto, *Manga wo Kaibo Suru* (Dissecting manga) (Tokyo: Chikuma Shinsho, 2004), 56–58.

67. Kure, *Gendai Manga*, 118–25.

68. Kure, *Gendai Manga*, 126.

69. Wright, *Comic Book Nation*, 155.

70. Gravett, *Manga: 60 Years*, 6–7.

71. Okada Toshio, *Otakugaku Nyūmon* (Introduction to otakuology) (Tokyo: Shinsho Oh! Bunko, 1996), 293–305.

72. Kure, *Gendai Manga*, 114.

73. Nakano Haruyuki, *Manga Sangyōron* (Theory of manga industry) (Tokyo: Chikuma Shobō, 2004).

74. Nakano, *Manga Sangyōron*, 25–28.

75. Nakano, *Manga Sangyōron*, 32–39.

76. Schodt, *Manga! Manga!*, 67.

77. Japan Economic Report. "Japanese Publishing Industry October-November, 2006," www.jetro.go.jp/en/market/trend/industrial/pdf/jer0611-2e.pdf (accessed September 12, 2007).

78. Nakano, *Manga Sangyōron*, 210–18.

79. Nakano, *Manga Sangyōron*, 256.

80. Schodt, *Manga! Manga!*, 62.

81. Gravett, *Manga: 60 Years*, 132–35.

82. Nakano, *Manga Sangyōron*, 53–55.

83. Naiki Toshio, "Kashihon Manga no Hakkō Nendo Kakutei no Hōhō Nitsuite" (A method for determining the publication dates for rental manga), *Manga Studies* 4 (2003): 180–89.

84. Hasegawa Yutaka, *Kashihonya no Boku wa Manga ni Muchūdatta* (Living in a book rental shop, I was obsessed with manga) (Tokyo: Sōshisha, 1999).

85. Naiki, "Kashihon Manga," 186.

86. Kure, *Gendai Manga*, 144–48.

87. Matt Alt and Hiroko Yoda, *Hello, Please! Very Helpful Super Kawaii Characters from Japan* (San Francisco: Chronicle Books LLC, 2007).

88. Sugiyama Akashi, "Komiketto 30 Shūnen Kinen Chōsa Kekka Hōkoku" (Comiket thirtieth anniversary survey results), in *Komikku Māketto 30's Fuairu* (Files from the thirtieth comic market), ed. Yonezawa Yasuhiro (Tokyo: Comiket, 2005), 290–305.

89. Ishida Kanta, "As Comic Market Grows, Its Focus Shifts," *Daily Yomiuri*, September 7, 2007, 13.

90. Hotta Junji, *Moe Moe Japan* (Moe moe of Japan) (Tokyo: Kodansha, 2005), 100–101.

91. Morinaga Takurō, *Moe Keizaigaku* (The economics of moe) (Tokyo: Kodansha, 2005), 45–58, 27–31.

92. Kubota Mitsuyoshi, *Dōjin Yōgo Jiten* (Dictionary of dōjin terminology) (Tokyo: Hidekazu System, 2004) 283.

93. Fujimoto Junko, "Kankeisei Kara Miru BL no Genzai" (BL today in terms of relationships), *Eureka: Poetry and Criticism* 39, no. 16 (2007): 89–95.

94. Mary Kennard, "Amateur Manga Flourishing," *Daily Yomiuri*, January 26, 2002, 11.

95. Kaneda Junko, "Yaoi Izu Araibu" (Yaoi is alive), *Eureka: Poetry and Criticism* 38, no. 1 (2006): 166–78.

96. Kazuko Suzuki, "Pornography or Therapy? Japanese Girls Creating the Yaoi Phenonenon," in *Millennium Girls: Today's Girls Around the World*, ed. Sherrie A. Inness (Lanham, MD: Rowman & Littlefield, 1998), 243–67.

97. Kaneda, "Yaoi Izu Araibu," 175–76.

98. Yamada Tomoko, "Boizu Rabu to Nakanaori: Shitataka ni Ikiru Manga no Naka no Gei Kyarakutātachi" (Reconciling with boys love: Tough living gay characters in manga), *Eureka: Poetry and Criticism* 39, no. 16 (2007): 82–88; Yoshimoto Fumiko, "Gei Manga to BL Manga no Ekkyō" (Crossing the boundaries between gay manga and BL manga), *Eureka: Poetry and Criticism* 39, no. 16 (2007): 247–48.

99. Dai Amon, *TAIZO MOTE KING SAGA* (Tokyo: SHUEISHA INC., 2005), 42; Araki Hirohiko, *JOJO'S BIZARRE ADVENTURE* (Tokyo: SHUEISHA INC., 1986), 46; and Minagawa Hiroshi, "*Jojo no Kimyō na Bōken*: Parodī-Inyō" (Parody and allusion in *Jojo's Bizarre Adventure*) (bachelor's thesis, Meisei University, 2007).

100. Kubota, *Dōjin Yōgo*, 259–60.

101. Yonezawa Yasuhiro, *Manga to Chosakuken: Parody to Inyō to Dōjinshi to* (Manga and copyright: Parody, citing, and *dōjinshi*) (Tokyo: Comiket, 2001), 6–11, 19–22.

102. Kubota, *Dōjin Yōgo*, 180–82.

103. Fukuda Makoto, "*Doraemon* Fanzine Ignites Copyright Alarms," *Daily Yomiuri*, June 17, 2007, 22.

104. MoruB (Tsuremoru), "Jojo to Ongaku no Kimyō na Kankei" (The bizarre relationship between Jojo and music), homepage3.nifty.com/supermalts/jojotop.htm (accessed May 2, 2008); Minagawa, "Jojo no Kimyō."

105. Bongco, *Reading Comics*, 14–15.

106. Kinsella, *Adult Manga*, 101.

107. Natsume Fusanosuke and Kure Tomofusa, "Jōdan Kara Koma: Manga Hyō? Manga Ron? Manga Gaku?" (From jokes to panels: Manga discourse, manga criticism, manga studies), *Manga Studies* 1 (2002): 6–39; Natsume Fusanosuke, *Mangagaku Eno Chōsen* (The challenge to manga studies) (Tokyo: NTT, 2004a).

108. Hosogaya Atsushi and Jacqueline Berndt, *A Guide to Books on Japanese Manga* (Yokohama: Asian *Manga* Summit Japan Executive Committee, 2002).

109. Ishinomori Shōtarō, *Ishinomori Shōtarō no Manga-ka Nyōmon* (Ishinomori Shōtarō's manga artist course) (Tokyo: Akita Shoten, 1998); Hart, *Manga Mania*.

110. Hart, *Manga Mania*, 5–17; McCloud, *Understanding Comics*, 24–59.

111. Aihara and Takekuma, *Even a Monkey*, 3–17; Ishinomori, *Ishinomori Shōtarō*, 39–41; Saitō, "Hajime ni 'Sen' Ariki," 26–37; and Tezuka, *Manga no Kokoro*, 45–63.

112. Natsume, *Mangagaku*, 24–26; Kaneda Junko, "Manga Dōjinshi: Kaishaku Kyōdōtai no Poritikusu" (Manga *dōjinshi*: The interpretive community's politics), in *Bunka no Shakaigaku* (The sociology of culture), ed. Sato Kenji and Yoshimi Shunya (Tokyo: Yuhikaku Arma, 2007), 186; and Okada Toshio, *Otaku wa Sude ni Shindeiru* (The *otaku* have already died) (Tokyo: Shinshosha, 2008).

113. Norman Fairclough, *Analyzing Discourse: Textual Analysis for Social Research* (London: Routledge, 2003), 35; Kawamata Takanori, "The Aftermath of an Accident of a Uranium Processing Plant: A Critical Discourse Analysis of Public Briefing Minutes," *Annual Bulletin of the Graduate School of Humanities and Social Sciences, Meisei University* 4 (2006): 12.

114. Nippon Otaku Taishō Jikkō Iinkai, *Nippon Otaku Taishō 2003* (Nippon Otaku Award 2003) (Tokyo: Fusosha); Nippon Otaku Taishō Jikkō Iinkai, *Nippon Otaku Taishō 2004* (Nippon Otaku Award 2004).

115. For example, *Manga yawa*; Natsume, *Mangagaku*, 18–23, 28–33.

116. For example, Fujimoto Yukari, Murakami Tomohiko and Yumemakura Baku, *Tatsujin ga Erabu Josei Notameno Manga Bunko 100* (The experts' choice of 100 manga for women) (Tokyo: Hakusensha, 2004); and Inoue Manabu, *Kono Manga ga Sugoi* (These manga are awesome) (Tokyo: Takarajimasha, 1996).

117. Murakami Takashi, "Earth in My Window," in *Little Boy: The Arts of Japan's Exploding Subculture*, ed. Takashi Murakami (New York: The Japan Society/New Haven, CT: Yale University Press, 2005), 98–149.

118. Makino Keiichi and Ueshima Yutaka, *Shikaku to Manga Hyōgen: Kagaku to Manga no Nabegēshon* (Perception and manga expression: Navigating science and manga) (Kyoto: Rinkawa Shoten, 2007).

119. Itō himself provided this English title. The book is *Tezuka izu Deddo: Hirakareta Manga Hyōgenron e* (Tokyo: NTT Shuppan, 2005).

120. Saitō, "Manga no Kōzo," 220–23.

121. Azuma Hiroki, *Dobutsu-ka Suru Posuto Modān: Otaku Kara Mita Nihon Shakai* (Postmodernism with animal instincts: Japanese society as seen by *otakus*) (Tokyo: Kodansha, 2001), 71–94; Ōtsuka Eiji, *Monogatari Shōmetsuron: Kyarakutāka Suru "Watashi," Ideorogikā Suru "Monogatari"* (The destruction of narrative: "Me" as becoming a character, "the story" as becoming ideology) (Tokyo: Kadokawashoten, 2004), 56–58.

122. Yokota-Murakami Takayuki, *Manga wa Yokubō Suru* (Manga do desire) (Tokyo: Chikuma Shobō, 2006), 176–80.

123. Natsume, *Mangagaku*, 50–59

124. Natsume, *Mangagaku*, 70–177.

125. Natsume, *Manga no Fuka-Yomi,* 93–101.

126. Nakano himself provided this English title. The book is *Manga Sangyōron.*

127. Kinsella, *Adult Manga*, 50–69, 162–201.

128. Yonezawa Yasuhiro, *Komikku Māketto 30's Fuairu* (Files from the thirtieth comic market) (Tokyo: Comiket, 2005); Kaneda, "Manga Dōjinshi," 163–190; and Morinaga, *Moe Keizaigaku.*

129. Ishida Saeko, "Dare no Tame no Manga Shakaigaku: Manga Dokusharon Saikō" (Sociology of manga for whom? Reconsidering the theory of manga readers), in *Manga no Shakaigaku* (The sociology of manga), ed. Miyahara Kōjiro and Ogino Masahiro (Kyoto: Shakaishisōsha, 2001), 157–87; Yokota-Murakami Takayuki, "Manga to Manga Hihyō: Riron to Sakuhin no Kankei no Kaitai ni Mukete" (Manga and manga criticism: Toward an understanding of the relationship between theory and the work), in *Manga no Shakaigaku* (The sociology of manga), ed. Miyahara Kōjiro and Ogino Masahiro (Kyoto: Shakaishisōsha, 2001), 34–67.

130. Natsume Fusanosuke, *Manga no Ibasho* (The place of manga) (Tokyo: NTT, 2003), 242–43.

131. Natsume Fusanosuke, Miyamoto Hirohito, and Itō Gō, "Kyara no Kindai—Manga no Kigen: Tezuka izu Deddo wo Megutte" (The *kyara* of today—the origins of manga: Regarding *Tezuka is Dead*), *Eureka: Poetry and Criticism* 38, no. 1 (2006): 53.

132. Yokota-Murakami, *Manga wa Yokubō*, 8–10.

133. Morikawa Keiichiro, "Sūji de Miru Fujoshi" (*Fujoshi* through the numbers), *Eureka: Poetry and Criticism* 39, no. 16 (2007): 128–29.

134. "Fujoshi Manga Taikei" (*Fujoshi* manga as super category), *Eureka: Poetry and Criticism* 39, no. 7 (2007): 1–206; "BL Sutadīzu" (Boys love studies), *Eureka: Poetry and Criticism* 39, no. 16 (2007): 1–270.

135. The review is in Kaneda Junko, "Yaoiron, Asuno Tameni Sono 2" (*Yaoi* theory for tomorrow 2), *Eureka: Poetry and Criticism* 39, no. 16 (2007): 48–54. The six positions are in Kaneda, "Manga Dōjinshi," 168–69.

136. Mark McHarry, "Yaoi: Redrawing Male Love," www.guidemag.com/temp/yaoi/a/mcharry_yaoi.html (accessed November 12, 2007); Mark McLelland, "Local Meanings in Global Space: A Case Study of Women's 'Boy Love' Web Sites in Japanese and English," *Mots Pluriels* 19 (2001): 1–22.

137. Mark McLelland, *Queer Japan from the Pacific War to the Internet Age* (Lanham, MD: Rowman & Littlefield, 2005), 16–35.

138. Fujimoto Yukari, "Shonen Ai/Yaoi-BL: 2007 Nen Genzai no Shiten Kara" (*Shonen* love/*Yaoi*-BL: From the perspective of 2007), *Eureka: Poetry and Criticism* 39, no. 16 (2007): 36–47.

139. Kaneda, "Manga Dōjinshi," 184–90.

140. *Dokusho Yoronchōsa 2008 Nenban* (2008 reading survey) (Tokyo: Mainichi Shimbun Tokyo Honsha Kōkokukyoku, 2008).

141. Hatano Kanji, "Children's Comics in Japan," in *Japanese Popular Culture*, ed. Hidetoshi Kato (Tokyo: Tuttle, 1959), 103–8.

142. Ōnishi Jun, "Kodomo to Manga: Kodomo Eno Ankēto Chōsa Kara" (Children and manga: From a survey to children), in *Kodomo to Manga: Manga Dokkairyoku wa Dō Hattatsu Suruka* (Children and manga: How manga comprehension develops), ed. Akashi Yōichi and Nakazawa Jun (Tokyo: Gendaijidōbunka Kenkyūkai, 1993), 11–54.

143. Takano Ryōko, "Hahaoya to Manga: Hahaoya Eno Ankēto Chōsa Kara" (Mothers and manga: A survey to mothers), in *Kodomo to Manga: Manga Dokkairyoku wa Dō Hattatsu Suruka* (Children and manga: How manga comprehension develops), ed. Akashi Yōichi and Nakazawa Jun (Tokyo: Gendaijidōbunka Kenkyūkai, 1993), 55–84.

144. Nakazawa Jun and Nakazawa Sayuri, "Manga Dokkairyoku no Hattatsu: Manga ga Wakaru Towa Nanika? Manga Dokkairyoku Chōsa Kara" (The development of manga comprehension: What does it mean to understand manga? Results from a Manga Comprehension Instrument), in *Kodomo to Manga: Manga Dokkairyoku wa Dō Hattatsu Suruka* (Children and manga: How manga comprehension develops), ed. Akashi Yōichi and Nakazawa Jun (Tokyo: Gendaijidōbunka Kenkyūkai, 1993), 85–189; Nakazawa Jun, "Manga no Koma no Yomi Riterashī no Hattatsu" (The development of manga panel reading literacy), *Manga Studies* 7 (2005): 6–21.

Manga in the History of Literacy 3

DISCOVERING THAT THE LITERACY OF manga texts involves almost all Japanese people at some point in their lives, the Chiba manga literacy researchers Akashi Yōichi and Nakazawa Jun remarked that any theory about the Japanese people must include manga.[1] In the previous chapter, we presented manga in terms of the history of graphic representation, from playful animals on temple scrolls and social dramas in woodblock print publications through to modern cartooning. We also presented manga in terms of the history of popular publishing, particularly the history of manga's development since the end of World War II. In this chapter, we explain manga in terms of the history of literacy, particularly the development of literacy in Japan.

Literacy has traditionally been defined as the ability to read and write. Once these skills have been mechanically learned, it is assumed that they can be applied across a range of texts since literacy is considered to be a transferable skill. Part of the function of schooling is mastering this ability to read and write. The mechanical nature of literacy is especially apparent in the texts used in school. The meaning of these texts is believed to be accessible, as the readers only have to understand, that is, recognize and decode the words on the page. Moreover, because written text often relies less on contextual features such as facial features and shared information, the meaning in the text is regarded as sufficiently self-evident.[2] Brian Street has described this perspective as the "autonomous model of literacy."[3] This autonomous model of literacy is further exemplified by the way reading is tested.[4] On examinations, reading passages are generally short, anonymous, and decontextualized, which test takers are supposed to understand by virtue of paying attention to the linguistic code. Admittedly, reading passages take on these features because brevity, anonymity, and decontextualization are seen to keep the test fair and free from bias. Moreover, readers encounter these texts only once. However, this interpretation of literacy, particularly the kind of literacy skills that are capable of being measured on conventional tests, is limited and does not account for a range of realities.[5]

To begin with, literacy takes place in a social context.[6] People learn to read and write so that they may communicate with others. In recent years, there has been an emphasis in literacy studies on examining how people use literacy in their daily lives.[7] This shift in interest to the users and the contexts of everyday literacy tasks recognizes that there are many kinds of literacies, depending on the medium, the purpose of engagement, and the social environment. The idea of a single all-embracing literacy has been replaced by the terms multiple literacies or multiliteracies.[8] The change in terminology reflects recognition of the enormous diversity of the types of media and the texts they contain that are currently available. The change also reflects an awareness of how language and power are interrelated in the texts. Shirley Brice Heath focused on the ways texts were used in the home and school among several communities of readers.[9] For Heath, the home and school were two key contexts or domains of use. She found that for some users, literacy in these two domains was unrelated, so much so that literacy practices in the home were seen as hindering success in school. Her work highlighted how attitudes to the roles of literacy and literacy practices vary, particularly in relation to social class and race. It also emphasized that some literacy skills and practices are more valued than others, especially in view of power relations in society.

The literacy skills needed for popular culture literacy such as for light novels, comics, and video games are not highly valued. Drawing on the work of Basil Bernstein, Gemma Moss argues that informal literacies are very different from school literacy.[10] They differ in the ways they are learned, how they are organized, and their functions. Although numerous people have raised the differences between school literacies and popular culture literacies, both are interrelated. In this chapter, we describe the kind of literacies that are acquired in school to explain how school literacy supports manga literacy. In the following chapters, we attempt the opposite, demonstrating how manga literacy might impact school literacy.

In spite of the complexities of its written scripts, Japan has long been considered a highly literate nation. The reasons for this are multiple and involve a complex history of linguistic borrowing, gendered literacy practices, and urbanization. The relationship between social contexts of Japan's history of literacy development and the kinds of literacy skills and practices people engaged in are closely linked to what we describe as "manga literacy."

Literacy in Japan

"Literacy" is conceptualized in Japanese educational circles most often as *yomikaki nōryoku* 読み書き能力 (the ability to read and write) or simply *literashī* リテラシー. Yet *literashī* is most usually collocated with *joho* 情報 (information), so therefore it refers more to the "new literacies" rather than to conventional reading and writing. Still, in non-educational contexts, literacy is conceptualized merely as the ability to decode scripts. The term *shikiji* 識字 reflects this focus and so does the term for literacy rates, *shikijiritsu* 識字率. Indeed, English-language newspapers are still referred to as *eiji shimbun* 英字新聞 (English-script newspapers). Modern Japanese makes use of four different scripts, thus it is not surprising that the initial skills of decoding appear to be prominent over other literacy skills. We have described earlier how the four scripts are actively exploited in manga for literary and graphic effects. A skill limited to decoding would miss a great deal of the message and the delights of rule-breaking pragmatics. The rules for specific script use are based on historical development and have evolved through the centuries.

Development of Scripts

Although the exact date is unclear, by the seventh-century Chinese orthography and texts in Chinese had arrived in Japan via Korea.[11] Later, some linguistic influence came directly from the Yangzi delta region. Through the texts on Confucianism and Buddhism, the Japanese aristocracy came to understand the kinds of texts that were to be valued. The necessary literacy skills were acquired with a goal to read these genres of texts. Since these Confucian and Buddhist texts contained a great deal of moral teaching, it was quickly assumed that those who could access them would be influenced by them and therefore become exemplary moral beings. Their literacy skills and thus their sense of judgment, learned from the texts, made the readers qualified for bureaucratic positions.

The high value of literacy prompted the emperor to establish in Kyoto the *Daigakuryō* 大学寮 (school of great learning), where the sons of aristocrats and high officials learned to read and write. There they studied Chinese literature and Confucian texts.[12] To learn to read and write Chinese was not easy. Chinese and Japanese languages are unrelated in any typological sense; Chinese is part of the Sino-Tibetan language family, while Japanese is widely regarded to be related to the Altaic language family that also includes Korean and Mongolian.[13] Although some scholars dispute this typology, most recognize the relationship between Japanese and Korean. Despite the enormous differences between Japanese and Chinese, Chinese characters (*kanji*) were adopted by the Japanese. This was not a practical decision linguistically nor a wise decision educationally, but such was the prestige of Chinese culture. As Florian Coulmas points out, the borrowing of a script even when it is based on an unrelated language is not unprecedented, as illustrated by the continued adoption of the Sumerian script by Sumeria's various conquerors and neighbors, even after the use of spoken Sumerian had disappeared by 1900 BCE.[14]

The Japanese borrowed a writing system and in doing so had to deal with new concepts and grammatical differences. There were several ways in which *kanji* were adapted into Japanese and since these patterns were based on the actual practices of users rather than authoritative prescriptive rules, the variations have contributed to the complexity of reading and writing in Japanese. Moreover, the influence from China came at different historical periods and from different regions, thereby reflecting divergent language varieties.

Texts could be written according to the patterns of Chinese writing, without reflecting the Japanese language. To mitigate this problem, one approach was to use the Chinese characters, yet written in such a way that they could be understood in

Japanese.[15] This led to a writing style called *kanbun* 漢文 in which only Chinese characters were used, but with markers added to indicate Japanese syntax. Although there were some variations of *kanbun*, it became the most highly regarded writing style and, as such, was used in official documents and educating the elite.[16]

Another approach to developing a writing system was to borrow Chinese characters on the basis of pronunciation. Characters that had a similar sound to a Japanese word were used, regardless of their meaning. Here pronunciation was the driving force. Using symbols to represent sounds rather than meaning is known as the *rebus* principle, which Coulmas maintains is an important step in the development of writing systems, as demonstrated by writing in Egypt and Sumeria.[17] A rebus is a symbol with both a phonological value and a semantic value, but takes on only the phonological value. Since any language has a finite set of sounds and syllables, a script that represents these sets would be more efficient because fewer symbols would be needed.

The custom of assigning to certain characters a phonological value was already practiced in China. Buddhist texts, for instance, contained sutras transliterated from Sanskrit. The following example contains the first few syllables of a prayer expressing belief in the Amitaabha (Amida) Buddha. The characters all have meanings of their own, but here they are used solely as phonological markers:

	南	無	阿	彌	陀	佛		南	無	阿	彌	陀	佛
Chinese	nan	wu	a	mi	to	fo	*Japanese*	na	mu	a	mi	da	butsu

The Chinese pronunciation above is written in *Hanyu Pinyin* based on contemporary *Putonghua*, and thus would not represent the historical Chinese varieties that Japanese borrowed from. Yet there are some syllables that indicate a similarity. Gradually, Chinese characters were selected to represent Japanese phonological sounds. This is how *manyōgana* 万葉仮名 evolved and became popular in the writing of poetry.[18]

By the ninth century, *manyōgana* was streamlined, leading to the development of a new script, *katakana*. Derived from parts of Chinese characters and in some instances retaining the same pronunciation, *katakana* was a set of symbols representing syllables in Japanese and was used alongside Chinese characters. Content words were written in *kanji*, while the function words were written in *katakana*. This combination of *kanji* and *katakana* meant that texts could be annotated and ideas written and understood more easily.

At the same time and based on similar principles of using certain *kanji* to represent Japanese syllables, another script, *hiragana*, was developed. Unlike *katakana*, *hiragana* was used for private or informal texts, such as letters and diaries. Although *hiragana* is often called women's script, as it came to be widely used by women, Christopher Seeley maintains that both men and women wrote in *hiragana*.[19] Most of the texts using *hiragana* did not have the same social currency as those written in *kanji* because of their informal function. Ki no Tsurayuki, in writing his tenth-century travelogue *Tosa Nikki*, posed as a woman and wrote the work in *hiragana*. Later in the eleventh century, a woman aristocrat, Murasaki Shikibu, wrote the novel-like epic, *The Tale of the Genji*, in *hiragana*.

Gradually different writing styles developed, in which *kanji* was combined with either *katakana* or *hiragana*. For instance, *sōrōbun* 候文 was the name of a style generally used in letters and semi-official documents. It combined *kanji* and *kana* scripts and was thus easier to read and write.[20] Although some texts did use *kanji* together with the two *kana* scripts, generally there was a distinction between when to use the latter. Seeley claims that *katakana* was more often used by men in formal texts, such as legal documents, commentaries, and dictionaries.[21] On the other hand, *hiragana* was more frequently used in informal or private texts, such as letters, diaries, poetry, and prose, especially by women. Thus the writing styles differed in terms of formality and function. However, this distinction was only a general one and became increasingly blurred through the centuries, as texts would be written in *kanji* together with the two *kana* scripts.

By the early twentieth century, *katakana* was used for certain brand names and women's names. Today, it is used mainly to indicate words that have a foreign origin. In addition, the script is used for emphasis and innuendo, such as in manga speech balloons or casual discourse. *Katakana* is thus the marked form. On the other hand, *hiragana* is used for grammatical markers, *furigana*, unmarked speech, and, like *katakana*, some proper names.

The introduction of *kanji* and the development of Japanese scripts also influenced the ways the texts could be read. Words could be read aloud in two ways, *on yomi* 音読み and *kun yomi* 訓読み. *On yomi* reflects more closely the Chinese origin of a word and would be represented by its Sino-Japanese equivalent. This reading tends to stand for single syllables, not independent words. These syllables or morphemes are called bound forms, thus appearing in texts with other characters in compound or polysyllabic words. Because the *on yomi* was used in Chinese style texts like *kanbun*, even today the *on yomi* evokes a more formal register. In contrast, *kun yomi* represents the local Japanese pronunciation and these readings tend to be free forms, as words that can stand alone, usually in polysyllabic form.[22]

However, Chinese characters continued to be borrowed and adapted into Japanese throughout the centuries and so pronunciation patterns, as well as the meanings assigned to *kanji*, varied.[23] Some characters that came via Korea were pronounced in ways that imitated the patterns in northern China filtered through Korean. Other pronunciations came directly from the Yangzi Delta and were pronounced in ways that imitated the Wu variety of Chinese used in the delta region. But even this distinction was not clear cut, as there were also pronunciations that came from northern China via the Grand Canal to the Yangzi Delta and then directly over to Japan. The various pronunciation patterns made it difficult to read *kanji*, since a character could have several different *on* readings. In addition, there could also be multiple *kun* readings as Japanese changed over time. As a result, individual words could be read in a number of ways. In the following example, there are multiple *on yomi* and *kun yomi*. The bound forms are indicated by hyphens.

上   (up, high)

on yomi	kun yomi
jo-	ue
sho-	kami
	nobo-
	a-
	age-

This example has two *on* readings and five *kun* readings. Writers of literary texts, especially poets—and manga creators—take great liberties by assigning their own readings to *kanji*. Most will add *furigana* to indicate the pronunciation of their unique readings. These extra readings are often used in given names. We have found the simple task of typing a student name list can be extremely time consuming. Most word processing software contain only the accepted *on* and *kun* readings. If we know the usual *on* and *kun* readings that is fine, but for the many low frequency *kanji* often used in given names, a dictionary needs to be consulted for each one.

Today, the basic list of approximately two thousand *kanji* that has to be learned by the end of middle school has about four thousand *on* and *kun* readings.[24] Becoming literate in Japanese is thus a complex process. Seeley maintains that currently three thousand to three thousand five hundred *kanji* are used in texts found in daily life, such as newspapers and popular magazines, considerably more than the amount taught in school.[25] Yet this is less than the number of *kanji* used before the script reforms following World War II. Despite the difficulties of becoming literate in Japanese, many people made the effort and they have been doing so for several centuries, particularly during the Edo period (1603–1868).

Spread of Literacy

Although literacy in Japan was initially confined to the elite, it slowly filtered down to the other social classes, especially with the use of styles such as *sōrōbun* which combined *kanji* and *kana* scripts. This was clearly seen during the Edo period with the expansion of the publishing industry and growth of a reading public. Mary Elizabeth Berry gives the example of a group of Kyoto publishing companies that had, in 1692, seven thousand titles organized into forty-six categories.[26] Peter Kornicki points out that this growth in publishing was also evident in the provinces and so was not confined to large cities such as Edo (present-day Tokyo), Kyoto, and Osaka.[27] During this period, literacy was important as a means of political control, as well as providing access for self-improvement and pleasure. The reason literacy was seen as a tool for maintaining political power was the ideology contained in the texts. The Tokugawa rulers actively encouraged Confucianism and the underlying ethical system of human relationships and social classes.[28] The ideology contained in the texts supported the positions of those in power. Brian Street, based on his work with Koranic readers in northeastern Iran, describes literacy as taught and acquired for ideological purposes.[29] Around the world, many societies that place religious texts as central to their ethos also promote an ideological model of literacy. Reading Confucian texts in East Asia was seen as influencing the reader's moral-ity.[30] This understanding of literacy provided legitimacy to the civil servants who passed the centuries-old Chinese civil service examinations. At the same time, the efforts toward ideological uniformity in Japan were largely indirect. The Tokugawa government did not frequently engage in overt censorship and, at the same time, rarely employed the burgeoning commercial publishing industry to promote its own ends.[31] Perhaps it was the industry itself that promoted the ideology. Berry makes the following observation: "Cultural literacy and collective identities, nation, and popular histories—these were projections not of the state but of commercial publications."[32]

Under the Tokugawa rulers, each feudal lord was expected to build an elite school (*hankō* 藩校) to educate his sons and those of the samurai. Although the emphasis was on Confucian texts and therefore the study of *kanji* and formal styles, Richard Rubinger maintains that there was most likely wide variation in literacy levels among the upper classes.[33] At the same time, during this period, a large urban middle class composed mainly of shopkeepers and skilled artisans grew, especially in Edo. They were in the economic position to hire tutors for their sons. In addition to private tutors, there were also local schools called *terakoya* 寺子屋, or temple schools. These had been in existence since the fifteenth century and were initially run by Buddhist priests. However, by the seventeenth century, the *terakoya* became secular and run by commoners.[34] Estimates on the number of *terakoya* vary, but Byron K. Marshall claims that there were about 15,500 such schools throughout Japan, with 1,200 in Edo alone.[35] Recently, it has been suggested that the numbers have been underestimated and that, in fact, there may have been many more such schools. Despite differences in numbers, it is quite clear that the number of *terakoya* grew exponentially in the nine-teenth century.[36] In addition to the *terakoya*, there were *shijuku* 私塾 (special private schools) for further education.[37] These schools taught a wide range of subjects includ-ing Confucianism, military studies, medicine, and, toward the end of the eighteenth century, Dutch studies. (Holland was the only Western contact in this period and its traders were confined to Nagasaki.) Students, mostly men, were generally of a higher social class and older, as the texts were more demanding.

Both boys and girls could attend *terakoya*. Boys usually studied for four years and the girls for five years.[38] The main purposes of the *terakoya* were to teach children to read, write, and learn basic arithmetic. Girls could also learn domestic skills, such as sewing and flower arranging. The schools were generally small and run by one teacher with a class of thirty to sixty students. Although there were male and female teach-ers, the majority were men. The students did not need to go every day, so attendance varied. Most of the day was spent silently practicing writing. At the end of the day, the students practiced reading or went over their arithmetic as they sat in groups around the teacher. The Tokugawa authorities were more interested in the education of the upper classes, so the *terakoya* teachers were free to use their own methods and materials. Since the students represented a range of ages and background, much of

Figure 3.1.   *Terakoya* Classroom (Excerpt from the *Ehoneikashu* by Katsukawa Shunsho. Reprinted with permission of Tokyo Metropolitan Foundation for History and Culture Image Archives.)

the curriculum was individualized.[39] Children began with learning to write the *kana* scripts, numbers, and the characters for common personal names. As they became more skilled, they learned more difficult *kanji*. They studied by practicing calligraphy in copybooks, following the models provided by teachers as in the 1790 woodblock print above (see figure 3.1). In addition to literacy, there was a wide range of subjects offered. These included the abacus, ethics, law, history, and geography, all with vocabulary lists, thereby emphasizing the practical nature of the education. Ichikawa Hiroaki and Ishiyama Hidekazu point out that there were three kinds of testing.[40] One was on the exactness of calligraphy. The second was vocabulary, with school children expected to memorize the corresponding *kanji*. The third was both a presentation and a test at an event held three times a year. These were formal occasions, at which the teacher and students wore their best clothes. The families and community were also invited.

The *terakoya* were not centrally organized, but they had a curriculum, textbooks, tests, and teachers. The schools varied considerably, depending on the teachers and geographical location. The earliest surviving curriculum dates from 1710. There were a huge variety of textbooks, over seven thousand, many of which were written by the teachers themselves. Most of the books, called *ōraimono* 往来物, had illustrations and text in the three scripts. The books with illustrations were published much like the *kibyōshi* described in chapter 2. Illustrations together with a short story were used in books and cards to teach the *kana* scripts and *kanji*. The combination of illustrations, text, and cards or panels emphasizes similarities to manga. The stories generally had a strong moral message. Ronald Dore describes how one of the most popular copybooks, *Teikin Ōrai* 庭訓往来, was based on a set of letters written by aristocrats hundreds of years earlier.[41] The letters contained a great deal of moral teaching for a variety of situations. Students learned to "read" the book by memorization rather than by understanding the context. Part of this moral emphasis was due to a revival of Confucian and Neo-Confucian studies. Since these texts would be difficult to read

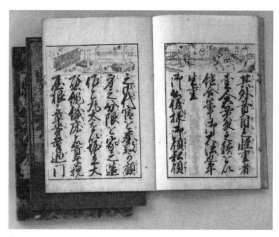

Figure 3.2.   *Shōsoku Ōrai* (Reprinted with permission of Tokyo Metropolitan Foundation for History and Culture Image Archives.)

because of the greater use of *kanji*, this in turn lead to widespread use of *furigana*, which provided pronunciation glosses of *kanji* in *kana*, thus ensuring, as they do today, access to reading material of a higher level and often more interesting content.[42] In figure 3.2 above, there is an example of the *Shōsoku Ōrai* 消息往来 that also presented letters, but instead of focusing on the moral content of the letters, the emphasis was on the rhetorical aspects of letter writing.[43] Notice the ubiquitous use of *furigana*.

Thanks to the *terakoya*, literacy gradually spread throughout Japan. Dore maintains that by 1660, all village headmen had to be literate, that is, be able to read official notices.[44] However, since there were mainly economic differences between the urban and rural areas, the richer urban areas provided more opportunities. In the urban areas, text was ubiquitous: on shop signs, on names of inns, in account books, in almanacs, and in official notices about town duties such as fire prevention. There were bookshops, used bookshops, and lending libraries, all of which indicate that literacy was not just confined to the upper classes. It is estimated that by the 1830s, there were 800 lending libraries in Edo, about 1 for every 1,250 inhabitants.[45] Most of the commercial publishing was of prose text, generally fiction, and, on average, three thousand titles were published annually.[46] However, many of these publications were also in the multimodal *kibyōshi* format. Books were published in "simple vernacular language with phonetic glosses of less familiar characters"—in other words, with *furigana*.[47] This would make them accessible to a large number of readers outside of the elite. Together with the circulating libraries and thus the sharing of books, it would suggest that in the late Edo period, literacy was more widespread than indicated by publishing figures alone.

Nevertheless, literacy aptitude levels varied, such as being able to comprehend text with multiple scripts, being able to write, and being able to read short texts that accompanied illustrations that were commonly used to clarify the moral message in stories. There were many who could not comprehend any text, especially in the remote rural areas. To emphasize the different kinds of literacies that were more likely available, Marshall Unger is critical about the claims of widespread literacy in Japan during the Edo period.[48] He maintains that the reading of *kanji* was greatly facilitated by the use of *furigana*, rather than there being widespread skill in both reading and writing. Furthermore, being able to read and write *kanji* depended more on social class, profession, and access to continued schooling and reading materials. Unger believes that there was a range of literacy proficiency and that low-level literacy skills were more common. His claims illustrate the difficulty of assessing literacy levels in early modern Japan. Most estimates are measured indirectly by consulting attendance records at *terakoya* and other schools, with little information on the actual abilities of people. Yet since attendance at *terakoya* varied, this would make estimates of literacy difficult to determine. On the other hand, foreign observers were impressed by literacy standards in Japan, although Rubinger points out this was probably *kana* literacy.[49] For instance, toward the end of the Edo period, a member of the Prussian government mission to Japan, Friedrich Albrecht Graf zu Eulenberg, was surprised by the easy access to books and the high levels of literacy, even among the lower classes. A British visitor, Bishop George Smith of Victoria, Hong Kong, who was able to visit a number of schools and observed classes, made similar comments.[50]

The Edo period did lead to a rise in literacy across the social classes, but it was during the next period, the Meiji era (1868–1912), that a centralized education system was formed and, as a result, a greater promotion of literacy. With the restoration of the emperor in 1868 and the creation of a constitutional government, an aggressive modernization program was implemented. The new rulers viewed an educated populace as essential for economic development, which in turn would lead to a strong modern Japan capable of resisting foreign imperialistic powers. Meiji leaders such as Mori Arinori stressed the importance of economic wealth and a strong military. Thus all children had to attend school initially for four years, which was then later extended to six years. There they learned the standard language. The new national educational system in 1871 enabled the establishment of public schools all over the country.

The Meiji government was able to build on the schools and literacy levels that had developed in the Edo period. This meant that many of the *terakoya* and teachers continued to function since the state was unable to supply buildings and teachers. But as Rubinger points out, literacy levels varied widely and this situation continued well into the twentieth century.[51] He bases his claims on the results of army literacy tests. With the introduction of conscription in 1889, the army tested the literacy levels of all conscripts. The results were used to determine the appropriate training for the conscripts. Conscription and testing continued to the end of World War II. The lowest levels of the literacy test were below elementary school levels and included categories such as having some or no ability to read and write one's name. Conscripts did not fail the test, as they could not leave the army. Instead, they were directed to different kinds of training. Rubinger maintains that at least in the early part of twentieth century, even after the introduction of compulsory education, regional differences continued. These differences were more influential on literacy levels than gender. In more remote parts of Japan such as in Kyushu and Hokkaido, literacy levels were low for both men and women. Peter Kornicki refers to an assessment of literacy levels in a village in rural Nagano in 1881.[52] In spite of the introduction of compulsory education, only 23 percent of the village men could write more than their names and addresses. This assessment indicates a gap of educational opportunities between cities and rural areas and also a gap in opportunities to use literacy skills.

Despite the regional variation, gradually in the twentieth century, more and more children attended school and literacy rates improved. This was not necessarily good news. As literacy levels rose, the authorities became concerned about what young people were reading. The army and the education ministry felt that young people were becoming morally decadent because of the kinds of texts they were reading. Carol Gluck describes how the education ministry wanted teachers to "scrutinize the contents of books read by students and pupils. Those that were deemed beneficial should be encouraged, while those likely to arouse unwholesome results . . . should be strictly prohibited both in and out of school."[53] Popular literacy such as newspapers, magazines, and novels were seen to be leading young people astray. The ministry wanted to control reading through promoting the building of libraries and lectures on social education. Patriotism with stories about war heroes was to be encouraged, rather than thrillers and romances. However, as Gluck points out, this was impossible because of the continued expansion of the publishing industry, the increasing use of the written vernacular language, and the growth of education and literacy. By 1911, for instance, there were 236 newspapers published in Japan.[54] Although they used *kanji*, the newspapers also used *furigana* so they could be read by a wide audience.

Over the years, there were changes in the kinds of texts to be read, the number of *kanji* taught in school, and the ways of writing. Regarding the latter, a new, more colloquial writing style that reflected a closer relationship between spoken and written Japanese developed and, by the 1940s, was considered acceptable enough to be used in official government documents.[55] Yet the path to literacy was not easy, especially learning *kanji*. This prompted some critics to demand script reforms that included abolishing *kanji*. One of the most persistent critics of using *kanji* was the army training department, as they had to work with conscripts who had varying levels of literacy. Other critics, such as newspaper companies, wanted a limit on the amount of *kanji* that could be used so that a wider audience could read the papers. The *Osaka Asahi Shimbun* inserted *furigana* for all instances of *kanji*.[56] This action was in response to the reality that the *kanji* used in newspapers could only be read by a minority. Newspapers continued to use varying amounts of *furigana* until the post–World War II script reforms. For the most part, the demands for script reform were strongly rejected by the government, especially before 1945. Even so, by 1940, the military had to restrict the number of *kanji* and increase the use of *kana* in training manuals and for weapons when faced with increasing numbers of less educated conscripts.[57]

Despite the difficulties of reforming the scripts, literacy was a considered a distinct set of skills, as well as a set of beliefs that reflected Japanese values and culture.

For those in power, national identity and literacy were interrelated. Being literate was more than being able to read and write because literacy was seen to promote the nation's strength and future. So strongly did the Japanese government believe in the ideological role of literacy, it made certain that literacy in Japanese was enforced in its colonial empire. In Taiwan, Korea, and later in the territories occupied during World War II, such as present-day Indonesia and Hong Kong, all schoolchildren were required to learn to read and write Japanese and take Japanese names.[58] Being part of the Japanese empire meant becoming literate in Japanese and sharing the same values, including one's name. Teachers and materials were sent from Japan to the colonies and occupied territories to ensure that these standards were met.

With its defeat in 1945, Japan lost its colonial empire and became an occupied nation until 1952. The occupying powers moved quickly to reform what they believed had caused Japan to go astray. One of the key areas targeted for change was education and thus literacy.[59] The allied occupation powers believed that unless there was script reform, it would not be possible to educate the populace to function in a democratic society. Some reformers suggested the abolition of *kanji*, so that all Japanese could be able to read the constitution, laws, and official documents. Literacy skills were seen to facilitate democracy and freedom. However, there was much disagreement about the actual nature of the script reforms, especially the role of *kanji*. In the end, it was decided to leave the details of the reforms to the Japanese government.[60]

On one level, the changes were radical and contentious. School textbooks were revised to ensure that the prewar militaristic ideas were replaced by more democratic values. The *kanji* script was retained and simplified. The script reform also led to changes in the reduction of the number of *kanji* that had to be learned in school.[61] However, on another level, there was continuity: literacy was still viewed as embodying certain accepted beliefs as well as being a set of skills to be taught in school. Furthermore, it was the role of public education to ensure that all pupils achieved the stated level of literacy. Much depended on how literacy was defined. Surveys in 1948 and later in 1955–1956 found that when literacy was defined in terms of being able to read and write *kanji*, there were large numbers of adults who were unable to do this effectively. Marshall Unger claims that because of these difficulties, it would be more practical to use the term restricted literacy. During the early postwar years, levels of *kanji* proficiency were still determined by social class and access to education.[62] The government continues to define the skills necessary to be considered literate and this has become a source of disagreement. For instance, the number of *kanji* to be learned in school was increased in 1973 and 1981.[63] At the same time, the hours spent in classes were reduced and English has been introduced into elementary school. Recent changes in the government have led to a reversal of some of these reforms and moves to increase the numbers of hours spent in school.

Throughout the twentieth century and even today in the twenty-first century, opinions have varied on just how many *kanji* children are expected to learn in school, that is, how many they should be able to recognize and actually write. These changes emphasize the varying criteria used to define literacy in Japan. As described in chapter 1, there is a sense of a crisis and growing concern over declining levels of literacy skills. Results of a survey conducted in 2006 by the National Institute for Educational Policy Research revealed that elementary and junior high school children have difficulties in reading and writing, especially *kanji*. Problems included misreading similar looking *kanji*, mispronouncing *kanji*, and not being able to recognize *kanji* that are not commonly used. Some of the reasons given for these difficulties were that as students grow older, they spend less time studying *kanji* at home, as well as the kinds of methods used for teaching *kanji*. An official was quoted as saying: "Schools should increase students' interest by using *kanji* in sentences."[64] In terms of its origins, *kanji* is a borrowed script and the *kana* scripts are indigenous yet derived from *kanji*. In spite of this history, *kanji* retains its prestige and is seen as an essential vessel of Japanese culture, so any decline in literacy skills is taken seriously.

What about *kanji* in manga? In children's manga magazines like Shogakukan's monthly *COROCORO*, almost all instances of *kanji* are rubied with *furigana*. In contrast, the *dōjinshi* parodies of well-known manga do not have any *furigana* for the *kanji*. Most commercially published manga have some *furigana*. In spite of our repeated efforts to obtain policy guidelines from publishers, we were not successful. We cannot say whether guidelines exist or not, nor that some publishers have them and others do not. As regular readers of *Morning* we do notice a variation among works, with some having more *furigana* than others. We did notice that the *komikku* version of *Doraemon*, a title that was serialized in *COROCORO*, has few instances of *furigana*. One junior editor of a large publisher mentioned that in the process of making the *komikku* versions, the size of panels must be reduced, thus making it difficult to print *furigana*. At the same time, many *komikkusu* do have *furigana*.

Many of these questions could be answered through methods of corpus linguistics. The problem is, manga cannot be scanned for print data in the way other texts can. That means all the textual data must be entered manually before the indexing and concordancing can begin. This would be a task as laborious as transcribing oral data.

Learning to Read

Given the complexity of Japanese literacy, how do children learn to read and write? In most cases, the process begins at home. Beginning with picture books, many children learn to read with their mothers at an early age at home,[65] as illustrated by this mother talking about her son.

> Interviewer: [So you started to read a picture book at four years old, did you?]
>
> Mother: [No. He started a picture book when he was one year old.]
>
> Interviewer: [I see. You read to X. And when did he read by himself?]
>
> Mother: [At four years old.]

These picture books would be mainly written in *hiragana* and, together with other kinds of children's books, are also readily available in local libraries. However, picture books, as well as children's manga, are bought by parents. It is only when they are older and receive an allowance that children can exercise greater choice in what they read. By the time children go to elementary school, Lois Peak maintains that many children would be able to read *hiragana* and simple stories.[66] With a knowledge of *hiragana*, the child would be able to also read the *furigana*, the rubies on the top or to the side of *kanji*. Here is another example of a child learning to read with a picture book.

Interviewer: [When did you start to read?] (*Addressing the child.*)

Mother: [She was two years old.]

Interviewer: [What did you read?] (*Addressing the child.*)

Mother: [It was the picture book *Nyantan.* And a cat book, don't you remember?]

Daughter: [Impossible.]

Although a number of our informants who were parents reported that they read to their children, it is questionable how widespread this practice is. As pointed out in chapter 2, Takano Ryōko found in her survey of parents that only little more than 50 percent of the respondents reported reading to their children.[67] A much larger proportion of parents watched television with their children. Indeed, the longest-running children's program on NHK, the government-sponsored channel, is called *Okāsan to Issho* [Together with Mother] to help mothers teach their children to engage in reading readiness.[68]

By the time they go to preschool, the majority of children have learned to read *hiragana* and also their name in *kanji*. There is a wide range of children's books and picture books on DVD available in bookshops and libraries. In explaining how she taught her son to read, one mother used a number of different kinds of children's books, both Japanese and translated ones. She also had to deal with different scripts.

Interviewer: [When did you start to read? Maybe your mother knows.]

Mother: [Is just a word OK? For example, Anpan-man?]

Interviewer: [Yes, that's OK.]

Mother: [He was three years old, I guess.]

Interviewer: [Was it in kindergarten or a day-care center?]

Mother: [No, it was before that.]

Interviewer: [Did you make a positive effort to teach him?]

Mother: [He wanted to know the name of a monster in Ultra-man.]

Interviewer: [I see, the name, wasn't it?]

Mother: [Yes.]

Interviewer: [So he learned hiragana?]

Mother: [Yes, hiragana and katakana. Both because a katakana word is also written in hiragana.]

Figure 3.3.   *Doraemon* (Excerpt from *Doraemon 21* by Fujiko F. Fujio. © 1981 by Tentōmushi Comics. Reprinted with permission of Shogakukan.)

Interviewer: [Oh, I see. You started with picture books.]

Mother: [Yes.]

Interviewer: [Was the first picture book Anpan-man?]

Mother: [Yes, it was, and Anpan-man, Doraemon, and another was Thomas the Train. It comes from England and the names are James and Gordon.]

Many public libraries have special activities for young children, reflecting the assumption that parents, especially mothers, are expected to encourage their children to read. For instance, at our local library in eastern Tokyo, these sessions are in the morning from 10:00 AM to 12:00 AM. Because of these hours, attending such sessions is often not possible for working mothers. At preschool, the emphasis is not on explicit language learning, but rather on training children to work together in groups.[69] However, we did find a six-year-old girl who was learning to write the *kana* scripts at her day-care center. This is how she described learning to read and write at the center:

Interviewer: [Where did you learn to read?]

Girl: [The day-care center is teaching us to read.]

Interviewer: [Does the center teach writing?]

Girl: [Yes. The teacher writes something on the blackboard and we write just one line in our notebook. Then I show my notebook to the teacher after I have written. So the teacher writes "Good work" after she checks my notebook.]

Interviewer: [Do you also learn *kanji*?]

Girl: [*Kanji* would be at school.]

Interviewer: [I see. So does the teacher teach *hiragana* and *katakana*?]

Girl: [Yes. They pass out a sheet of *katakana* and I do it.]

Figure 3.4.   Japanese Scripts in Urban Neighborhoods.

Figure 3.5.   Examples of Iconic *Kanji* in an Elementary School Textbook (Excerpt from *Hirogaru Kotoba: Shōgaku Kokugo 1 Jyō* by Kinoshita Junji and Imanishi Yuyuki. © 2007 by Kyōiku Shuppan. Reprinted with permission of Kyōikutosho Kyōkai.)

Even if this is an exceptional day-care center, children are surrounded by text at kindergartens and day-care centers. There are signs on doors, notices on the chalkboard, and children's names are written on their belongings. Both in and out of school, they would see multiple scripts, not only *kanji*, *hiragana*, and *katakana* but also in words in *romaji*, English, and possibly other languages. Figure 3.4 shows a range of signs and scripts that can be seen in an urban neighborhood.

Once children enter elementary school, the learning of *kanji* begins in earnest. As the girl in the day-care center told us, *kanji* is learned formally and only at school. In grade 1, the children have to study eighty *kanji*, beginning with the ones that seem the most iconic.[70] Examples include *ki* 木 (tree), *tsuki* 月 (moon), and *yama* 山 (mountain). A recent textbook provides the example seen in figure 3.5.[71] These are similar to the ones used in a comparable language textbook for first-year Chinese children.[72] At each grade level, the amount of *kanji* to be learned increases. By the end of grade 4, children are expected to have mastered 640 *kanji*, as well as *katakana*.[73] In grade 4, they are also taught *rōmaji*. By the end of elementary school, children would be expected to have learned 1,006 *kanji*, of which 90 percent are used in newspapers.[74] After elementary school, children move to junior high school for three more years of compulsory education. By the time they have completed these years, they are expected to know 1,945 *kanji*. Those students who continue for three more years in senior high school would spend time deepening their knowledge of Japanese through studying modern and classical literature and translating classical texts.

Although many children begin to become literate at home, school is still considered to be the place where children really "learn" to be literate, since literacy (and arithmetic) is seen as the main function of the first years of schooling. This is particularly important in Japan with the learning of *kanji*. As a result, teachers often disregard what children have learned at home, since this is not part of school literacy. This pattern of ignoring learning obtained outside of formal schooling is not unusual. For instance, in her work with Native American children, Elizabeth Noll described the gap between literacy practices in and out of school and the teachers' lack of awareness of the students' abilities.[75]

School literacy is described as a set of discrete skills that can be taught and tested, as well as a vehicle for learning appropriate values and beliefs.[76] We have already described how the link between literacy, schooling, and ideology was made in Meiji Japan. In her analysis of the rise of compulsory state schooling in sixteenth-century Germany, Carmen Luke describes how literacy was considered to be fundamental to implementing Christianity, in particular Lutheranism.[77] With ready access to the printing press, schoolbooks were able to be mass-produced. These factors led to the development of public schooling, and with it, the ranking of students by ability, curricula, and examinations. Literacy was hierarchically organized as a set of skills so that there was a steady development of skills. What was learned in one year became the basis for the next, and this hierarchical organization was reflected in the curriculum and teaching materials. Centuries later, these practices are still part of modern public schooling throughout the world, and the way literacy is defined and taught in Japan reflects this kind of approach. By being defined in such quantitative terms, school literacy becomes formalized and thus the dominant literacy, as it is the basis for success in school and, by extension, success in the work world. Poor performance in reading tests is seen as a failure on the part of the institution or even the education system as a whole to fulfill its task. This can be seen in recent proposals to increase the amount of time spent studying Japanese, in response to the low-ranking performance on international surveys of academic abilities.[78]

By becoming a standard for success, school literacy marginalizes other kinds of literacy since these are considered unimportant. Yet these other literacies do not disappear and can continue both at home and in school. For instance, the books, comics, and magazines children read at home may also be brought unofficially to school and shared with friends.[79] Indeed, one of the current themes in literacy studies is finding out what children do read out of school so that teachers may have a more accurate understanding of the range of reading skills their students actually possess. It is assumed that this knowledge would then lead to more successful teaching by enabling teachers to build on skills students already have.[80] In Japan, for example, the widely held belief that school children are not reading enough is seen as one of the main reasons for the decline of literacy, especially logical thinking and reading *kanji*.[81] Hence reading in and out of school has been actively promoted in recent years.[82]

As researchers have begun to focus on how children use literacy in their daily lives, there has been a shift from school literacy to other kinds of literacies. Rather than emphasizing the divide between literacy in school and at home, literacy is instead reconceptualized as being used in different domains such as home, friends, school, and peers. These domains may or may not overlap. Basil Bernstein distinguishes between formal, hierarchical literacy in school and informal literacy engaged in by children outside of school.[83] He maintains that the school focuses on different kinds of knowledge and skills, and, similar to the sixteenth-century German schools described by Carmen Luke, these skills are developmentally organized and the content carefully regulated. He views school literacy as on a vertical plane, in contrast to informal literacies that are on a horizontal plane where neither the texts nor skills are graded. Informal literacy is temporary in that it is subject to changes in fashion and popularity. As children's interests change, so do the kinds of knowledge and expertise they may acquire. For Bernstein, these skills are dependent on their context and so would not transfer to the school context.

There is a fundamental difference between school literacy and popular culture literacy. School literacy must be transferable to other contexts, whereas popular culture literacies like manga literacy do not have to be. Indeed, educational reform movements are often triggered by evidence of school literacy not being transferable, that is, lacking in relevance. In the following chapters, we will describe how school literacy skills do transfer to manga literacy. But the transfer is not sequential. Children engage in manga literacy before their school literacy skills are well developed. Moreover, our informants provide examples where manga literacy skills have transferred to school literacy.

Summary

Becoming literate in Japanese is a complex process not only in terms of the number of scripts that have to be learned but also because of the difficulties created by the scripts, especially *kanji*. Regardless of the differences between the Chinese and Japanese languages, the Japanese ruling class adopted Chinese characters because they valued the prestige of Chinese civilization that the script represented. Over the centuries, the uses of *kanji* developed through patterns of practice rather than prescriptive rules. This led to variations in the ways the characters could be read and pronounced. Despite these complexities, many people learned to read and write. During 250 peaceful years of the Tokugawa rule, urbanization and commercialization facilitated a vibrant publishing industry. Literacy rates began to increase not just among the elite but also in other social classes. In addition to schools for the elite, there were a wide variety of schools for commoners. This provided a basis for the creation of a national system of public schools, starting in the late nineteenth century with the new Meiji government. Education and literacy were considered to be essential for the formation of a modern industrialized state and thus had to be centrally organized. In addition, schooling and therefore literacy were also thought to be essential for the promotion of official ideology.

The end of World War II led to a reevaluation of the education system. Among the changes were script reforms, such as the simplification of certain *kanji*, changes in the number of *kanji* to be learned by the end of compulsory schooling, and changes in the content of the school texts. However, the role of the state in deciding the ways literacy is to be taught, the content of textbooks, and literacy standards continues. This emphasizes the relationship between literacy, schooling, and ideology, a relationship that exists in Japan and in most countries. Yet in spite of the emphasis on school literacy to provide collective identities and ideological conditioning, the popular media can be just as effective in constructing shared beliefs and shared senses of the past.

Unlike school literacy, popular culture literacies, like manga literacy, are not conceived in terms of "skills" and are not tested. They are engaged in by the agency of readers themselves and not imposed by power structures, although social pressures can exist. The agency of individual readers can also be driven by ideology. Manga literacy, like school literacy, is engaged in social contexts. While school literacy is scaffolded by institutions and ideology, manga literacy is scaffolded by individual agency and communities of other readers.

Notes

1. Akashi Yōichi, "Hajimeni: Kenkyū no Izu (Introduction: Research intent) in *Kodomo to Manga: Manga Dokkairyoku wa Dō Hattatsu Suruka* (Children and manga: How manga comprehension develops), ed. Akashi Yōichi and Nakazawa Jun (Tokyo: Gendaijidōbunka Kenkyūkai, 1993), 1.

2. David R. Olson, "From Utterance to Text: The Bias of Language in Speech and Writing," *Harvard Educational Review* 47, no. 3 (1977): 257–81.

3. Brian V. Street, *Literacy in Theory and Practice* (Cambridge: Cambridge University Press, 1984), 19–65.

4. Clifford Hill and Kate Parry, "The Models of Literacy: The Nature of Reading Tests," in *From Testing to Assessment: English as an International Language*, ed. Clifford Hill and Kate Parry (New York: Longman, 1994), 7–34.

5. Jenny Cook-Gumperz, "Introduction: The Social Construction of Literacy," in *The Social Construction of Literacy*, ed. Jenny Cook-Gumperz (Cambridge: Cambridge University Press, 1986), 1–15; New London Group, "A Pedagogy of Multiliteracies: Designing Social Futures," *Harvard Educational Review* 66 (1996): 60–92; J. Elspeth Stuckey, *The Violence of Literacy* (Portsmouth, NH: Boynton/Cook Publishers, 1991), 21–61; and Robert Y. Yagelski, *Literacy Matters: Writing and Reading the Social Self* (New York: Teachers College Press, 1999), 28–32.

6. For example, David Barton, *Literacy: An Introduction to the Ecology of the Written Language* (Oxford: Blackwell, 1994); Shirley Brice Heath, *Ways With Words: Language, Life, and Work in Communities and Classrooms* (Cambridge: Cambridge University Press, 1983); Sylvia Scribner and Michael Cole, *The Psychology of Literacy* (Cambridge, MA: Harvard University

Press, 1981); Brian V. Street, *Literacy in Theory and Practice* (Cambridge: Cambridge University Press, 1984); Brian V. Street, "Introduction: The New Literacy Studies," in *Cross-Cultural Approaches to Literacy*, ed. Brian V. Street (Cambridge: Cambridge University Press, 1993), 1–22; Michael Stubbs, *Language and Literacy: The Sociolinguistics of Reading and Writing* (London: Routledge & Kegan Paul, 1980), 91–115; and Allan Luke and Peter Freebody, "Critical Literacy and the Question of Normativity: An Introduction," in *Constructing Critical Literacies: Teaching and Learning Textual Practice*, ed. Sandy Muspratt, Allan Luke, and Peter Freebody (Cresskill, NJ: Hampton Press, 1997), 1–18.

7. For example, David Barton and Mary Hamilton, "Literacy Practices," in *Situated Literacies*, ed. David Barton, Mary Hamilton, and Roz Ivanič (London: Routledge, 2000), 7–15; Mike Baynham, *Literacy Practices: Investigating Literacy in Social Contexts* (Harlow, UK: Longman, 1995), 38–72; Shirley Brice Heath, *Ways With Words: Language, Life, and Work in Communities and Classrooms* (Cambridge: Cambridge University Press, 1983); and Janice Radway, *Reading the Romance: Women, Patriarchy, and Popular Literature* (Chapel Hill: The University of North Carolina Press, 1984).

8. "Multiple literacies" in Street, *Literacy in Theory*, 8; "multiliteracies" in New London Group, "A Pedagogy of Multiliteracies," 60–92.

9. Heath, *Ways With Words*.

10. Gemma Moss, "On Literacy and the Social Organisation of Knowledge Inside and Outside School," *Language and Education* 15, nos. 2 and 3 (2001): 146–61; Gemma Moss, "Informal Literacies and Pedagogic Practice," *Linguistics and Education* 11, no. 1 (2000): 47–64.

11. Florian Coulmas, *The Writing Systems of the World* (Oxford: Blackwell Publishers, 1991), 122–23; William C. Hannas, *Asia's Orthographic Dilemma* (Honolulu: University of Hawai'i Press, 1997), 32; and Christopher Seeley, *A History of Writing in Japan* (Honolulu: University of Hawai'i Press, 2000), 4–6.

12. Seeley, *A History of Writing*, 40.

13. Roy A. Miller, *Japanese and Other Altaic Languages* (Chicago: The University of Chicago Press, 1971), 1–47; Hannas, *Asia's Orthographic Dilemma*, 27.

14. Coulmas, *The Writing Systems*, 79.

15. Seeley, *A History of Writing*, 25–26 and note 33.

16. Coulmas, *The Writing Systems*, 79–89; Nanette Gottlieb, *Language and Society in Japan* (Cambridge: University of Cambridge Press, 2005), 123–24.

17. Coulmas, *The Writing Systems*, 30–32.

18. Coulmas, *The Writing Systems*, 124; Hannas, *Asia's Orthographic Dilemma*, 37; and Insup Taylor and M. Martin Taylor, *Writing and Literacy in Chinese, Korean and Japanese* (Amsterdam: John Benjamins Publishing Company, 1995), 306–7.

19. Seeley, *A History of Writing*, 78–79 and note 61.

20. Richard Rubinger, *Popular Literacy in Early Modern Japan* (Honolulu: University of Hawai'i Press, 2007), 10–11.

21. Seeley, *A History of Writing*, 100.

22. Hannas, *Asia's Orthographic Dilemma*, 29–31.

23. J. Marshall Unger, *Literacy and Script Reform in Occupation Japan: Reading Between the Lines* (New York: Oxford University Press, 1996), 18–21.

24. Taylor and Taylor, *Writing and Literacy*, 301.

25. Seeley, *A History of Writing*, 2.

26. Mary Elizabeth Berry, *Japan in Print: Information and Nation in the Early Modern Period* (Berkeley: University of California Press, 2006), 1.

27. Peter F. Kornicki, "Obiya Ihei, a Japanese Provincial Publisher," *British Library Journal* 11 (1985): 131–42.

28. Ichikawa Hiroaki and Ishiyama Hidekazu, *Edo no Manabi* (Learning in Edo) (Tokyo: Kawade Shobo Shinsha, 2006).

29. Street, *Literacy in Theory*, 95–125; Street, "Introduction," 1–22.

30. John E. Ingulsrud and Kate Allen, *Learning to Read in China: Sociolinguistic Perspectives on the Acquisition of Literacy* (Lewiston, NY: The Edward Mellen Press, 1999), 3.

31. Peter F. Kornicki, *The Book in Japan: A Cultural History From the Beginnings to the Nineteenth Century* (Leiden, The Netherlands: Koninklijke Brill NV, 1998), 12–13.

32. Berry, *Japan in Print*, 251.

33. Rubinger, *Popular Literacy*, 16–17.

34. Ronald P. Dore, *Education in Tokugawa Japan* (Berkeley: University of California Press, 1965), 254–60; Herbert Passin, *Society and Education in Japan* (New York: Teachers College Press, 1965), 27, 30.

35. Byron K. Marshall, *Learning to be Modern: Japanese Political Discourse on Education* (Boulder, CO: Westview Press, 1994), 18.

36. Ichikawa and Ishiyama, *Edo no Manabi*, 6–7.

37. Richard Rubinger, *Private Academies of Tokugawa Japan* (Princeton, NJ: Princeton University Press, 1982), 8–14.

38. Dore, *Education in Tokugawa Japan*, 254, 320; Passin, *Society and Education*, 31.

39. Dore, *Education in Tokugawa Japan*, 271–90; Ichikawa and Ishiyama, *Edo no Manabi*, 31.

40. Ichikawa and Ishiyama, *Edo no Manabi*, 32–33.

41. Dore, *Education in Tokugawa Japan*, 276–78.

42. Seeley, *A History of Writing*, 101–2.

43. Ichikawa and Ishiyama, *Edo no Manabi*, 20.

44. Dore, *Education in Tokugawa Japan*, 21.

45. Marshall, *Learning to be Modern*, 8; see also David Pollack's description of widespread advertising in Edo, as well as "Literacy Pills," in "Marketing Desire: Advertising and Sexuality in Edo Literature, Drama and Art," in *Gender and Power in the Japanese Visual Field*, ed. Joshua S. Mostow, Norman Bryson, and Maribeth Graybill (Honolulu: University of Hawai'i Press, 2003, 71–88.

46. Kornicki, *The Book in Japan,* 140.

47. Berry, *Japan in Print*, 32.

48. Unger, *Literacy and Script Reform*, 24–35.

49. Rubinger, *Popular Literacy*, 135–42.

50. Kornicki, "Literacy Revisited: Some Reflections on Richard Rubinger's Findings," *Monumenta Nipponica* 56, no. 3 (2001): 381–94.

51. Richard Rubinger, "Who Can't Read and Write? Illiteracy in Meiji Japan," *Monumenta Nipponica* 55, no. 2 (2000): 163–98; Richard Rubinger, "Comments," *Monumenta Nipponica* 56, no. 3 (2001): 395; and Rubinger, *Popular Literacy*, 162–95.

52. Kornicki, *The Book in Japan*, 275–76.

53. Carol Gluck, *Japan's Modern Myths: Ideology in the Late Meiji Period* (Princeton, NJ: Princeton University Press, 1985), 170.

54. Gluck, *Japan's Modern Myths*, 171.

55. Gottlieb, *Language and Society*, 44.

56. Seeley, *A History of Writing in Japan*, 145.

57. Unger, *Literacy and Script Reform*, 36; Seeley, *A History of Writing*, 150.

58. Leo T. S. Ching, *Becoming "Japanese": Colonial Taiwan and the Politics of Identity Formation* (Berkeley: University of California Press, 2001), 92–97; Jennifer Robertson, *Takarazuka: Sexual Politics and Popular Culture in Modern Japan* (Berkeley: University of California Press, 1998), 89–138; and Susan C. Townsend, *Yanaihara Tadao and Japanese Colonial Policy: Redeeming Empire* (Richmond, UK: Curzon, 2000), 83, 131–34, 200–201.

59. Kaori Okano and Motonori Tsuchiya, *Education in Contemporary Japan: Inequality and Diversity* (Cambridge: Cambridge University Press, 1999), 30–33.

60. Unger, *Literacy and Script Reform*, 58.

61. Gottlieb, *Language and Society in Japan*, 60; Seeley, *A History of Writing in Japan*, 152–59.

62. Unger, *Literacy and Script Reform*, 36–43.

63. Seeley, *A History of Writing in Japan*, 165–67.

64. Tomidokoro Kosuke, "Survey: Students Still Lacking Basic Skills," *Daily Yomiuri*, July 19, 2006, 4.

65. Masahiko Minami, *Culture-Specific Language Styles: The Development of Oral Narrative and Literacy* (Clevedon, UK: Multilingual Matters, 2002), 238–58.

66. Lois Peak, *Learning to Go to School in Japan: The Transition From Home to Preschool Life* (Berkeley: University of California Press, 1991), 65–66.

67. Takano Ryōko, "Hahaoya to Manga: Hahaoya Eno Ankēto Chōsa Kara" (Mothers and manga: A survey to mothers), in *Kodomo to Manga: Manga Dokkairyoku wa Dō Hattatsu Suruka* (Children and manga: How manga comprehension develops), ed. Akashi Yōichi and Nakazawa Jun (Tokyo: Gendaijidōbunka Kenkyūkai, 1993), 55–84.

68. John E. Ingulsrud and Kimiko Kai, "A Lexical Analysis of Children's TV Programs in Japan," *Visio* 24 (1997): 157–64.

69. Peak, *Learning to Go to School*, 63–65.

70. MEXT (Ministry of Education, Culture, Sports, Science, and Technology), *Shōgakkō Shidō Yōryō Kaisetsu (Kokugohen)* (Elementary school curriculum notes [national language volume]) (Tokyo: Tōyōkan, 1999).

71. Kinoshita Junji and Imanishi Yuyuki, *Hirogaru Kotoba: Shogaku Kokugo 1 Jyo* (Increasing vocabulary: Elementary Japanese 1a) (Tokyo: Kyoiku Shuppan, 2007), 84.

72. Ingulsrud and Allen, *Learning to Read*, 116.

73. MEXT, *Shōgakkō Shidō*.

74. Gottlieb, *Language and Society*, 82.

75. Elizabeth Noll, "Literacy and American Indian Students: Meaning Making through Multiple Sign Systems," in *What Counts as Literacy: Challenging the School Standard*, ed. Margaret A. Gallego and Sandra Hollingsworth (New York: Teachers College Press, 2000), 213–28.

76. Barton, *Literacy: An Introduction*, 11–12; Bernardo M. Ferdman, "Literacy and Cultural Identity," *Harvard Educational Review* 60, no. 2 (1990): 181–204.

77. Carmen Luke, *Pedagogy, Printing, and Protestantism: The Discourse on Childhood* (Albany: State University of New York Press, 1989), 3–5, 133–36.

78. "Panel: Increase Study Hours for Japanese, Math, Science," *Daily Yomiuri*, February 10, 2006, 2.

79. David G. O'Brien, "Multiple Literacies in a High-School Program for 'At-Risk' Adolescents," in *Reconceptualizing the Literacies in Adolescents Lives*, ed. Donna E. Alvermann, Kathleen A. Hinchman, David W. Moore, Stephen F. Phelps, and Diane R. Waff (Mahwah, NJ: Lawrence Erlbaum Associates, 1998), 27–50; Kate Allen and John E. Ingulsrud, "*Manga* Literacy: Popular Culture and the Reading Habits of Japanese College Students," *Journal of*

Adolescent & Adult Literacy 46, no. 8 (2003): 674–83.

80. Donna E. Alvermann, Jennifer S. Moon, and Margaret C. Hagood, *Popular Culture in the Classroom: Teaching and Researching Critical Media Literacy* (Newark, DE: International Reading Association, 1999), 22–40; Margaret A. Gallego and Sandra Hollingsworth, "Introduction: The Idea of Multiple Literacies," in *What Counts as Literacy: Challenging the School Standard*, ed. Margaret A. Gallego and Sandra Hollingsworth (New York: Teachers College Press, 2000), 1–23; Jackie Marsh and Elaine Millard, *Literacy and Popular Culture: Using Children's Culture in the Classroom* (London: Paul Chapman Publishing, 2000), 1–9; Muriel Robinson, *Children Reading Print and Television* (London: The Falmer Press, 1997), 176–86; and Adam Schwartz and Elaine Rubinstein-Avila, "Understanding the Manga Hype: Uncovering the Multi-Modality of Comic-Book Literacies," *Journal of Adolescent & Adult Literacy* 50, no. 2 (2006): 40–49.

81. "Kids Found Lacking in Logic Skills," *Daily Yomiuri*, July 15, 2006, 2.

82. "Ministry to Assign More Full-Time Librarians," *Daily Yomiuri*, October 24, 2005, 2.

83. Basil Bernstein, *Pedagogy, Symbolic Control and Identity: Theory, Research, Critique* (London: Taylor & Francis, 1996), 169–80.

The Literacy Practices of Reading Manga   4

R EADING MANGA IS WIDELY PERCEIVED AS an individual activity. We have mentioned the observation that readers of all ages read manga on public transportation. We have also referred to the practice of *tachiyomi*, browsing in shops, which appears to be an individual activity. In our surveys, we found that among young people, the preferred place to read manga is at home, thus implying manga is read alone. Indeed, mass media descriptions of *otaku* as obsessive consumers of manga and its kindred media depict them behaving so as individuals. This is not surprising as the consumption of popular culture is closely linked with individual taste, interest, and preference. For these reasons, we have described the reading of manga as involving "personal" literacies.[1]

Yet manga literacy practices as an individual activity does not fully represent the way readers engage with text. What is less well known is that reading manga is also a communal activity. We have found that even in the developmental process of learning to read manga, children learn to read in the context of other readers. We have repeatedly asserted that children learn to read manga on their own. What we mean by this is that children are not trained in a formal way, such as in school. They learn by informal means, and these informal and personal patterns of learning are often acquired in communities of practice with other readers.

In this chapter, we describe how children learn to become manga readers. We present the factors that foster children's learning, beginning with family members, then anime, and finally friends. We have put friends last because it is in the context of friends as readers that leads to a variety of literacy practices. We have included anime because the reading of manga is not done in isolation from other media. Like family members, the "kindred" media of anime, video games, light novels, and toys are connected with the reading of manga in terms of learning literacy skills, understanding stories, and appreciating characters. We focus in the chapter on watching anime, illustrating how the medium relates to the development of manga literacy. Let us first explain how we obtained our findings.

For the last ten years, we have been surveying reading practices. We were interested in the kinds of things our students read for pleasure and also how much time they actually spent on reading. The students, male and female, attended a small liberal arts college in southwestern Japan. After three years of surveys and interviews, we narrowed the focus to the reading of manga. To the interviews, we invited students whom we knew were enthusiastic manga readers. We also made it known that we were interested in interviewing anyone who wanted to share their ideas on manga. In addition to the invited students, we asked friends to recommend readers. Sometimes students came together with their friend or the friend came alone later. The interviews were mainly in Japanese, and students brought their favorite manga to share with us. Later, when we moved to Tokyo, we were able to interview more college students about their manga reading. Some of the students were members of manga clubs. All were enthusiastic manga readers.

As our interest in finding out more about manga readers deepened, we then interviewed children and their parents, both in the Tokyo area and other parts of Japan. Even those who were not keen manga readers were invited to share their experiences. The children, male and female, ranged in age from six to seventeen years. In all the interviews, we asked the readers to talk about their reading practices and their favorite manga. Parents also participated and shared their own histories of reading manga. In addition to parents, we interviewed a number of adult manga readers, both those who continued to read manga as well as those who had stopped.

Apart from these interviews and college surveys, we were later able to survey three junior high schools in two prefectures near Tokyo. The students, male and female, were all in the second and third years of public junior high school. We were unable to interview these students, but they were encouraged to write comments about their reading in open-ended questions at the end of the survey. The final survey we conducted was of senior high school students at a prestigious, competitive high school in another prefecture near Tokyo. This survey we have included in the appendix. The students, male and female, were encouraged to sign up for interviews to share their manga reading practices. These interviews were in English and/or Japanese, depending on which language the respondents wanted to use.

Throughout this period, we have focused on several areas: how readers begin learning to read manga, why they continue reading manga, and what kinds of manga they read. We have interviewed readers from six to fifty years old, male and female. We found that there is no single profile of a manga reader, but the information we have gathered, together with our own experience of reading manga, has helped us acquire a general understanding about the kind of reading done outside of the formal institution of school. This has led to an awareness of the range of literacy practices engaged in by students and thus the nature of manga literacy.

Becoming a Manga Reader

Among the respondents and interviewees, there was a variety of answers explaining how they became manga readers. For some, it was through their parents or a sibling.

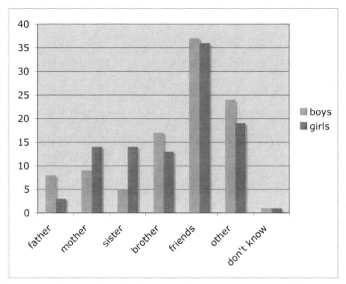

Figure 4.1.   People Who First Introduced Manga (Boys n=376; Girls n=402.)

For others, it was through friends. There were a few who indicated that they started reading on their own, yet for most, it was someone else, thus indicating that children became manga readers in a community. Even though some stated that they were not directly introduced to manga by others, the fact that manga were lying around and available suggests that the children were part of a community of readers. This indicates there can be varying degrees of involvement and agency in a community of readers. Figure 4.1 provides junior and senior high school survey results, in percentage, of the people who introduced readers to manga. It should be pointed out that the information is based on respondents remembering their first encounters with manga and that this was not possible for some of them. The results show that a community of readers is instrumental in initiating manga literacy. The community also plays a role in maintaining that literacy. For most children, reading starts in the home, which is their initial reading community.

Learning to Read Manga at Home with Parents

Once children have begun to read picture books, often with parents as described in the previous chapter, reading manga becomes another option. Most of the readers in the surveys and interviews indicated that they first started to read manga at home. Sometimes manga were lying round the house, so children picked them up to read. Manga are therefore familiar and part of the literacy practices in most homes. In a survey on reading practices, Takano Ryōko found that 90 percent of parents did not mind their children reading manga.[2] This is illustrated by a mother describing how her elementary school son began reading manga.

> Mother: [We just had *Kyojin no Hoshi* at home when he watched the anime. His dad had read it. He's (the son) read manga since starting grade 6. Haven't you?]

Son: [Yes, I have.]

Mother: [The others are manga that his dad used to have.]

Son: [*Judo Ichokusen* and only *COROCORO*, I guess. No others.]

A high school student we interviewed described how she found her favorite manga at home and her grandmother's.

Student: Yeah. I have a *Touch*, which is my mother's. When I go to my grandmother's house, found it, and I take back.

Interviewer: So you have many manga at home?

Student: Yes, my mother's bookshelf. And I research that.

Since manga were available at home, this suggests that parents were not opposed to reading them. Whether or not a family member deliberately encouraged manga reading, the fact that this kind of literacy exists in the home is evidence for its encouragement. Today in people their fifties and sixties remember frequenting the book rental shops. Parents in their thirties and forties were part of the generation that could afford to buy their own manga. They all grew up reading manga such as *Tetsuwan Atomu* (Mighty atom)[3] and later *Doraemon*.[4]

Some parents actively promoted manga to their children. One college student described how her mother was an avid fan of gothic mystery manga and so bought this kind of manga for her young daughter.

[M]y mother likes horrible stories. One day I went to a bookstore with my parents, my mother bought this book. This book looks like a horrible and my mother bought it. I didn't understand this story for the first time, but I could understand it more and more.

The daughter was only in elementary school and had difficulty comprehending the manga, but her mother insisted on buying and reading it together. Gradually, the daughter came to appreciate and then share her mother's enthusiasm for this type of manga.[5] In this instance, the daughter was invited to participate in her mother's enjoyment. A parent can also encourage children to read manga so that they identify with the characters, as we found when we interviewed a high school student about her favorite manga.

Student: [After seeing the anime on TV, my mother recommended reading the manga. The reason is that the main characters of *Touch* are twins. And so am I.]

Interviewer: [Oh, you are a twin. Do you have a twin brother or sister?]

Student: [We are twin sisters.]

Interviewer: [So your mother recommended it to you because of the story. Does your sister read it?]

Student: [Yes, she does. Tatsuya and Kazuya who are the main characters in *Touch* play baseball with each other.]

Figure 4.2. *Touch* (Excerpt from *Touch 1* by Adachi Mitsuru. © 1981 by Shōnen Sunday Comics. Reprinted with permission of Shogakukan.)

Yet not all parents are happy about their children reading manga. Instead, they would much prefer their children to read books, particularly as manga literacy is not acknowledged in school and thus seen not to be contributing to academic success. However, as this mother pointed out, she was unsuccessful in trying to control what her children read:

> [I didn't want them to read (manga) before going to school. I gave them a picture book or an ordinary book as a good thing to read. I thought manga are not good for children, but they like manga. They found *COROCORO* and others in their friends' house by themselves.]

She had wanted her children to learn to like reading books while they were still at home. Once they went to school, she knew they would become more interested in reading manga. She was able to keep manga out of the home until her oldest child went to school. When he began to going to school, he borrowed manga and brought them home. His younger sisters then started reading the manga, preferring them to books.

Mother: [Y was in first grade. She started to read with her brother.]

Interviewer: [So Y, did you read your brother's manga?]

Daughter: [Yes.]

Interviewer: [What was the first manga you read from your brother?]

Daughter: [It was *COROCORO*.]

Interviewer: [Did your brother allow you to read it?]

Daughter: [Yes.]

Faced with this situation when teaching her two young daughters to read, the mother selected suitable manga, as well as books, for her children. As a parent, she made a decision to buy appropriate manga since she knew her son would probably continue borrowing manga and bringing them home to read. Parents who try to control their children reading manga do exist, as illustrated by this mother writing about what she and her husband did:

> It became apparent when Sean began to learn to read Japanese that he could easily become a *manga* (comic book) addict. My husband was not keen on the content of *manga* targeted at elementary school boys, and limited *manga* in our house to those dealing with history or the lives of famous people.[6]

These parents all value reading, but the content of the reading matter is more important than the child's enjoyment. Manga are not highly regarded by some parents and, as a result, children may be actively discouraged from reading them. Reading, especially comics and in this case manga, is not a neutral practice and carries social class values.[7] Although most Japanese parents allow their children to read manga, few parents would equate reading manga with reading books.

Learning to Read Manga at Home with Siblings

As much as parents may be instrumental in introducing manga to children, siblings play a more influential role. Older siblings tend to have access to manga, as they can borrow them from friends or buy them. When they bring the manga home, younger siblings can read them. In a newspaper article celebrating her career, Takahashi Rumiko, the creator of several popular *shōnen* manga including *Inuyasha* and *Ranma ½*, described how she began reading *shōnen* manga as a small girl because of her older brother.[8] In our surveys of junior high school girls, if a sister introduced manga to her younger sister, it tended to be a *shōjo* manga. On the other hand, if a brother introduced manga to a younger sister, it tended to be a *shōnen* manga. It was through her sister that this college student became interested in manga:

> Student: When I was in high school, I bought and my sister bought those. My sister likes manga very much and she has about six hundred manga in her room. When I go back to home, I read hers.
>
> Interviewer: Right. Now why do you like manga?
>
> Student: I don't know, but I've learned to read manga since I was ten. And my friend and my sister read, so I read.

In the interviews, there was only one example of a boy who was introduced to *shōjo* manga by his sister. This was the case of an adult who described how his older sisters read *Berusaiyu no Bara* (The Rose of Versailles).[9] It is a story about Marie Antoinette and the French Revolution, and since he was interested in history, he began reading the manga as well. However, this reading was only done at home and not shared with friends at school.

When we interviewed an elementary school boy and his two sisters, the girls explained that they read manga because of their brother. This was especially true of the younger sister. Although only six years old and in the first year of elementary school, she insisted on talking to us about her favorite manga and then showing us how she was able to read it. The manga was her brother's and much too difficult for her because she did not know the *kanji* nor the serialized story. Even though her mother and siblings told her that she would not be able to understand, she pretended to do so. As she turned the pages, she talked about the story, making it up as she went along. Reading manga and being interviewed about reading were things her older brother and sister had done, so she was not going to be left out.

Siblings are not only helpful for introducing manga, they can also join in the pleasure of reading through sharing. For example, one elementary school reader told us how she shared the amusing parts of the manga with her older sister: "Like I show her the funny parts."

Learning to Read Manga at Home and Watching Television

In the home, aside from parents and siblings, the other main reason for starting to read manga is television. In her study of the literacy practices of second- and third-grade children in a Californian school, Anne Haas Dyson found that the children had a thorough knowledge of popular culture, much of which was gained through watching television, reading comics, and playing video games.[10] She considers this knowledge central to what she calls contemporary childhood. Similarly, children in Japan gain access to popular culture through television. Surveys have consistently shown, over the years, high rates of television viewing among all age groups.[11] However, unlike in the United States, television viewing in Japan can also be an important prompt to reading manga. Takano Ryōko reports that parents watched anime with their children almost as much as they watched other kinds of children's programs.[12] Many successful manga are made into anime, even for very young children, and can become very popular, as this six-year-old told us. (At the time, we had no idea of the wide range of anime and watched a number of them after the interview.)

Interviewer: [So did you first see this as an anime?]

Daughter: [Yes. I thought it was fun after I watched it on TV. It was from 7:30 to 8:00. *Tokyo Mew Mew* is after *Cobby* and after that is *Mirumo de Pon*.]

Interviewer: [What channels are they on?]

Daughter: [*Cobby* is Channel 6, *Tokyo Mew Mew* is Channel 12, and *Mirumo de Pon* too.]

Mother: [What day are they on?]

Daughter: [It's Saturday.]

Interviewer: [Is it in the evening?]

Daughter: [No, in the morning.]

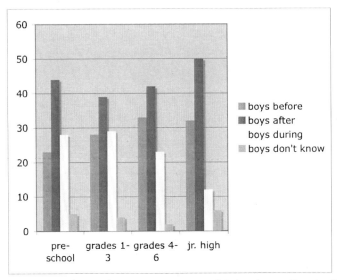

Figure 4.3.   The Relationship Between Manga and Anime Among Boys (n=90)

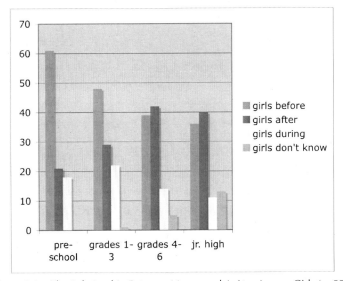

Figure 4.4.   The Relationship Between Manga and Anime Among Girls (n=93)

Anime such as *Ninpen Manmaru* (Manmaru the ninja penguin)[13] and *Mikan e Nikki* (Mikan's illustrated diary)[14] are directed at parents and their young children. As presented in figures 4.3 and 4.4, many senior high school readers began reading manga because of anime or a television program based on a manga. A note of caution needs to be made because some students did not answer the question if there was no anime based on their favorite manga. Despite this limitation, some patterns did emerge for this particular group of high school students.

When girls started reading manga and during the first few years of elementary school, they remember watching the anime before reading their favorite manga. Anime were thus important prompts to reading manga. By the time they reached upper elementary school, the pattern changed and they tended to read manga first and later watched the anime version. On the other hand, the boys differ in that they were more likely to find and read their favorite manga before watching the anime version. In comparison with the girls, it seems that watching anime is not so important a prompt for reading manga. As the readers become older, especially junior high school boys, it is not surprising that watching an anime does not trigger the initial reading of the manga because by then students are generally reading a wide range of titles. This particular group of senior high school students indicated that they were currently reading 123 different titles. The list does not include manga magazines with multiple stories, such as *SHŪKAN SHŌNEN JUMP*,[15] nor overlapping categories, such as girls reading *shōnen* manga. In spite of the growth in volume of anime shown on television, most of the manga titles these older students were reading did not have anime versions.

However, for many initial readers, especially the girls, the surveys show a close relationship between watching an anime and then reading the related manga. One explanation is that a large number of young children's anime are based on manga, such as *Doraemon, Janguru Taitei* (Jungle emperor),[16] and *Bonobono*.[17] This was how an elementary school boy found a favorite manga, *ONE PIECE*[18]: ["I watched the first story on TV and it was fun, so I started to read the manga"]. A high school student was influenced by both the anime and her friends: ["Actually I saw the anime too. I saw it first and I borrowed the manga from my friends later"]. A junior high school reader described how he found his favorite manga, *DRAGON BALL*,[19] through anime: "Well, first I saw it on TV. And then we had this really crappy TV and I sort of flipped the channels. One had *DRAGON BALL* on, so I watched it and cool."

Another junior high school reader started to read a certain manga, *ONE PIECE*, after seeing it on television. Since the production of anime is slower than the pace of publication of new episodes in the serial, the student explained why he turned to the manga: ["I wanted to read the story before the anime came out"].

The influence of anime is not necessarily immediate. One college student we interviewed stated that when he first saw, as an elementary school student, the anime *Akira*, he was not interested. The story is a complex science fiction account of the collapse of Japanese society.[20] However, years later in high school, he remembered the anime and decided to read the manga, which then became his favorite:

> When I elementary school, I watched TV and *Akira*. But it was not interested. But very, very surprised. Liked the picture. So I am a high school student, I remember *Akira*. I read. And I interested in manga so I remember *Akira*. I bought *Akira* manga. I'm fever it.

Some readers became interested in watching the related anime once they had begun to read the manga or varied their patterns, as explained by this junior high school boy when talking about his two favorite manga: ["I saw the anime first. After watching the anime, I read the manga. In the case of *ONE PIECE*, I read the manga first."]. On the other hand, more readers maintained that the relationship between anime and manga was almost simultaneous; they saw the anime and, at the same time, they began to read the manga. A high school student shared a similar experience when talking about how he began reading *Doraemon*.

Interviewer: Did you read the manga first or did you see the anime first?

Student: I see. [I wonder which one I saw first. I saw both of them.]

Interviewer: [You saw both of them at the same time?]

Student: Both.

Anime seem to be very influential in encouraging people to read manga. This influence might be even stronger for manga readers outside of Japan. For instance, the South African magazine *Otaku* devotes more space to reviewing anime and games than to manga.[21] With access to a twenty-four-hour anime satellite channel, anime have become the primary source of introduction to Japanese popular culture for South Africans. When watching anime in Japan, children will see advertisements for manga and so be further encouraged to read them. Although she tried to control her son's reading, one mother described how she bought her son's first manga. He had seen an advertisement for the manga on television when watching an anime and wanted to read it. She wanted him to read books, but she knew he would borrow manga from his friends. Rather than read manga she disapproved of, she bought ones she thought more appropriate.

[I did not want him to read a particular type of manga. But there were commercials on TV. For example, TV magazines or similar manga commercials were broadcast when we watched something like *Kamen Raidā* on TV. And he said, "I want that! I want that!" So I bought one tentatively.]

The relationship between anime and manga is complex. Although most anime are based on manga, the two are different media and these differences can affect readers and viewers.[22] Some readers could only express the connection in negative terms: ["Even if the drama or the anime is made, I won't accept them. It would harm my image of the manga. I have my own image"]. A similar opinion was expressed by this high school student when asked if she would like to watch a drama or anime based on her favorite manga: ["No, I wouldn't. I'm afraid that my own image of the manga would be harmed"].

There are a number of possible explanations for the readers' negative reactions to the animated version of their favorite manga. To begin with, when changing a serialized manga to an anime, the story is shortened. It can be irritating for the reader, as this high school student told us:

Interviewer: [Is there a drama of *Fruits Basket*?]

Student: [No. There was an anime, but it was cut short so I didn't like it that much.]

On the other hand, deleting parts of the story can be helpful. For instance, one elementary school reader found the anime version much easier to understand than the actual manga.

Interviewer: [How about *Meitantei Conan?*]

Daughter: [I'm interested in the anime, but I don't understand the manga.]

Mother: [She enjoys watching it on TV.]

Interviewer: [So it's hard to read the manga, is it?]

Daughter: [Yeah.]

Although manga and anime are both based on illustrations, there are differences, which readers may not like. For instance, a junior high school boy maintained that ["manga is more fun than anime. . . . Illustrations, I thought manga is better"]. Another high school manga reader pointed out that in anime, the graphics and the pace of the presentation could be disconcerting:

[When we see anime, I can't help but pay attention to a speaking character. But in terms of manga, not only the main character but also other people have lines too. Since I can take my time to look at details closely, I can find something interesting that anime doesn't have. For instance, you can see one person who is doing something here, but another person is doing something else at the same time.]

In addition to the changes in the length, the plot, and the graphics, the strongest reason we found for disliking anime was auditory, as indicated by this elementary school boy who explained why he did not like the voices in the anime of his favorite manga: ["I felt they are different from my imagination. My imaginary voices are more agreeable. I make it a rule to imagine their voices when I read manga"]. A high school student, who was also critical, had this to say about the effects of the voices in the anime:

[The pictures of a manga and an anime don't change at all, but the voices become high-pitched. So I feel they are strange because the characters' mental age seems to be lower than that of the original characters. I feel the strangeness of the voices too. The looks of the characters are similar to the original ones, but the voices are different. I can see a manga or an anime as different works.]

College students we interviewed also reported that voices in anime seemed at a higher pitch than they had imagined. The differences between the voices in the anime and the readers' own imagined voices of the manga characters can be more disturbing than the cuts that would result from converting a long-running serial into a shorter anime. This can be seen in the following student's criticisms of the anime version of her favorite manga, *Fruits Basket.*[23]

Student: [Well, I thought the voices of the actors didn't match. I wanted to hear deeper voices. That's because I have my own image.]

Interviewer: [So you felt the voices were fake?]

Student: [Yes, I felt so. And if the actors had starred in another anime, I would be more disappointed. I don't like it. Everybody has their own imaginary voices, I think. So some people become disappointed when a manga becomes an anime or a drama. But sometimes other people say they prefer anime to manga. Therefore it depends on the people.]

The impact of the voices used in an anime seems to be more influential when the readers have already created their own imagined ones. One first-year, junior high school boy shared this opinion, but not when it came to seeing a full-length movie based on the manga. This was how he described finding out about the manga *ONE PIECE*:

[I went to see the movie of *ONE PIECE* last March with my friends. I watched the movie first. I accepted it (the voices) from the beginning. If I had read the manga first and watched the anime after that, I would have been disappointed in the differences between the voices and my imaginary ones. However, in my case, I watched the movie first and started to read the manga. So I imagine Luffy's voice every time when I read.]

The same reader preferred the anime version of *ONE PIECE* rather than the manga because the former was clearer. This is not surprising as the manga, *ONE PIECE*, is one of the more complex in layout and has been serialized for a long time:

[I prefer the anime because it has voices and this makes it easier to understand who is talking and what kind of situation it is like. For example, when the scene is at sea, the sound of waves or music in the background can describe how calm it is. That's why I can easily recognize when the scene is calm or tense.]

The voices used in anime are important, particularly as anime can have long runs and thus relate closely to the character's image. For instance, the popular children's anime *Doraemon* has been aired for more than twenty-five years. Based on the manga of the same name, the characters are easily recognizable and used in other contexts, such as advertising, thereby signifying their *kyara* status, that is, when a character transcends the narrative in which it was cast.[24] When the theme songs were changed in 2002, it prompted outpourings of regret and dismay in the national media as generations had grown up with the anime.[25] Later when the voice actors were changed, many viewers were further upset. This is how one college student described her reaction to the voice changes in *Doraemon*: "I was very shocked when I heard the news. I could not imagine the different voice for *Doraemon* and other main characters."

As they read manga, readers build up an imaginary world of characters that they "know" by the way they look and speak. Thus, when a manga is made into an anime with the addition of sound and motion, readers can be disappointed. They do not want to watch it because of the discrepancies between the anime and how they imagined the characters in the manga. Yet for some readers, particularly the younger ones, the shortened anime was easier to understand than the longer serialized manga. In addition, the nature of anime, especially the use of sound, can be helpful. On the other hand, the older students found the cuts in the plot irritating.

Furthermore, the differences between how they imagined the voices of the manga characters and the ways these were realized in the anime seemed disconcerting. The age of the readers, the complexity of the story, especially in a long-running serial, and the media features of anime are factors can influence whether or not the anime adds to or detracts from enjoyment of the manga.

Reading Manga at School and with Friends

Once children go to school, children's reading patterns change. Even though by kindergarten many children may know the *kana* scripts and thus would be able to read books with simple *kanji* and additional *furigana*, elementary school expands their reading horizons. They begin seriously to learn *kanji* and, by the end of grade 4, would be expected to know 640.[26] Knowing this amount of *kanji*, in addition to the *kana* scripts and the roman alphabet, provides students with a greater range of reading material, including manga. As indicated in figure 4.5, there is an increase in the percentage of children starting to read manga, especially between the ages of six and eight. This is when school literacy begins to make an impact on manga literacy.

Some students reported that their elementary and junior high school libraries offered manga, not just historical-literary books in manga format but also manga such as *Burakku Jakku* (Black Jack) by Tezuka Osamu,[27] *Ashita no Jo* (Rocky Joe) by Chiba Tetsuya and Takamori Asao,[28] or *Nausicaä of the Valley of the Wind* by Miyazaki Hayao.[29] These were generally donated by students. In interviews, the students pointed out that since their teachers read and appreciated manga, they saw no reason to discourage their students. For instance, a college student told us how her brother was introduced to Tezuka's *Burakku Jakku* by his elementary school teacher and that it was through her brother she began to read the manga: "My brother's elementary school teacher

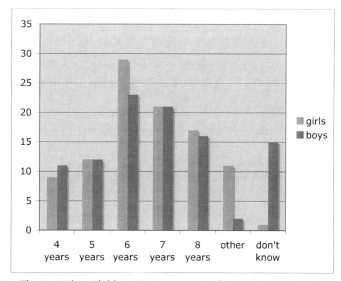

Figure 4.5.   The Age When Children First Began to Read Manga (Boys n=373; Girls n=361)

gave *Burakku Jakku* to my brother. Then I read. The manga is very famous." In addition, while she read her brother's *shōnen* manga, she also pointed out that he did not read her *shōjo* manga. A junior high school boy similarly described how his sports' teacher introduced him to manga in elementary school:

> [When I was in fourth grade in elementary school, I joined a club. I joined the basketball club and a teacher in the club told me about *Slam Dunk*, which is a manga. That's when I started reading manga. The teacher said, "This is a good manga you should read."]

Although school can play a key role in introducing children to manga, this was not the experience of most of our informants. When asked if she read manga at elementary school, a student replied: ["Manga are not allowed in school"]. Rather than for having supportive teachers and manga in the library, school is more important as being a venue for meeting people, and thus it offers the reader the possibility of having wider circles of friends.

Communities of Readers

One way of looking at children's uses of literacy is in terms of "readership networks,"[30] or communities of readers. These communities arise when readers with similar interests talk about and share their interests. Readers can belong to more than one community, thus relating to different domains such as home, school, and friends. The communities may be short-lived, as they depend on a shared interest. Once this interest wanes, the community is likely to change or disperse. These readership networks or communities of readers share similarities with the communities of practice described by Etienne Wenger. He explains a community of practice in terms of three dimensions: mutual engagement, a joint enterprise, and a shared repertoire.[31] Mutual engagement refers to the community members doing things together and the relationships that are built up through this participation. A joint enterprise focuses directly on the kind of work that the community engages in. A shared repertoire describes the stories, actions, and ways of thinking that members of a community can develop through working together.

This concept of a community of practice can be applied to the communities created by manga readers. For instance, in "lady's" comics, readers are actively encouraged to suggest plot lines, which are then used by the writers. Some of these manga include readers' comments and photographs in the margins of the stories,[32] thereby emphasizing the sense of community created by readers and writers. Our survey and interview data indicate that there were communities of manga readers. Readers share a common interest in manga and in certain titles. They may borrow and lend manga. They may read them together at friends' homes, on the way to school, or *tachiyomi* in a convenience store. They may talk about the stories and characters. They may collect and exchange manga. All of these practices correspond to Wenger's three dimensions, particularly his notion of a shared repertoire. Readers may vary in how many practices they engage in at different ages, yet belonging to a community of readers is an important part of developing their literacy skills.

In his survey of fourth, sixth, and eighth graders, Ōnishi Jun asked his respondents what topics they talked about.[33] The three top categories were very close in number. The most popular topic was talking about friends. The second was television and the third was manga. From our earlier discussion of anime, we can assume that there is a large degree of overlap between the second and the third topic. To take part in these conversations, the child needs access to television and manga.

Being part of a community of readers is one of the ways children become proficient readers. As they talk about texts, they learn ways of interpreting texts and can also get assistance when they do not understand. Since communities of readers are built around shared interests, children can gain status within the group, depending on their knowledge of the texts. In her study of children watching horror videos, Gemma Moss described the ways children used their often-limited knowledge of horror videos to establish themselves as experts in their readership network and also to build up their knowledge of the genre because most of the children were not allowed to watch these kinds of videos.[34] We also have observed that possessing access to manga, which friends may read or borrow, can provide status in their communities.

Borrowing and Lending
By creating communities of readers, children find a space and friends for sharing reading. For many young children, such as in Britain, the United States, and Japan, comics are an important shared text and can be the basis of a community of readers.[35] Having friends who read manga and thus share the same interest is important. Figures 4.6 and 4.7 summarize, in percentages, the information provided by the junior and senior high school students about their friends who read manga.

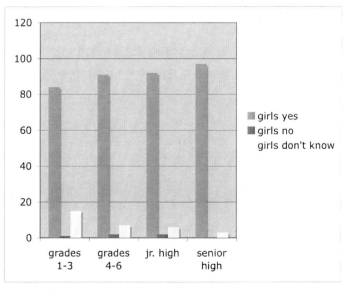

Figure 4.6. Girls With Friends Reading Manga (n=389)

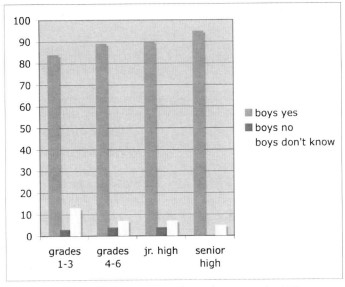

Figure 4.7.   Boys With Friends Reading Manga (n=378)

Throughout their years in school, most boys and girls claim to have friends who read manga, and this network would provide the basis of a community of readers. We found, in the surveys and interviews, that friends introduce manga by talking about and sharing them, as shown by an elementary school reader describing how he found his favorite manga: ["I found an interesting and fun manga that another friend had read when I visited his house. So I started to buy it after that"]. This was how one mother described her son finding his favorite manga: ["He visited his friend's house and he read *COROCORO*. Then he wanted it"]. In the same way, a college student discovered his favorite manga when he was in junior high school: "My friend told me that this manga is interesting." Being able to go to friends' homes is a useful way of finding manga, especially for young children, who may not have access to manga if their parents disapprove of them.

Friends are important not only for talking about manga but also for providing access to them, as explained by this high school reader: ["First, I watched a TV program that showed a book report about it (manga) and I became interested in it at that time. After that, it turned out that a friend of mine had the manga. So I borrowed it"]. Borrowing manga is an important way of finding out if you like the manga before you buy it, so borrowing is a key reason for belonging to a community of readers. This is illustrated by a junior high school boy's comments: ["Most of my friends have the *ONE PIECE* series. If a friend has the newest volume and I haven't read it yet, I would ask to see it and read it while at my friend's house"]. Borrowing is also an economical way of reading, as some readers do not have to buy many manga, such as explained by this high school student: ["I don't have so many, but I often read manga by borrowing from my friends"]. This approach was used by another high school reader: ["Actually, I borrow manga from my friends.

I only borrow from them. I return them and borrow another one when a friend tells me about an interesting manga. My friends introduce me to an interesting manga, which they have recently read"]. This same reader was very particular about her borrowing patterns in that she would only borrow published *komikkusu*, rather than read a magazine serial because she was unable to wait for each episode to be published. Being able to borrow the sequential volumes of the bound *komikkusu* also shows that her friends were serious collectors.

> [If I read a series, I become anxious to read the next episode. And if the release date is delayed, I get the urge to read it more and more. So I make it a rule to borrow complete sets, those manga which are already published. In other words, I prefer all the volumes in the set, which my friends have.]

One reason for lending manga is to get other readers interested in your favorite one. A college student explained that by lending her manga, she was able to talk about them with her friends: "When I buy new manga, I lend them and talk about the manga." She talked about the story and the jokes rather than the illustrations. Through lending manga, readers can find ways to build communities of readers and strengthen friendships. This is clearly described by another high school student who actively borrowed and lent her *shōjo* manga, *TENSHI NANKAJANAI* (I'm not an angel).

> Interviewer: [Do you lend them (your manga) to people?]
>
> Student: [Yes, I do. I want everyone to read my favorite manga. I want to share, I want to share this feeling. And I want them to have fun by reading the interesting manga. I want to talk about it with them (my friends). I lend most of the manga I have because I can chat with them, something like "What will happen next?" and so on. I borrow a lot too.]

Sharing and encouraging others to read the same type of manga is thus a way to deepen the friendship and strengthen the reading community, since it would provide common topics to talk about. As the above reader points out, having a common interest is important for her because she would be able to participate in the group. Furthermore, since the manga is her favorite, she would most likely be able to exhibit her expert status by knowing details about the characters and stories. Being able to talk knowledgably about the shared texts is a central practice of belonging to a community of readers.

For some readers, having manga that others want to borrow gives them status or social currency. Friends come to their house, read, and then borrow manga as described by a junior high school student:

> [At a certain age I was reading *Slam Dunk* and I had collected thirty-one volumes. There weren't many friends who had read the series, so when they came to my house, they would often ask if they could read it.]

An elementary school student described a similar situation. Her friends did not have manga, so they came to her house to read hers.

Interviewer: [Have you ever read manga at a friend's house?]

Student: [My friends don't have them so I don't read them.]

Interviewer: [Do they come here (her home) to read?]

Student: [Yes, they do.]

While having access to manga can provide status, being part of the community of readers is not without pressure, as this elementary school student described about his reading of manga in fourth grade.

Student: [Oh, but there were many manga which my friends talked about and I hadn't read.]

Interviewer: [And how do you feel about not having read them?]

Student: [I wanted to read them.]

Being part of a community of readers can also mean you have to know what you are talking about. A senior high school student told us that he reread *DRAGON BALL* to make sure he could keep up with his friends: ["Well, the details can remain fresh in my mind by rereading. And I can talk with my friends about it, so I like rereading"]. Rereading to prepare for conversations with friends is a point also made by Merry White in her study of Japanese teenagers.[36]

Yet, as we found in an interview with an elementary student, these communities of readers can be exclusive. One young girl read manga at home because she borrowed her brother's *shōnen* manga. The boys around her at the after-school day-care center read and talked about manga she knew, but she did not join in. She also did not talk about manga with her friends because they did not read them.

Mother: [Do you have time to talk about manga?]

Daughter: [Boys talk about them at my after-school day-care center.]

Mother: [Do you join them?]

Daughter: [No, I don't. I just listen because I play with my friends.]

Mother: [Do you talk about manga with (friend)?]

Daughter: [No, we don't.]

The influence of friends can, however, become a form of peer pressure, as we found in one of our interviews. One particular boy was friend of an avid manga reader and they were also in the same school swimming club. The manga reader invited his friend along to our interview. In addition to questions about reading practices and preferences, we asked our interviewees to read a part of their favorite manga and trace their eye movements with a marker. Although we had prepared a manga that he had said he liked, he became tired after reading the third page. His junior high school friends were all manga readers and discussed them enthusiastically. We surmised that rather than be left out of the group, the boy claimed to be a manga fan and selected one that was easier than most because of the clear story line. More importantly, since the manga had been televised as a long-running anime, he was able to maintain some knowledge in the group.

Peer pressure can operate in a number of ways as this mother discovered when she described how her son became interested in Pokémon[37]—the game, anime, and manga.

> [I remember when he was in first grade elementary school. I thought he didn't know about Pokémon at all and I didn't know either. When he went to school, his friends told him that the game was fun, I guess. At that time, I hadn't talked about it with him so I didn't know about it. But when I went to the first parents' open day, his teacher let the pupils introduce themselves. Actually they needed to talk about their name and their favorite things. And my son said, "My favorite is Pokémon." I thought he hadn't seen it before. I just thought he copied the others. A lot of them did (said they liked Pokémon) that day. Soon after that, the anime came on TV and the manga also came out.]

Although some of our interview data suggest that children are active lenders and borrowers, the survey results present a mixed picture. Figures 4.8 and 4.9 show the borrowing and lending patterns for the combined junior and senior high school students. While lending and borrowing increase with age for both groups, the boys lag behind the girls, especially from upper elementary school to senior high school. This was confirmed by statistical analysis in that the differences between the girls and boys were significant from the grade 4 and upward, becoming most pronounced at the high school level.[38] A high school student described how his reading changed as he grew older: ["I used to do it (read at a friend's house) in the past, but not now. When I was in junior high school"]. A similar change in pattern was given by this

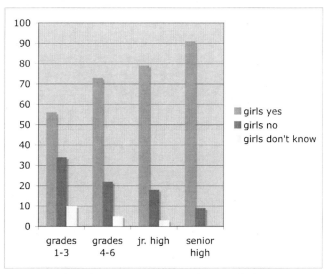

Figure 4.8.   Borrowing and Lending Patterns Among Girls (Junior high n=196; Senior high n=164)

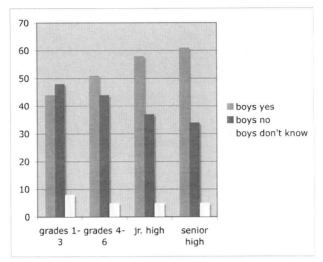

Figure 4.9.   Borrowing and Lending Patterns Among Boys (Junior high n=211; Senior high n=128)

male college student: ["I did share, especially in the upper elementary grades, not so much in the lower grades. But I tended to borrow more than lend"]. Unlike boys, girls are more likely to share their manga with their friends. Furthermore, the surveys show that the sharing of manga among girls increases in high school. It seems that girls are more actively engaged in being part of communities of readers. We also found this to be the case among college students in the Tokyo area.

In their study of junior high school students, Rebecca Fukuzawa and Gerald Le-Tendre found that by the third year, the boys tended to concentrate on video games, while the girls shared their reading as well as borrowed and lent books.[39] This pattern is similar to gendered reading practices in Canada, Britain, and Australia, where sharing books is a preferred female activity.[40] Among the students we studied, the girls were more active in sharing their reading, but it was manga, not books, that were circulated.

Although there are differences in the actual size of proportions when compared with our results, the practice of more girls than boys borrowing and lending is also evident in Ōnishi Jun's survey results.[41] He found that nearly 30 percent of junior high school girls borrowed and lent, while less than 15 percent of the boys did so. On the other hand, in a survey by Takano Ryōko of mothers reflecting on their practices when they were in school, she found that close to 75 percent borrowed and lent manga.[42] This level is similar to the results we found. Citing Ōnishi, Takano concludes that, over the years, patterns of borrowing and lending are declining and that due to affluence, children prefer to buy their own copies. Yet our respondents report strong patterns of borrowing and lending, perhaps because these practices are a central part of belonging to communities of readers.

Parents react in different ways to their children borrowing and lending manga. One mother told us that she did not mind friends coming to the home and borrowing her son's manga because she knew where her son was and what he was doing. However, not all parents accepted the borrowing and lending, as one junior high school boy explained:

Interviewer: [Then do you borrow manga too?]

Student: [No. If I borrow my mum will get angry. So I read at friends' homes.]

Interviewer: [So your mum doesn't get angry if you lend manga to your friends?]

Student: [Yes, she does get angry in that case too.]

Tachiyomi and Preferred Places to Read Manga

Sharing in the community of readers is not only borrowing and lending the manga or talking about them. It can also include the reading experience, such as reading at a friend's house. However, in Japan there is also another kind of shared reading practice and that is *tachiyomi*. *Tachiyomi* refers to standing and browsing in bookshops or convenience stores and it involves specific literacy practices. While it can be done individually or in groups, most of the students we interviewed stated that they browsed with friends, especially junior high school friends.

Regarding the practice of *tachiyomi*, Japanese bookstores have no difficulty attracting customers to stand and browse. Their challenge is to get the customers to buy. That is why coffee shops within bookshops are rarely seen. In our interviews, students stated that on the way home from school, they regularly go into convenience stores to browse rather than to bookshops because the latter tend to bind popular manga in plastic or with rubber bands to discourage *tachiyomi*. Here is how one junior high school boy described *tachiyomi*: ["I often *tachiyomi* on my way home from practice. My (male) friends and I go to the convenience store together"]. An advantage of *tachiyomi* is that readers can find a manga series they like and then later go and buy it.

Figure 4.10.   *Tachiyomi* in a Bookshop

Even though some bookshops try to discourage *tachiyomi* by binding manga in string or wrapping them in plastic, the term *tachiyomi* is now used on websites by a number of publishing companies to invite people to read sample chapters. However, not all manga are available for online *tachiyomi*, and the chapters that can be accessed are limited. Similar to many bookshops, publishers of online manga want readers to buy.

The surveys and interviews indicated that many of the readers actively borrowed and lent manga and thus belong to communities of readers. Yet, as table 4.1 shows, when asked about where they liked to read, it seems that reading is not always a shared experience. Reading manga is something that is also enjoyed when alone.

The overwhelmingly preferred place to read manga is at home. Since a family member is the person most likely to introduce children to manga (see figure 4.1), the family member as agent reinforces the home as the space for reading manga. In addition, the home has an important role in enabling children to develop their personal literacy practices.[43] Ōnishi's survey results also show this tendency.[44] Furthermore, while reading at home perhaps implies that manga reading is done individually, this does not rule out sharing with family members. Finally, although we have not asked this question, we would suspect that most likely, the practice of rereading manga, which is explored in chapter 5, is done at home.

Yet to gain access to new material, children have to go out of the home, and this is where being part of communities of readers is helpful since they can find different kinds of manga. Friends can provide information about new titles and also lend manga. Thus manga readers have different literacy practices as they move to different places. They may prefer to read alone at home. Outside home, they have more opportunities to be with friends while they commute to school, *tachiyomi*, or visit friends' homes.

Table 4.1 shows that when students enter senior high school, there are changes in where they like to read manga. Among the boys, while *tachiyomi* is still important, reading at school is more popular than reading at a friend's home. For the girls, reading at a friend's home is even less popular. One possible reason is that many students

Table 4.1: Preferred Places to Read Manga

	First	*Second*	*Third*	*Fourth*	*Fifth*	*Sixth*
Jr. High Boys n=228	Home	*Tachiyomi*	Friend's home	Train	School	Other
Senior High Boys n=150	Home	*Tachiyomi*	School	Friend's	Train	Other
Jr. High Girls n=217	Home	*Tachiyomi*	Friend's	Train	School	Other
Senior High Girls n=171	Home	School	*Tachiyomi*	Train	Friend's	Other

change schools at the end of junior high school, the last year of compulsory education in Japan. When they enter high school, decisions have to be made about the type of high school, usually in terms of academic achievement. For instance, those students interested in entering a key university compete in the entrance examination to gain a place at a well-known high school. For many students, going to high school means leaving behind old friends, moving to a bigger institution, a longer commute, and with it the task of making new friends for the final three years of secondary school. This indicates there are fewer opportunities to read at friends' homes. Other reasons for not reading at friends' homes may be developmental. White observed that high school students preferred to keep home and their friends separate.[45]

Another difference between girls and boys is that senior high school girls are less likely to *tachiyomi*. *Tachiyomi* seems to be especially popular with boys from junior high school through to college and possibly beyond. For girls, on the other hand, *tachiyomi* is popular at junior high school. One college student explained that boys were more successful at *tachiyomi* because girls felt pressured to buy manga, whereas the boys did not. In our earlier surveys of college students, we found that by the time they enter college, women begin to shift their reading preferences from manga to magazines. Moreover, in comparison with men, we found that fewer college women indicated that they engaged in the practice of *tachiyomi*, even for magazines. Unlike boys, it seemed that girls become more sensitive to social norms as they grow older, and so move from reading manga to more socially acceptable magazines. Yet results from our later surveys suggest that these reading habits had changed over the years.

In a 2007 survey of college students, ranging from first to fourth year, we found different results compared with our earlier surveys of college readers. Among the female students, 76 percent actively borrowed and lent manga in high school. This then dropped to 59 percent who continued these practices at college. Despite this decline in the number of readers, there are still many female manga readers at college. This contrasts with the patterns for the male readers at college and high school. 47 percent of the college students stated they read and lent manga at high school. This then declined to 43 percent who continued to do so at college. While the overall number of manga readers declines at college, in comparison to the female readers, the men are not so actively engaged. When the female and male patterns of sharing of were statistically compared, there was a significant difference (Chi-square, .05 and .01) between them. Being part of a community of readers seems to be more important to the female college students, similar to the senior high school students we surveyed. Our initial surveys and interviews of college students were conducted in a provincial city. The latest survey was administered in the Tokyo area. Given these reading practices, it seems that students in Tokyo, particularly females, continue to enjoy manga. The data indicated that despite a general decline in manga sales, the high school students were actively engaged in reading manga and that this practice persisted into college.

There is evidence of other changes among manga readers. As companies are putting manga on mobile phones, they are discovering that the viewers are mainly females, from ten to thirty years old. The intended audience had been salary men, commuting to work. As a result of this increased female readership, more *shōjo* manga have been made available for viewing.[46] The privacy of reading manga on a mobile phone seems to be promoting readership, as it mitigates the obviousness of reading manga in print form. The increased female readership is similar to the readership patterns of manga in the United States, where 60 percent of the manga readers are female.[47] This contrasts with the predominantly male readership of comics.

The surveys and interviews all show varying patterns of reading, as being a manga reader can be both an individual and a communal practice. This is how a junior high school boy, who also engaged in *tachiyomi* with his friends and actively shared manga, described his daily reading of manga:

> [I often read manga in my spare time. When I get up early in the morning, I eat breakfast, and since I walk to school with my friends, I read while waiting for them and I also read a little when I get home. In short, I read every day. Since it is not good to have an *ofuro* [Japanese hot bath] right after dinner, I often read then. Again, after I finish my homework and if I am not too sleepy, I read manga before going to bed.]

Readers as Manga Collectors

As has been described, for many members, being part of communities of readers means being able to borrow or lend manga. Having a popular series can give readers status in their communities. Friends want to borrow their manga or come to their home and read them. It means that collecting manga is another kind of literacy practice. This was reflected in the data, which showed that large numbers of readers have at one time or another built collections of their favorite manga (see table 4.2). These collections may range from a few volumes to six hundred or more. A college student introduced himself by saying his hobbies were playing soccer and collecting manga. He had nineteen hundred manga in his bedroom. Being a collector is yet another sign of being a passionate manga reader. Elementary and junior high school seem to be typical periods when readers collect manga. Once students enter high school, except for the very committed collectors, most readers stopped collecting. This pattern is reflected in the following high school student's comments:

> [I started collecting manga when I was in elementary school and then to junior high school. And I've bought some volumes of the series and added them to my collection. But I haven't bought new volumes since I entered high school. Not so many. I mean I buy a new volume that I've been collecting, but I don't buy a new series from volume one.]

Table 4.2:   Senior High School Readers as Manga Collectors

	Girls n=168				Boys n=132		
Yes	No	Used to			Yes	No	Used to
54%	19%	27%			59%	19%	22%

A high school boy had a similar pattern of collecting only in junior high school: "Now, I don't collect, but junior high school. When I was in junior high school, I collected them."

Readers varied in the kinds of manga they collected. For instance, one college student told us that he had wanted to be a police officer since he was a junior high student. This lead to him reading and then collecting the manga *Kochira Katsushika-ku Kameari Kōen Mae Hashutsujo* (The police station in front of Kameari Park in Katsushika), which is based on a police officer.[48] He had collected all the volumes and that was the only manga he was interested in: "I want to be a policeman. I started to read this manga when I was thirteen years old. I have all (volumes). All. From 1 to 116."

Identifying with the hero of a manga was also the reason why another junior high school student collected *DRAGON BALL*. This manga is based on the quest of Son Goku, a boy from outer space, to find seven magic dragon balls. During his journeys, he becomes skilled in martial arts and has numerous adventures. The manga first came out before the reader was born, so he combed secondhand bookshops to find back copies. Similar to the hero in the series, the boy practiced karate. Another reason he had for collecting this particular manga was the artwork, especially back spines of the *komikkusu*. The volumes could be placed together and form a picture:

> 42 volumes. I like these martial sort of things. I like this flying, that sort of stuff. I do karate, so it sort of have a little bit in common. The manga first come out like 1985, that was like before I was born. I went to the secondhand bookshops so they didn't have all of them, which was sometimes I had to skip that book that wasn't there and get the next one. And when it came out, then I would get that one and read what was missing. I like the illustrations. Like these sort of pictures, like in the beginning or the front cover, he does a picture and I like the cover and stuff. If you buy all of them, it makes a big picture, a big long picture going this way.

Figure 4.11 is a photocopy of the illustrations when all the volumes are purchased. As this collector of *DRAGON BALL* has described, creators can promote interest in collecting manga.

Figure 4.11.   Graphic on the Spines of *DRAGON BALL* (From *DRAGON BALL* © 1984 by Bird Studio/ SHUEISHA Inc.)

When describing why he collected a particular series, a college student told us that he did not enjoy current manga and was more interested in older ones, which he felt had more text and therefore more complex stories. For this reader, older manga were those of the 1970s. His favorite manga was *Uchū Kaizoku Kyaputen Hārokku* (Space pirate Captain Harlock).[49] This is the story of space pirates, in particular, the adventures of Captain Harlock. Since the student had a part-time job in a secondhand bookshop, he was easily able to buy back copies to add to his collection.

Secondhand bookshops, especially national chains such as *Book Off*, are important for collectors because they have a wide range of the bound *komikkusu* at very reasonable prices. These bookshops also buy used books and a number of students stated that they had sold their used manga there. People can go into these bookshops and *tachiyomi*, without the pressure of having to buy. More importantly, the *komikkusu* are not wrapped in plastic, which makes it easier for customers to find ones they like. Using these kinds of shops was how the above *DRAGON BALL* reader built up his collection:

> I didn't have much money so I had to buy them from the *chūko* (second hand), the place they sell them like a hundred yen. I go to school in X, but we used to live in Y, and in this bookshop that I bought these. It's like right in front of the station. So when I came home, off the train from school, I'd sort of go there and read a little and buy some. This place is, they are all *chūko*, so they don't really care if they *tachiyomi*.

The collectors we interviewed emphasized that they regularly reread their manga. Each time they did so, they were able to find something new and thus continue to enjoy the experience. A number of studies have been done on girls reading teen romance series.[50] These kinds of book series have been criticized for the sameness of the stories and that the repetition leads to passive reading. When asked about their favorite book, the readers are unable to name a particular title; instead, they give the name of the series. Yet it could be argued that with a series, readers are introduced to an overall narrative, in which the characters face different situations in each book. This repetition of the individual stories does not lead to boredom. In his description of readers of comics in the United States, Matthew Pustz maintains that comics build up continuity and that over the years writers are able to develop complex characters through the various stories.[51] This knowledge, which depends on intertextual links between the different stories, would be familiar to long-term readers. An attraction to parody comes out of this intimate knowledge of a series.

We found similarities with manga collectors. In a series, the creator is able to develop characters as they experience various situations. This makes it important to collect, or have access to, a number of episodes so that readers can note the changes and share the information in communities of readers. As if to emphasize this, one college reader stated that she had read for more than nine years the manga *YUKAN KURABU*,[52] serialized in the weekly magazine *Ribon*.[53] This manga is based on the adventures of a group of young rich students who solve various mysteries. She also enjoyed reading the *shōnen* manga, *HUNTER X HUNTER*,[54] based on the main

Figure 4.12.   *YUKAN KURABU* (Excerpt from *YUKAN KURABU* © 1981 by Yukari Ichijō/SHUEISHA Inc.)

character's search for his father. Combining science fiction and martial arts, it is an action/adventure story, very different from the *YUKAN KURABU*. As a reader of long-running serials, she pointed out that readers of serials have to be patient. For instance, the creator of *HUNTER X HUNTER* had difficulty meeting publishing deadlines, so it was not easy to follow the story. She did not blame the creator, as she sympathized with the difficulties of trying to produce a good story and graphics:

> The manga, the writer is very clever. The manga is very interesting. When I'm reading it, I have to think. The writer is a perfectionist. He is obsessed with the manga. He thinks of the story very hard. And he can't draw by the date. He often misses the deadline.

We have focused on reading practices of manga readers. Some of the readers identified themselves as having created manga, another literacy practice.

Readers as Manga Creators

While collecting manga was a popular practice, creating them was not, as shown in table 4.3. The difference between the girls and boys was statistically significant. One of the most common reasons for not creating manga was the belief of being bad at drawing, as expressed by a high school reader: ["I'm not good at drawing"]. The importance of good artwork was also a reason given by a mother, who told

Table 4.3:   Senior High School Readers as Manga Creators

Girls n=166				Boys n=136		
Yes	No	Don't remember		Yes	No	Don't remember
29%*	69%	2%		8%	90%	2%

$p < .05$

us about her experience of creating manga when she was in elementary school: ["I used to draw a manga on my own. (But then) I drew a manga including a story with my three girl friends when we were third- or fourth-year students"]. When asked if she had sent in her manga to any of the publishers' competitions, she replied: ["No. I was bad at drawing pictures. I knew that I was bad at it. I thought my drawings were terrible"].

A high school student who was a keen reader and collector of manga described how, together with her friend, she had also created manga in elementary school. Like the above readers, she emphasized the importance of being a good artist. Even though she no longer creates manga, she felt that the experience of trying to create had given her added understanding of the medium.

> [I wanted to be a manga artist when I was young. I had a friend who was good at drawing pictures. Either she or I made a story and we drew pictures together in a notebook. I was about a third or fourth grade student in elementary school. She was really good at drawing. At that time I borrowed manga a lot and I drew too. But I don't know where the notebook has gone. If I could read it now, I'd be terribly embarrassed. "I wrote these things!" There are special techniques to create manga. I sometimes notice how techniques are used in manga when I read them.]

We interviewed another adult who had created a manga while in high school and in the first year of college. Like the above high school student, her best friend had helped her develop her art skills. She had sent in two of her manga to a publisher's competition and got highly recommended. However, she gave up creating because of parental pressure. She was encouraged to go to college rather than become a manga creator. She is still a committed manga reader and continues collecting them.

One of the few active manga creators we interviewed was a college student, who had also formed a writing club. She and her friends met regularly to share and talk about manga. She had sent a manga to a Tokyo publishing company, but received no response. Despite this lack of publishing success, she continued to create, sharing her work with the group and encouraging others to create as well. However, she was the only manga creator, since the others preferred to write poetry or not write at all. When asked about her work, she told us that she had changed over the years and no longer drew panels. Instead, she now drew pictures of the characters so that she had a clear idea of what they looked like and what clothes they wore. Once she had done this, she would then begin writing the story. The pictures were her props. Rather than using the traditional manga format of integrating panels and text, she had moved to writing text with some illustrations, as in light novels. Her stories were long and detailed, all with science fiction themes. Even though she spent much time on her drawing, she emphasized that the writing was more critical. Indeed, she complained about the lack of feedback from her group. She was a keen manga reader and collector, buying on average thirty different manga a month.

The only male creator we interviewed was also a college student, who stated that he tried to work daily: "Two hours or three hours. But almost everyday I write something." He was, however, only recognized by his classmates as being a good artist, so much so that they kept asking him to draw posters for their clubs and bedrooms. Unlike the woman we interviewed, he worked alone and did not talk about getting any help from his friends. However, since he felt no one was interested in his favorite manga, he was active in sharing it so as to get other students to read it. Both of these college students were creators, although one was more successful than the other in involving friends and building a community of readers.

Even though there were only a few students in the interviews who said they had created manga, most of them were women. Moreover, most of them created manga at elementary school, the time when manga reading begins to expand. They were all readers and collectors. In addition, they relied on a community of readers and shared the creating experience. One high school boy gave a reason for the apparent lack of interest in creating manga: ["I think boys don't create manga so much. I think women like to do it more than men"]. For him, creating manga was a gendered practice. In the commercial world of manga, the *shōnen* manga outnumber *shōjo* and most creators are male. While there are some male *shōjo* creators, most of the creators are women. Yet the innovations in manga, such as the *yaoi* and *moe* themes, are largely the result of women creators. These innovations have actually come out of the amateur world of the *dōjinshi*. The term *dōjinshi* means a magazine created together and so the name itself emphasizes communities of practice.

Perhaps in recognition of the increasing worldwide interest in manga, the government has introduced manga drawing in the junior high school curriculum. Under the new curriculum, time is spent in the art class learning some techniques of manga illustration. However, the emphasis is on drawing and mastering basic techniques rather than on how to write a story. One student described how her junior high art teacher had the students create a manga. They were encouraged to base the story on a common theme, such as a school event or their daily life. While this recognizes the importance of having a familiar context for the readers, which is similar to many of the most popular manga for our readers, it also suggests that the story is not primary. Since it was an exercise in an art class, this dismissal of the plot is not surprising.

> [I had an art class, which had students write manga in my junior high school. We could do that because of the new educational ministry guidelines. Actually we didn't have to write a story. The teacher told us that we could write anything we wanted. For example, it was OK to write about sports day or our daily lives. The teacher gave us paper, pens, and some sheets of screentone (shading). The teacher told us that we should practice these techniques for a while and write a manga.]

When we asked the student if she learned about the special symbols used in manga, such as sweat drops, the student replied: ["No, I didn't. I learned normal skills"]. This student was an avid manga reader and collector who enthusiastically shared her ideas with us. Yet, apart from the art class exercise, she had never created a manga and did not want to. It would seem that the step from being a reader and collector to creating manga is one that is taken by very few. After all, how many of those who enjoy reading novels actually write any?

Summary

Our findings indicate that many manga readers belong to communities of readers. In these communities, readers share their ideas, develop social skills, and use manga to find topics to talk about with their friends. Through their reading of manga, they build up friendships because their reading practices can be a reason for initiating and maintaining relationships. Furthermore, if the manga is a personal favorite that they can lend, individual members would probably gain expert status by knowing details about the characters and stories. Members of a community are expected to possess, or be in the process of gaining, knowledge of the shared manga. The communities of readers can vary since manga may be shared with family members, as well as friends in and out of school, and in friends' homes.

Although most readers in the interviews and surveys started learning to read at home, it was not until they went to elementary school that they seriously began to read manga. It is at school that their literacy skills become stronger, thereby enabling them to read manga on their own. It is also at school that children have greater access to manga through their friends. In addition, older children have more allowance, which means they can buy manga. As they become more familiar with reading manga, the number of titles being read increases—ones they buy themselves and ones they borrow from friends. We also found that the senior high school girls were more active readers than the boys. This pattern continued even when the women entered college, though this may depend on geographical location.

Regarding the relationship between reading manga and watching the anime version, there were variations. For instance, among the girls, watching the anime before reading the related manga clearly declined with age. In addition, seeing the anime after reading the manga peaked at upper elementary school and then declined. For boys, the patterns are less clear. However, reading the manga first and then later watching the anime was the dominant practice, although there were differences related to the ages of the readers. In junior high school, both boys and girls read the manga before watching the related anime. As they became older, such as in senior high school and college, readers' preferences diversified, since they read titles that have no anime versions. Thus the connection between watching anime and reading manga becomes less relevant with age.

Many manga readers reported collecting manga. The collections serve the readers' desire to reread their favorite manga and become more involved with the stories and characters. The collections also serve as resources for sharing manga, thereby providing the reader agency and status within his or her community of readers. A much smaller number of readers reported that they engaged in creating manga. Still, approximately three times as many girls claimed to have created manga. While professional manga creators are still mostly men, amateur activity, including activity at *Comiket*, is largely engaged in by women.

Notes

1. Kate Allen and John E. Ingulsrud, "Reading *Manga*: Patterns of Personal Literacies among Adolescents," *Language and Education* 19, no. 4 (2005): 265–80.

2. Takano Ryōko, "Hahaoya to Manga: Hahaoya Eno Ankēto Chōsa Kara" (Mothers and manga: A survey to mothers), in *Kodomo to Manga: Manga Dokkairyoku wa Dō Hattatsu Suruka* (Children and manga: How manga comprehension develops), ed. Akashi Yōichi and Nakazawa Jun (Tokyo: Gendaijidōbunka Kenkyūkai, 1993), 55–84.

3. Tezuka Osamu, *Tetsuwan Atomu* (Mighty atom) (Tokyo: Kobunsha, 1952).

4. Fujio F. Fujiko, *Doraemon* (Tokyo: Shogakukan, 1969).

5. Kate Allen and John E. Ingulsrud, "*Manga* Literacy: Popular Culture and the Reading Habits of Japanese College Students," *Journal of Adolescent & Adult Literacy* 46, no. 8 (2003): 674–83.

6. Mary S. Noguchi, "An American Sabbatical Experience," *Bilingual Japan* 15, no. 3 (2006), 21.

7. Mel Gibson, "Reading as Rebellion: The Case of the Girls' Comic in Britain," *International Journal of Comic Art* 2, no. 2 (2000): 135–51; Jackie Marsh and Elaine Millard, *Literacy and Popular Culture* (London: Paul Chapman Publishing, 2000), 101–17; Jo Worth, Megan Moorman, and Margo Turner, "What Johnny Likes To Read Is Hard To Find In School," *Reading Research Quarterly* 34, no. 1 (1999): 12–27; and Allan Luke, "Series Editor's Introduction," in *Texts of Desire: Essays on Fiction, Femininity and Schooling*, ed. Linda K. Christian-Smith (London: The Falmer Press, 1993), vii–xiv. See also Gesine Foljanty-Jost, who in her study of deviance in a Japanese city, described how the neighborhood committees used as a sign of potential delinquency children wearing school uniforms doing *tachiyomi*, that is, reading manga in bookshops, in "Heartful Guidance: Strategies of Preventing Deviance in Japanese Schools," paper presented at the JSAA 2001, Japan Studies Association of Australia, Biennial Conference, Sydney, Australia, June 27–30, 2001.

8. Ishida Kanta, "'Inuyasha' Creator marks 30 Yrs in Manga Biz," *Daily Yomiuri*, August 15, 2008, 15.

9. Ikeda Riyoko, *Berusaiyu no Bara* (Rose of Versailles) (Tokyo: Shueisha, 1972).

10. Anne Haas Dyson, *Writing Superheroes: Contemporary Childhood, Popular Culture, and Classroom Literacy* (New York: Teachers College Press, 1997), see especially chapter 1, 10–28.

11. Nihon Shimbun Kyōkai, "Mediabetsu Setsuzoku Jōkyō" (The situation of access according to media), www.pressnet.or.jp/adarc/data/1br/14.html (accessed March 6, 2007).

12. Takano, "Hahaoya to Manga," 55–84.

13. *Ninpen Manmaru* (Manmaru the ninja penguin) (Tokyo: Shinei Video and TV Asahi, 1997) (animation).

14. *Mikan e Nikki* (Mikan's illustrated diary) (Tokyo: Nippon Animation, 1992). Animation.

15. *SHŪKAN SHŌNEN JUMP* (Tokyo: Shueisha, 1969).

16. Tezuka Osamu, *Janguru Taitei* (Jungle emperor) (Tokyo: Gakudosha, 1950).

17. Igarashi Mikio, *Bonobono* (Tokyo: Takeshobo, 1986).

18. *ONE PIECE* © 1997 by Eiichiro Oda/SHUEISHA Inc.

19. Toriyama Akira, *DRAGON BALL* © 1984 by Bird Studio/SHUEISHA Inc.

20. Otomo Katsuhiro, *Akira* (Tokyo: Kodansha, 1982).

21. *Otaku* (Johannesburg: Xvolve, 2005).

22. Susan J. Napier, *Anime from Akira to Princess Mononoke: Experiencing Contemporary Japanese Animation* (New York: Palgrave, 2000), 20.

124 CHAPTER 4

23. Takaya Natsuki, *Fruits Basket* (Tokyo: Hakusensha, 1999).

24. Itō Gō, *Tezuka izu Deddo: Hirakareta Manga Hyōgenron e* (Tezuka is dead: Postmodernist and modernist approaches to Japanese manga) (Tokyo: NTT Shuppan, 2005).

25. Wm. Penn, "'Doraemon' Gets Facelift to the Displeasure of Viewers," Televiews, *Daily Yomiuri*, November 29, 2002, 12.

26. MEXT (Ministry of Education, Culture, Sports, Science, and Technology), *Shōgakkō Shidō Yōryō* (Elementary school curriculum), www.mext.go.jp/b_menu/shuppan/sonota/990301/03122601/002.htm (accessed March 4, 2007).

27. Tezuka Osamu, *Burakku Jakku* (Black Jack) (Tokyo: Akita Shoten, 1973).

28. Chiba Tetsuya and Takamori Asao, *Ashita no Jo* (Rocky Joe) (Tokyo: Kodansha, 1968).

29. Miyazaki Hayao, *Nausicaä of the Valley of the Wind* (Tokyo: Takuma Shoten, 1982).

30. Gemma Moss, "Children Talk Horror Videos: Reading as a Social Performance," *Australian Journal of Education* 37, no. 2 (1993): 169–81; Muriel Robinson, *Children Reading Print and Television* (London: The Falmer Press, 1997), 24, 185–86.

31. Etienne Wenger, *Communities of Practice: Learning, Meaning, and Identity* (Cambridge: Cambridge University Press, 1999).

32. Gretchen I. Jones, "Bad Girls Like to Watch: Writing and Reading Ladies' Comics," in *Bad Girls of Japan*, ed. Laura Miller and Jan Bardsley (New York: Palgrave Macmillan, 2005), 97–109.

33. Ōnishi Jun, "Kodomo to Manga: Kodomo Eno Ankēto Chōsa Kara" (Children and manga: From a survey to children), in *Kodomo to Manga: Manga Dokkairyoku wa Dō Hattatsu Suruka* (Children and manga: How manga comprehension develops), ed. Akashi Yōichi and Nakazawa Jun (Tokyo: Gendaijidōbunka Kenkyūkai, 1993), 11–54.

34. Moss, "Children Talk," 169–81.

35. For example, Martin Coles and Christine Hall, "Taking Comics Seriously: Children's Periodical Reading in England in the 1990s," *Reading* (November 1997): 50–54.

36. Merry White, *The Material Child: Coming of Age in Japan and America* (Berkeley: University of California Press, 1994), 132. See also Rebecca Erwin Fukuzawa and Gerald K. LeTendre, *Intense Years: How Japanese Adolescents Balance School, Family, and Friends* (New York: RoutledgeFalmer, 2001), 49, on how a knowledge of manga is an important feature of group membership.

37. Tajiri Satoshi, *Poketto Monsutā* (Pokémon) (Tokyo: Nintendo, 1995) (video game).

38. Contrasts were run with two gender groups and four age groups, $p < .05$.

39. Fukuzawa and LeTendre, *Intense Years*, 62.

40. Meredith R. Cherland and Carole Edelsky, "Girls and Reading: The Desire for Agency and Horror of Helplessness in Fictional Encounters," in *Texts of Desire: Essays on Fiction, Femininity and Schooling*, ed. Linda K. Christian-Smith (London: The Falmer Press, 1993), 28–44; Elaine Millard, *Differently Literate: Boys, Girls and the Schooling of Literacy* (London: The Falmer Press, 1997), 85–87; and Anne Simpson, "Fictions and Facts: An Investigation of the Reading Practices of Girls and Boys," *English Education* 28, no. 4 (1996): 268–79.

41. Ōnishi, "Kodomo to Manga," 11–54.

42. Takano, "Hahaoya to Manga," 55–84.

43. Allen and Ingulsrud, "Reading *Manga*," 265–80.

44. Ōnishi, "Kodomo to Manga," 11–54.

45. White, *The Material Child*, 152–55. On the other hand, Fukuzawa and LeTendre (*Intense Years*, 45) suggest this can start in junior high school.

46. Matsushita Shuji, "Girls Love K-Tai," Mobile Ojisan, *Cnet Asia*, asia.cnet/reviews/

blog/mobileojisan/0,39050793,39358040,00.htm (accessed May 8, 2006).

47. Coco Masters, "America is Drawn to Manga," *Time* (August 10, 2006): A5.

48. Akimoto Osamu, *Kochira Katsushika-ku Kameari Kōen Mae Hashutsujo* (The police station in front of Kameari Park in Katsushika) (Tokyo: SHUEISHA Inc., 1976).

49. Matsumoto Leiji, *Uchū kaizoku Kyaputen Hārokku* (Space pirate Captain Harlock) (Tokyo: Akita Bunka, 1978).

50. An important work that influenced the study of girls' reading practices is Janice A. Radway, *Reading the Romance: Women, Patriarchy and Popular Literature* (Chapel Hill: University of North Carolina Press, 1984). The following examples have focused on young women: Gemma Moss, *Un/Popular Fictions* (London: Virago Press, 1989); Linda K. Christian-Smith, "Sweet Dreams: Gender and Desire in Teen Romance Novels," in *Texts of Desire: Essays on Fiction, Femininity and Schooling*, ed. Linda K. Christian-Smith (London: The Falmer Press, 1993), 45–68; Linda K. Christian-Smith, "Popular Texts and Young Women," in *Difference, Silence, and Textual Practice: Studies in Critical Literacy*, ed. Peter Freebody, Sandy Muspratt, and Bronywn Dwyer (Cresskill, NJ: Hampton Press, 2001), 189–207; John Willinsky and R. Mark Hunniford, "Reading the Romance Novel: The Mirrors and Fears of a Preparatory Literature," in *Texts of Desire: Essays on Fiction, Femininity and Schooling*, ed. Linda K. Christian-Smith (London: The Falmer Press, 1993), 45–68; and Norma Odom Pecora, "Identity by Design: The Corporate Construction of Teen Romance Novels," in *Growing Up Girls: Popular Culture and the Construction of Identity*, ed. Sharon R. Mazzarella and Norma Odom Pecora (New York: Peter Lang, 1999, 2001), 49–86.

51. Matthew J. Pustz, *Comic Book Culture: Fanboys and True Believers* (Jackson: University Press of Mississippi, 1999), 129.

52. *YUKAN KURABU* © 1981 by Yukari Ichijō/SHUEISHA Inc.

53. *Ribon* (Tokyo: Shueisha, 1955).

54. *HUNTER X HUNTER* © by POT (Yoshihiro Togashi) All rights reserved/ SHUEISHA Inc.

Strategies for Comprehending Manga   **5**

THE COMMUNITIES OF MANGA READERS, composed of friends and/or family members, provide a valuable space where readers can learn to read manga. As readers interact with each other, they develop their knowledge of manga genres and specific titles as well as acquire additional reading skills. Communities involve interaction, yet this "interaction" can also be viewed from another perspective, that is, the reading process itself can become interactive as readers engage with text to create meaning.[1]

Research into the reading process has been heavily influenced by cognitive psychology. This research has concentrated on decoding, word recognition, and comprehension. Many of these studies, conducted in the 1970s and 1980s, focused on describing models of reading, with an emphasis on cognitive processing. Accordingly, readers process the different kinds of information in a text, which is related to what they already know.[2] In their recent model of adolescent reading, Donald Deshler and Michael Hock explain the reading process in terms of three main strands—word recognition, language comprehension, and executive processes or reading strategies—thereby emphasizing the importance of simplicity.[3] Although all the researchers differ in their representation of the reading process, most describe reading as involving a kind of interaction. This idea was well established in the philosophical traditions of hermeneutics. For example, the "hermeneutic circle," proposed by the nineteenth-century philosopher Frederich Schleiermacher, stressed the relationship of understanding the text's parts to the understanding of the text as a whole and vice versa. Zygmunt Bauman further explains the "circle" as "an endless recapitulation and reassessment of collective memories."[4]

The metaphor of reading as interaction helps us understand the reading process. It takes us from the skills of decoding to the skills of comprehension and reading strategies. In doing so, the process involves numerous related and overlapping activities represented by different methodological approaches. For instance, there is the understanding of new information in terms of old information. There is the background or prior knowledge of the reader that relates to the reader's ability to access textual knowledge. At the same time, the recognition of textual knowledge is made significant by reflecting on the reader's prior knowledge. The memory of intertextual links, stimulated by the encounter with the text, provides the possibility of not only intelligibility but also an assessment of the significance of the information. This can also result in shared ways of understanding that can lead to new identities for the reader to embrace.

Through the various kinds of "interaction," reading is a process leading to comprehension. Yet comprehension does not function well as a goal. It can, in the context of testing, be a goal in terms of a perfect score. This is not a banal point, because tests serve as gatekeepers for almost anyone who experiences some form of schooling. Scoring highly on a high-stakes reading test, for example, can lead on to fortune while a low score can discourage a reader. Apart from testing, however, comprehension seems to dissolve into other motives such as pleasure, usefulness, and inspiration. Usually, the notion of comprehension is raised only when the reading process is not functioning adequately.

Interaction in the reading process can also vary for different reading purposes.[5] For instance, some may read quickly because they only want to understand the gist of the story. Others may read more slowly to gain a deeper understanding, especially when they read parts they think are important. Reading speed can also vary if readers encounter difficulties. They may slow down and try to solve the problem. On the other hand, they may decide to ignore the difficulty by reading on or even stop reading. Readers, particularly good readers, are thus continually making decisions about their reading, such as what aspects of the text to focus on or how to deal with parts they do not understand.[6] For much of the time, the decision-making can be automatic and this depends on the readers' proficiency. One of the purposes of schooling is to train students to become proficient readers by developing their skills to understand texts and deal with any difficulties. Yet Marilyn Chambliss has demonstrated that, by the end of high school, many students may still be considered poor readers, being unable to comprehend a text since they have a limited knowledge of text structure, which is one of the clues to a deeper understanding of a text.[7] In the case of manga readers, who learn to read manga outside of the classroom and thus lack a formally structured approach to learning to read, the social context of their reading is an essential part of the process of becoming a successful reader. Motivated by a strong desire to read manga, as independent learners, they are able to develop their reading skills by themselves and maintain their enthusiasm for the task through sustained practice.

In this chapter, we examine some of the ways readers interact with manga and the strategies they develop as they become experienced readers. Reading strategies involve decoding the structural features of manga, such as the text and speech balloons. As has been described earlier, readers tend to learn these manga literacy skills on their own, implying that they have little difficulty doing so. However, it is not always the case. Readers do encounter difficulties in comprehending manga. Yet our interviewees who reported difficulties also described strategies to deal with or compensate for the problems. One common strategy is to reread manga, expecting that subsequent readings would allow for further comprehension. However, the phenomenon of rereading is a complex one and is not just a strategy for comprehension. Rereading also relates to the multimodal nature of the medium and the multifaceted shape of the narratives, providing continued enjoyment in rereading the same work. Indeed, as described above, our notions of "comprehension" assume a school-based, more specifically, a test-based literacy. The motives and practices reported by readers do not correspond entirely with these assumptions.

Strategies Used to Read Manga

We have already described how we employed surveys and follow-up interviews to the surveys. In addition, we conducted further interviews in which readers were asked to complete certain tasks. Between 2002 and 2003, fourteen girls and boys ranging from grade 2 in elementary school to the third year of junior high school, as well as some of the parents, were interviewed about their reading of manga. These interviews were conducted in Japanese or English, depending on the wishes of the interviewees. We also asked ten of these readers, ranging from six to thirteen years old to perform a task. Before the interviews, we inquired about the title of their favorite manga. We purchased a copy, if possible, in the magazine format because it is printed on large (B5) sized paper. In the course of the interview, we then asked the readers to take a felt pen and trace their eye movements on the paper. By doing so, we intended to see what parts readers read and what parts they leave out. We also intended to see what readers deemed as salient in the text. In addition, the tracings acted as prompts for questions, so that we could find out about their patterns of reading because it is not easy for children to think of how they read and reasons for using particular strategies. Finally, by asking the children to read their favorite manga, they would have developed the necessary schemata or knowledge structures to understand the text, since they would be familiar with the story line and creator's techniques. As readers would be reading their favorite manga, we assumed that any difficulties they might have would not be a problem of a general unfamiliarity with the genre, but rather with that specific text being read in that particular situation.

These tasks were not conducted under experimental conditions. Although we tried to purchase the latest editions of the magazine wherever possible, so that the readers would have a purpose or motivation for reading, we did not control for them having read the episode or not. However, those who did participate stated that they had not read the installment in the magazine we had purchased. Another limitation is that tracing with a felt pen does not represent an accurate account of eye movements, only an approximation. Yet, more importantly, the task provided both the readers and us with a way of talking about the process of reading, a kind of mediated discourse.

Despite the weakness of the methodology employed in the tasks and interviews, we were able to observe patterns of reading behavior that went across the range of readers. Based on the data, we have analyzed two major kinds of reading strategies. One is a sequential pattern involving the order in which manga is read and the parts that are focused on, in contrast to the parts that are less emphasized. The second is a pattern of rereading. Rereading is done for a variety of reasons, involving different reading skills at each sitting.

Readers tended to ignore parts they thought were irrelevant and used a variety of reading strategies. These strategies involve decoding the structural features of manga, that is, the text, speech balloons, characters, background, panel shape, and order of arrangement. Some of the strategies were so common among readers that we are able to provide a tentative hierarchy. The most important is focusing on the text in the speech balloons. This is what virtually all our readers read. The second common point is studying the characters' faces, indicating that facial expression contains a great deal of information. The third common point is that the reader tends to follow the order of panels. The research setting may have influenced this sequential nature of reading. It could also be influenced by classroom training of reading, which emphasizes following the sequential order of a text.[8] As we discuss our findings, we focus first on the reading of written text in manga, then on the order of panels, and finally on rereading as a strategy.

Reading Printed Text

Our readers were flexible and exhibited a range of reading strategies. One twelve-year-old boy was a careful, focused reader. He had chosen the manga *ONE PIECE*[9] and told us, ["I simply look at the characters to see who is talking to whom"]. This reader deliberately skipped the commentary and focused directly on the speech balloons. Yet there were some panels where he paused. He did this when there was an unexpected turn in the story (see figure 5.1). The place where he paused was the center panel on the left. There he carefully traced the rim of the speech balloons. Another boy, age nine, also focused on the written content in the speech balloons. He had chosen the manga *Kochira Katsushika-ku Kameari Kōen Mae Hashutsujo* (The police station in front of Kameari Park in Katsushika).[10] Based on his tracing, he seemed to read every panel, character, and speech balloon. However, he pointed to one panel on a page and said, ["I usually don't read here"], referring to the background of panel scenes. This appears to be the case with most of our readers, as they skipped the panels without speech balloons. We suspect that many manga creators are aware of these reading strategies. Recently, it is rare to see manga with extensive commentary in panels or at the margins. Instead, the commentary is worked into the speech balloons. This is an example of interdiscursivity, where text genres are mixed.[11] Sometimes the dialogue in the speech balloons presents information that the characters plausibly already know. The inclusion of the expository material appears to be placed for the benefit of the reader, not for the characters in the story.

Reading Graphics

Many readers told us that the graphics are one of the main reasons why they read manga. They become familiar with different styles and some of the very young

Figure 5.1. Tracing an Episode from *ONE PIECE* (Excerpt from *ONE PIECE* © 1997 by Eiichiro Oda/ SHUEISHA Inc.)

readers we interviewed enjoy copying the pictures. This was illustrated by a mother talking about her elementary school daughter's favorite manga: ["Others are the Miyazaki Hayao series. She watched the anime. Then she bought his manga because she wanted to copy his drawings"]. The appeal of graphics is also true for older readers, even outside Japan. For instance, the South African magazine *Otaku*,[12] which focuses on Japanese anime, manga, and other related media, regularly interviews local artists, all of whom are influenced by anime and manga. The magazine also holds conventions that feature fan art competitions where fans copy the style of their favorite manga artist.

Like the speech balloons, the graphics convey information that readers need in order to understand fully the story. One young boy described how he taught himself to pay attention to the faces in his favorite manga, *Zettai Zetsumei Dangerous Jīsan*[13] and so learned to anticipate the humor (see the tracing in figure 5.2):

> [This is a fun panel and here and here. It's difficult, but I carefully read every panel in *Dangerous Jīsan* the first time I bought it. And I knew this manga was funny as I got used to it. I just look at a face because this face will be funny for sure. I understood after reading it three times, I guess. Such a face makes the story funny.]

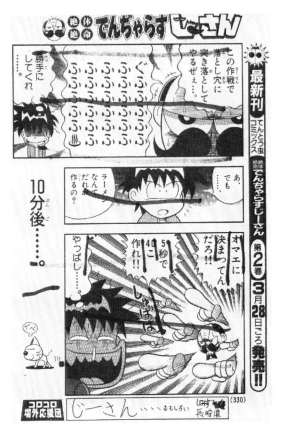

Figure 5.2. Tracing an Episode from *Zettai Zetsumei Dangerous Jīsan* (Excerpt from *Zettai Zetsumei Dangerous Jīsan* by Sōyama Kazutoshi. © 2003 by *COROCORO Komikku*. Reprinted with permission of Shogakukan.)

Similarly, a high school reader described how she studied the graphics in order to understand the story:

[But in the second reading, I can afford to read the pictures and the background slowly. That's because I've already read the lines. . . . I look at each line and the central characters' faces. Then I look at the small pictures in the corner. That's where there are fancy pictures.]

She particularly enjoyed the graphics in her favorite manga *ONE PIECE* because she thought ["the pictures are very elaborate"]. Another high school reader stated she found that ["sometimes it is easier to understand the content by looking at the pictures than rereading the explanation"]. The importance of the graphics in leading to an understanding of the story is recounted by a junior high school boy. When describing how he read while browsing in convenience stores, he explained that he focused on the graphics because there was not enough time to read the complete manga: ["In the case of *tachiyomi*, I read only the important parts. That means I don't necessarily read all of the panels, but I do look at the characters' faces"].

These comments demonstrate how the readers' ability to interpret graphics was learned informally. Visual literacy skills are developed through the experience of regularly reading. Manga readers have to learn by themselves how to interpret the graphics as well as the language and layout of the text. It is only when manga are translated into different languages that the texts might carry explanations of specific visual symbols, such as in manga published in English by the San Francisco–based manga publishing company, Viz MEDIA, LLC.

Managing Panel Order

The sequence of panels is an issue for readers and has to be learned through experience. In the English translations of *SHŌNEN JUMP*, the Viz editors provide an explanation and diagram to illustrate how to read the correct order of panels.[14] Such an explanation would not be found in manga in Japan since it is assumed readers already know this. As explained in chapter 2, there is wide variation in the panel order. In addition to differences of panel order that may be found in *shōnen* and *shōjo* manga, creators may vary the panel order in individual stories. Learning how to interpret the panel order takes much practice, as explained by the elementary school boy who liked *Zettai Zetsumei Dangerous Jīsan*:

> [I didn't know how to read, but I found out how to connect the panels while reading over and over again. I found out with no teacher. And if there are a few boring panels, a funny panel will soon come, so I'm sure to read and look at the panels. . . . The end panel is very important.]

In an earlier article, we explained the rhetorical pattern *ki-shō-ten-ketsu* as a convention for an arrangement of panels on each page.[15] We describe it in the following way: At the top of the right corner, the story begins (*ki-*). Then moving to the left and down, the story develops (*sho-*). Suddenly something unexpected happens (*ten-*). Finally, at the bottom of the page there is a resolution (*ketsu*). Although this was a common pattern used in manga in the past, most creators today deviate from it.[16] For instance, *shōjo* manga creators have been innovative in breaking traditional panel sequences by arranging characters and symbols in larger, often full-paged panels. In *shōnen* manga, the panel sequences generally become less obvious in action scenes. In one interview, an eight-year-old girl chose the *shōnen* manga *YU-GI-OH!*.[17] Although her tracing was much like that of the other readers—that is, with a focus on the speech balloons—the pages with the action scenes indicated a tentativeness with her tracing going in a circular, winding fashion. It seemed as though she needed time to process the images (see figure 5.3). Her confusing tracing reveals a limitation of our task. We were assigning a linear task in an action scene where a simultaneous set of actions was happening, instead of a sequence of single actions.

Coping with Difficulties

To understand the comprehension of manga, we were very interested in how readers dealt with reading difficulties. By collecting information from the surveys, as

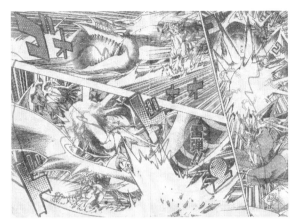

Figure 5.3.   Tracing an Episode from *YU-GI-OH!* (Excerpt from *YU-GI-OH!* © 1996 by Kazuki Taka-hashi/SHUEISHA Inc.)

well as from the readers who traced their reading patterns in the interview task, we intended to obtain a clearer understanding of the nature of reading difficulties. As readers reported on their difficulties, they could also demonstrate how they dealt with them when reading their favorite manga. Moreover, the combination of the different sources of information would go some way to illustrating readers' competence. Readers' descriptions of their difficulties and ways of dealing with them could be compared to what they did when they actually encountered problems reading the text. However, as Ann Brown has pointed out, it is not easy even for adults to analyze their reading processes.[18] The reading difficulties that were reported in the surveys and observed in the interviews were mainly those relating to vocabulary and panel sequences. Even though the readers might have had difficulty in remembering past reading difficulties and therefore given an approximation, their difficulties steadily declined over the years as the readers became more competent. Furthermore, the patterns for both the girls and boys are similar (see table 5.1).

Among those students that did report reading difficulties, we then inquired about the kind of help they sought. Table 5.2 shows the types of strategies the readers used in addressing their difficulties. For both boys and girls, rereading the difficult part is the most common way of dealing with reading difficulties, although by senior high school, girls seem to use this strategy less than the boys. Girls and boys also differ in their use of the other strategies. For example, girls in senior high school are more likely to ask someone for help than the boys. One reason for this might be that, as shown in chapter 4, girls are more actively engaged in their communities of readers well into senior high school. When borrowing and lending manga, they would therefore have more opportunities than the boys to talk about manga and perhaps deal with difficulties.

Reading widely is considered an important means of promoting vocabulary development and also comprehension.[19] Given the limited amount of explicit vocabulary instruction in formal classrooms in the United States, William Nagy

Table 5.1: Difficulties Reading Manga Among Junior and Senior High School Students

Level	Girls			Boys		
	Yes	No	DK	Yes	No	DK
Preschool Girls n = 357 Boys n = 331	48%	35%	17%	46%	37%	17%
Grades 1–3 Girls n = 330 Boys n = 335	39%	44%	17%	32%	52%	16%
Grades 4–6 Girls n = 344 Boys n = 338	31%	57%	12%	31%	59%	10%
Junior H. S. Girls n = 348 Boys n = 334	25%	68%	7%	32%	60%	8%
Senior H. S. Girls n = 158 Boys n = 125	21%	74%	5%	22%	70%	8%

Table 5.2: Strategies for Dealing with Reading Difficulties

		Preschool	Grades 1–3	Grades 4–6	Junior High	Senior High
Girls	Reread	60%	65%	77%	74%	35%
	Ask someone	22%	22%	13%	13%	29%
	Other strategies	18% (n=100)	13% (n=76)	10% (n=61)	13% (n=55)	36% (n=69)
Boys	Reread	60%	56%	66%	78%	60%
	Ask someone	32%	34.5%	24%	16%	19%
	Other strategies	8% (n=93)	9.5% (n=64)	10% (n=67)	6% (=64)	21% (n=58)

maintains that reading is crucial for language development because the texts provide a context for vocabulary.[20] As children learn to read manga informally, rereading is an important strategy for enabling readers to gain familiarity with the stories and styles. By continuing to read manga, their knowledge of vocabulary and visual techniques expands. For instance, one junior high school reader remarked, ["I understood how to read just after reading a lot of manga"]. Table 5.3 shows how often readers reread their favorite manga.

For both girls and boys, rereading manga is a common pattern. In addition, there is a sizable number who reread their favorite manga ten or more times. These results suggest that multiple rereadings are an important means of dealing with reading difficulties. For instance, as they reread, readers can use their knowledge of context to determine the meaning of unknown vocabulary. When making inferences, readers may draw on different kinds of knowledge, which Robert Ruddell and Richard Speaker describe as linguistic knowledge, world knowledge, and decoding knowledge.[21] Decoding knowledge and world knowledge, together with the linguistic knowledge of text structure, refer to the reader's knowledge of language, such as grammar and vocabulary. Knowledge could also be termed schemata, or "knowledge already stored

Table 5.3: Amount of Rereading of Manga by Junior and Senior High School Students

Level	1 Time	3+ Times	10+ Times
Preschool			
Girls	17%	58%	25%
(n=331)			
Boys	13%	54%	33%
(n=304)			
Grades 1–3			
Girls	12%	54%	34%
(n=252)			
Boys	8%	50%	42%
(n=268)			
Grades 4–6			
Girls	11%	57%	32%
(n=310)			
Boys	7%	53%	40%
(n=303)			
Junior H. S.			
Girls	11%	56%	33%
(n=304)			
Boys	8%	50%	42%
(n=308)			
Senior H. S.			
Girls	16%	51%	33%
(n=121)			
Boys	8%	58%	34%
(n=108)			

in memory."[22] This awareness of the ways language is used is developmental, beginning at an early age. By the time they enter elementary school, children have gained considerable control over their language.

How readers deal with vocabulary difficulties is illustrated by the eight-year-old elementary school girl we referred to earlier. She enjoyed reading *YU-GI-OH!*, but admitted ["it's a little difficult because it has a lot of *kanji*. I can't read *kanji*"]. At that age, she would have been in grade 3 and have learned approximately 240 *kanji* by the end of grade 2.[23] As she read the manga in the interview, she encountered words that she did not know. These words were written in *kanji* while the *furigana* was in *hiragana*. In one instance, she claimed to use her knowledge of context to solve the problem: ["I found a *kanji* I haven't learned yet, but it is just one *kanji*, so no problem. I look at the words around it or above and below and then I know"]. This particular word was not easy to understand, not only in terms of what it meant but also in the way it was glossed and the kinds of contextual clues that it was supposed to be anchored with (see the tracing in figures 5.4 and 5.5).

To begin with, the difficult word she referred to in the speech balloon was written in *kanji*, 「幻想の魔術師」 *gennsō no majutsushi* (illusory magician). Instead of the usual *furigana* in *kana* script, the word was glossed in *kanji* as 精霊 *seirei* or "spirit." This

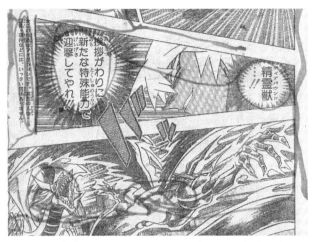

Figure 5.4. Tracing an Episode from *YU-GI-OH!* (Excerpt from *YU-GI-OH!* © 1996 by Kazuki Taka-hashi/SHUEISHA Inc.)

Figure 5.5. Tracing an Episode from *YU-GI-OH!* (Excerpt from *YU-GI-OH!* © 1996 by Kazuki Taka-hashi/SHUEISHA Inc.)

was not the pronunciation nor the meaning, but a lexical cohesive tie to the name of the spirit, Tiabaundo. This *kanji* compound had first appeared on the previous page, five panels earlier. In this instance, the *furigana* was in *katakana*, ティアバウンド, and indicated not the pronunciation of the *kanji*, but the personal name of this particular spirit, Tiabaundo, as 精霊獣 *seireijū* (possessed beast). Through this convention, the reader is supposed understand the nature of Tiabaundo. To further complicate the cross-referencing, the spirit was referred to by its personal name, Tiabaundo, in the speech balloon immediately preceding the balloon where the young reader encountered the vocabulary problem. The reader was thus expected to connect all these different associations in order to fully understand the meaning of the *kanji* compound 精霊. Figures 5.4 and 5.5 illustrate these three steps, beginning with the first mention

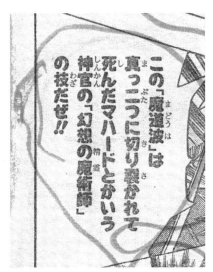

Figure 5.6.   Close-up of a Speech Balloon from *YU-GI-OH!* (Excerpt from *YU-GI-OH!* © 1996 by Kazuki Takahashi/SHUEISHA Inc.)

of the 精霊 in the larger compound, 精霊獣 with the *katakana* for Tiabaundo ティア バウンド, and then showing the other two speech balloons: one with Tiabaundo ティ アバウンド and the other with the *furigana* in *kanji*— 精霊. *Furigana* usually aids the reader in pronouncing the word, but here the *furigana* provides semantic clues—more specifically, cohesive ties. Because this was in such small font, we have provided a focus on the speech balloon so that the rubies can be seen (see figure 5.6).

When we reread the transcript and followed the reader's tracing, we tried to determine the meaning of the different *kanji* by paying close attention to the contextual clues indicated by the reader. Although this reader stated that she had understood the word by using contextual clues, perhaps it was more her motivation to read the manga, which she pointed out at the outset was difficult and beyond her *kanji* level, rather than specific use of contextual vocabulary clues that assisted her. However, as a reader, she believed that she could use contextual cues and thus solve vocabulary difficulties. Beginning in grade 1, Japanese language textbooks regularly use fill-in-the-blank type exercises to encourage readers to look at neighboring words and thus develop an awareness of contextual cues. But, as discussed earlier, readers have different purposes for reading, which could entail different levels of understanding.[24] In this situation, the reader wanted to read her favorite manga, in particular the latest installment. Perhaps she only wanted an overall understanding. She acknowledged that the story was difficult for her, but nevertheless she enjoyed it. Her brother, who had been interviewed earlier, reread his manga after finishing the interview, so perhaps she knew she would be able to reread the manga later.

By rereading, readers can solve difficulties at their own pace and in their own space. This is a key strategy to develop since manga readers are generally self-taught. There is another reason why rereading is so important as a strategy for dealing with difficulties. Many students stated in interviews that they did not like to admit having such difficulties, as explained by a junior high school boy:

> [When I don't know a word, I try to think of it in its context. For any word, I try to interpret the meaning on my own. I never ask anyone because I don't want to be told, "Don't you know that word?" I deal with problems myself.]

A high school reader described how she was embarrassed to admit to still reading manga and also to having problems. If she did not understand anything, she reread rather than asked for help:

> [Though I could ask questions when I was a child, now I don't do it any more. It's hard to say that I, a high school student, still read manga. They may think me childish for still reading manga. Everyone would look at me strangely because I'm in the third year.]

Since manga are considered easy to read, it is seen as embarrassing to acknowledge having any problems, especially among older children. Another junior high school reader highlighted this attitude. He did have an occasional problem and would solve it by rereading. He could ask his friends about difficulties in novels or a textbook, but not in manga.

> Interviewer: [Are there some places you are not sure when you read manga?]
>
> Student: [Ah yes, sometimes. But if I read well and think well, then I will understand. . . . Think about what I didn't understand.]
>
> Interviewer: [Have you ever asked your friends what it means when you don't understand manga?]
>
> Student: [Not with manga. I sometimes do it with novels or textbooks . . . I will think by myself.]

Yet the data from survey respondents summarized in table 5.2 indicate that there are times when readers do ask someone for assistance. The category of asking for assistance included asking a parent, sibling, or a friend, with parents being the largest group, followed by friends and then siblings. One mother described how her son asked for help with words he did not know: ["He often asks me questions about words he doesn't know. Because there is *furigana*, it is easy for him to ask. Recently, he asks about some pretty difficult words"]. With most of the *kanji* appearing with *furigana*, it is possible to pronounce the word and ask someone or look up words in a dictionary. However, manga vary in the amount of *furigana* they use and therefore in how many contextual clues they provide.

Other strategies for dealing with reading problems include ignoring the difficulty and reading on. For instance, the earlier reader of *YU-GI-OH!* who described how she used contextual clues to deal with reading problems also ignored unknown words and continued reading: ["I skip the boring ones"]. In one particular speech

Figure 5.7.   Tracing an Episode from *YU-GI-OH!* (Excerpt from *YU-GI-OH!* © 1996 by Kazuki Taka-hashi/SHUEISHA Inc.)

balloon, there was the word *gisei* 犠牲 (scapegoat) in *kanji* with *furigana* in *hiragana*: ぎせい, the pronunciation for *gisei* (see figure 5.7). *Gisei* is a difficult word, especially for an eight-year-old. When asked if she understood this word, she replied, ["I don't know the meaning, but it is not difficult. I skip words I don't know"]. In this instance, she skipped the word and instead focused on the graphics.

When asking for assistance, some readers made it clear that only certain kinds of assistance would be requested. For example, a junior high school boy stated, ["I get feedback from friends on the graphics, but not on the story"]. Two college-aged readers were also circumspect when asking for help. They described that rather than directly asking for help, they would approach the problem indirectly, such as by asking what their friends thought of a particular point in the story. This might then lead into a discussion of the difficulty. Another college reader told us that she sometimes looked at the anime to find an answer to her problem.

Depending on the situation, readers vary the strategies they use to deal with difficulties. Of the three that are presented in table 5.2, rereading is the most common. Yet rereading is not only a strategy for dealing with difficulties. It can be a strategy for enjoyment. One possible reason for this rereading, as pointed out earlier, is the manga text's multimodal nature. The interaction of panels, graphics, sound effects, and dialogue lend themselves to understanding the story more deeply with each reading. In addition, the content and characters may be attractive enough to sustain interest over multiple rereadings. Rereading thus seems to have various functions. It can be a way of learning how to read manga, a comprehension strategy to deal with reading difficulties, and it can also be used to further the enjoyment of reading.

Rereading at a Single Sitting

In order to discuss further the nature of the rereading, a distinction can be drawn between rereading at a single sitting compared with rereading at multiple sittings. In an interview, one reader, a fifth-grade boy, demonstrated his rereading strategy.

Figure 5.8.   Tracing an Episode from *Mr. FULLSWING* (Excerpt from *Mr. FULLSWING* © 2001 by Shinya Suzuki/SHUEISHA Inc.)

He traced the manga twice (at his suggestion), each time using a different color felt pen. The first time was with a light green pen and the second time was with a dark green pen. On his first reading of *Mr. FULLSWING*, he focused on the graphics and traced the characters' faces.[25] Unlike other readers, he skimmed most of the speech balloons (see figure 5.8). We are able to claim he skimmed because in this manga the text is written vertically. He read quickly—["I want to know the content sooner; I want to know the point"]. That was not the only reason: ["Well, I glanced around and I thought this and this might be interesting"]. For some of the panels he skipped, he said, ["I will read this later"]. This was a preparation for the second reading.

The strategy that this reader used is reminiscent of top-down processing. This involves first trying to comprehend the macrostructure or the general picture and then later moving down to comprehend the microstructure or the details, especially when faced with difficulties.[26] However, his reading process appears more complex than a top-down strategy. On the first reading, he read the panel with the commentary describing the episode in relation to past episodes. This behavior was different from some of our other readers who ignored any commentary outside the speech balloons.

On the boy's second reading, not all the speech balloons were read. Only selected ones were read, although they were read in sequence. He stated: ["Most of the interesting lines are written in bold; and I thought these (selected) panels were just interesting"]. When he did read a speech balloon, he traced each line. He later mentioned that the more interesting panels tended to be the larger ones. In the interviews with different readers, we were interested in whether the selected parts were necessary for the comprehension of the whole. That was less of a priority for this particular reader who was more interested in isolating interesting parts and finding the jokes. When investigating the skills required for manga literacy, we have tended to focus on the skills of understanding main ideas, the story line, and inferences, particularly in the gutter between the panels. We assumed that comprehending the whole story was a necessary prerequisite. Instead, we have found that readers focus on character dialogue, skip contextual commentary, skim for points of interest, and scan for jokes.

The strategy of rereading in one sitting may not be an isolated phenomenon. In an interview with a senior high school student, we found another reader who also used a variety of reading strategies when rereading at a single sitting. We described earlier how she uses graphics, but here we include a more detailed explanation of her reading strategies:

> [First, I read the lines generally. But in the second reading, I can afford to read the pictures and the background more slowly. That's because I've already read the lines. I sometimes skip in reading a new manga, so I can read many times to find out the part I haven't read yet. (In the second round) I look at each line and the main characters' faces.]

As this reader pointed out, rereading is done at varying speeds and for different purposes. Through rereading, the reader can gain a greater understanding and also an appreciation of the story.

Two college-age men reported that they read manga stories in a similar way, thus demonstrating flexible reading skills. First they skim the entire story and then later they go to back to the panels where:

a. Their interest is drawn, either by the size or the graphics in it.
b. There are movements in the narrative, such as a tension between characters and unexpected developments. In these panels, the speech balloons are read carefully.
c. There are gags or jokes. Even in serious manga stories, the dialogue can contain witty phrases, jokes, and puns.

In spite of the flaws of the tracing task, we found that readers are flexible, employing a variety of strategies. There was, however, one reader who did seem to try to read everything on a page. He gave up after a few pages. As pointed out in chapter 4, we later found out that he was a reluctant reader and only read manga to keep up with his friends, all of whom were avid manga readers. Frederik Schodt reports that manga readers read at an estimated speed of sixteen pages per minute.[27] It is misleading to compare this to the speed-reading of prose, which is always measured in terms of a comprehension test. The reading of manga is not tested. It is likely that readers read different stories at different speeds, reflecting their different purposes for reading. In a nearly five-hundred-page issue of the weekly *SHŪKAN SHONEN JUMP*, for instance, not all the stories would be of interest to all readers. Those that do not attract a particular reader would presumably be flipped through quickly. Those that are attractive would be read more carefully. However, even those stories of interest would be read selectively. The selectivity (and perhaps loss of memory) from reading in the first sitting leaves open the possibility of new material to be read in another sitting.

Rereading at Multiple Sittings

Many readers reread manga at different sittings. Repeatedly reading a favorite manga can help the readers become familiar with the creator's style, as described by this senior high school girl:

> [Actually, I couldn't understand them (symbols) when I was little. But I read my favorite manga so many times and it helped to understand them after that. If I read manga many times and know the subsequent story, it helps me to understand the previous part.]

The majority of readers learn to read manga informally in the first few years of elementary school. Rereading is one of the most common strategies to grasp how to do this. This was emphasized by one adult reader who said she had learned to read manga and was able to do so quickly, yet several of her friends, as well as her mother, "can't read, they don't know how to read manga," because they had never learned how. It was clear to her that manga literacy was more than just looking at pictures and reading words on a page. These reading skills had to be developed through practice.

However, rereading at a single or multiple sittings is not just a comprehension strategy but also a part of the pleasure of reading. This was true of elementary and high school readers, whether the manga was a serial or a single episode story. For instance, enjoyment was the reason a nine-year-old boy reread his favorite manga:

> [All of *COROCORO* and the others I've read over a hundred times. Yes, because it's fun. I've read it (*Dangerous Jīsan*) over one hundred times in my free time. . . . There are so many funny parts. I have read the current issue many times.]

Enjoyment is also cited as a reason for rereading manga by older readers, such as a senior high school girl when describing how she read manga, in this instance, one she had borrowed: ["I read it five or six times. I read it about twice in one night. I read it again and again. I can find something new when I read it many times"].

Apart from rereading to understand or enjoy the story, some readers reread to find additional, specific information related to another activity. One young boy was interested in video games and read the related manga. He reread the manga carefully because, as he told us, ["I read not only the story, but also the information. This information is useful for my game. I read almost everything. Yes, many times because I don't get all the information in the manga in the first few times"]. The close relationship between manga and kindred media such as video games motivates this kind of rereading.

Another reader had a different reason for rereading manga, but it also related to the need for a careful study of the text. He was a senior high school student and explained why he reread his favorite manga, *DRAGON BALL*:[28]

> [Well, the details can remain fresh in my mind by rereading. And I can talk with my friends about it so I like rereading. Yes, I can share the details with them. Because of this, I think I should read in more detail. I look at the pictures roughly and read the lines in the first reading. And I read in detail and burn them into my mind in the second reading. That's my pattern.]

For this reader, rereading was a way he could remember plot details and thus keep up with his friends. As described in chapter 4, many readers share their manga and talk about them in their communities of readers. Being able to keep up with the group is important, especially in elementary and junior high school, and rereading is a strategy to ensure that the readers have the necessary information to be an active member of the group.

Summary

Readers employ a variety of strategies when reading manga. Through the eye-movement tracing task, we were able to find that almost all readers focus on the speech balloons, that is, the print aspect. Most readers then focus on the faces of characters in order to understand emotions and reactions. Fewer readers focused on background and commentary. Although the task provided some indication of the order in which readers read manga, the task provided the unexpected advantage of serving as a talking point for readers to explain their strategies.

On the surveys, most readers reported that they never encountered difficulties while reading manga. While some asked family members and friends for help, most did not. Those readers we were able to interview explained that they were embarrassed to ask for help because it is assumed that reading manga is easy. Consequently, most readers who encountered difficulties had to deal with them on their own or ask indirectly by striking up a conversation on the manga's content.

The most common strategy to deal with difficulties is to ignore them and reread the manga in the hope that subsequent readings would clarify the difficulty. However, the practice of rereading is more than simply a strategy to cope with reading difficulties. More readers reported rereading their favorite manga than those readers who reported having difficulties. Furthermore, the majority of our respondents stated that they read their favorite manga multiple times. Rereading is considered to be highly pleasurable. Some readers reread in one sitting, using different kinds of strategies for each reading. Others reread on different occasions, reporting that they discover something new each time.

Notes

1. Terry Beers, "Commentary: Schema-Theoretic Models of Reading: Humanizing the Machine," *Reading Research Quarterly* 22, no. 3 (1987): 369–77; Walter Kintsch, "An Overview of Top-Down and Bottom-Up Effects in Comprehension," *Discourse Processes* 39 (2005): 125–28.

2. For example, Kenneth S. Goodman, "Reading: A Psycholinguistic Guessing Game," *Journal of the Reading Specialist* 6 (1967): 126–35; Walter Kintsch and Teun A. van Dijk, "Toward a Model of Text Comprehension and Production," *Psychological Review* 85 (1978): 363–94; and David E. Rumelhart, "Schemata: The Building Blocks of Cognition," in *Theoretical Issues in Reading Comprehension: Perspectives from Cognitive Psychology, Linguistics, Artificial Intelligence, and Education*, ed. Rand J. Spiro, Bertram C. Bruce, and William F. Brewer (Hillsdale, NJ: Lawrence Erlbaum Associates, 1980), 33–58.

3. Donald D. Deshler and Michael F. Hock, "Adolescent Literacy: Where We Are, Where We Need to Go," in *Shaping Literacy Achievement: Research We Have, Research We Need*, ed. Michael Pressley, Alison K. Billman, Kristen H. Perry, Kelly E. Reffitt, and Julia Moorhead Reynolds (New York: The Guildford Press, 2007), 98–128.

4. Zygmunt Bauman, *Hermeneutics and Social Science: Approaches to Understanding* (Aldershot, UK: Gregg Revivals, 1992).

5. Patricia A. Alexander and Tamara L. Jetton, "Learning from Text: A Multidimensional and Developmental Perspective," in *Handbook of Reading Research*, vol. 3, ed. Michael L. Kamil, Peter B. Mosenthal, P. David Pearson, and Rebecca Barr (Mahwah, NJ: Lawrence Erlbaum Associates, 2000), 285–310.

6. Susan R. Goldman and John A. Rakestraw, Jr. "Structural Aspects of Constructing Meaning from Text," in *Handbook of Reading Research*, vol. 3, ed. Michael J. Kamil, Peter B. Mosenthal, P. David Pearson, and Rebecca Barr (Mahwah, NJ: Lawrence Erlbaum Associates, 2000), 311–35.

7. Marylyn J. Chambliss, "Text Cues and Strategies Successful Readers Use to Construct the Gist of Lengthy Written Arguments," *Reading Research Quarterly* 30, no. 4 (1995): 778-807.

8. MEXT (Ministry of Education, Culture, Sports, Science, and Technology), *Shōgakkō Shidō Yōryō* (Elementary school curriculum), www.mext.go.jp/b_menu/shuppan/sonota/990301/03122601/002.htm (accessed March 4, 2007).

9. *ONE PIECE* © 1997 by Eiichiro Oda/SHUEISHA Inc.

10. Akimoto Osamu, *Kochira Katsushika-ku Kameari Kōen Mae Hashutsujo* (The police station in front of Kameari Park in Katsushika) (Tokyo: Shueisha, 1976).

11. Norman Fairclough, *Analyzing Discourse: Textual Analysis for Social Research* (London: Routledge, 2003), 218.

12. *Otaku* (Johannesburg, South Africa: Xvolve, 2005).

13. Sōyama Kazutoshi, *Zettai Zetsumei Dangerous Jīsan* (Dangerous *jīsan*) (Tokyo: Shogakukan, 2000**)**.

14. For example, *SHŌNEN JUMP*, February, vol. 1, no. 2 (2003): 328. At the same time and on the same page, readers are given another cultural lesson as they are informed that page 328 is not the first page of the magazine. Instead, it is the last page and the magazine should be read from right to left, as in Japan.

15. Kate Allen and John E. Ingulsrud, "*Manga* Literacy: Popular Culture and the Reading Habits of Japanese College Students," *Journal of Adolescent & Adult Literacy* 46, no. 8 (2003): 674–83.

16. Natsume Fusanosuke, "Manga Bumpō Niokeru Koma no Hōsoku" (Rules for frames in manga syntax: Categories and relationships between frame to frame and frame to page), in *Manga no Yomikata* (How to read manga), ed. Inoue Manabu (Tokyo: Takarajimasha, 1995), 196–205; Tezuka Osamu, *Manga no Kokoro: Hassō to Tekunikku* (The mind of manga: The inspiration and techniques) (Tokyo: Kobunsha, 1994).

17. *YU-GI-OH!* © 1996 by Kazuki Takahashi/SHUEISHA Inc.

18. Ann L. Brown, "Metacognition: The Development of Selective Attention Strategies for Learning from Texts," in *Theoretical Models and Processes of Reading*, third ed., ed. Harry Singer and Robert B. Ruddell (Newark, DE: International Reading Association, 1985), 501–26.

19. Karen Mezynski, "Issues Concerning the Acquisition of Knowledge: Effects of Vocabulary Training on Reading Comprehension," *Review of Educational Research* 53, no. 2 (1983): 253–79.

20. William Nagy, "On the Role of Context in First- and Second-Language Vocabulary Learning," in *Vocabulary: Description, Acquisition and Pedagogy*, ed. Norbert Schmitt and Michael McCarthy (Cambridge: Cambridge University Press, 1997), 64–83.

21. Robert B. Ruddell and Richard B. Speaker Jr., "The Interactive Reading Process: A Model," in *Theoretical Models and Processes of Reading*, third ed., ed. Harry Singer and Robert B. Ruddell (Newark, DE: International Reading Association, 1985), 751–93.

22. Richard C. Anderson and P. David Pearson, "A Schema-Theoretic View of Basic Processes in Reading Comprehension," in *Interactive Approaches to Second Language Reading*, ed. Patricia L. Carrell, Joanne Devine, and David E. Eskey (Cambridge: Cambridge University Press, 1988), 37–55.

23. MEXT (Ministry of Education, Culture, Sports, Science, and Technology), *Shōgakkō Shidō Yōryō* (Elementary school curriculum), www.mext.go.jp/b_menu/shuppan/sonota/990301/03122601/002.htm (accessed March 4, 2007).

24. Brown, "Metacognition," 501–26.

25. *Mr. FULLSWING* © 2001 by Shinya Suzuki/SHUEISHA Inc.

26. For example, Priscilla A. Drum, "Children's Understanding of Passages," in *Promoting Reading Comprehension*, ed. James Flood (Newark, DE: International Reading Association, 1984), 61–78; Marilyn J. Adams and Allan Collins, "A Schema-Theoretic View of Reading," in *Theoretical Models and Processes of Reading*, third ed., ed. Harry Singer and Robert B. Ruddell (Newark, DE: International Reading Association, 1985), 404–25.

27. Frederik L. Schodt, *Manga! Manga! The World of Japanese Comics* (Tokyo: Kodansha International, 1986), 18.

28. Toriyama Akira, *DRAGON BALL* © 1984 by Bird Studio/SHUEISHA Inc.

Reasons for Reading Manga 6

Just as there is no single reason why people start reading manga, there is also no single reason explaining why they continue. As readers interact with manga, they create their own meanings, thus there can be different meanings for different readers. However, as we found in the surveys and interviews, there were patterns among the readers, and the most consistent reason why people read manga is that they enjoy doing so. The pleasures that readers derive from manga operate at many levels and are realized in various ways. To begin with, manga can take readers into a different world that stimulates their imagination, as described by high school students: ["There is a world view that is not in movies or other media"]; ["Manga provide worlds different from reality"].

Reading Manga for Pleasure and Unintentional Learning

Among the college students, both males and females frequently offered the word "dreams" as a reason for reading manga:

> ["I like manga because they give dreams and pleasure to readers."]
> ["There are dreams and they (manga) are a far-off world."]
> ["There is a plot, dreams, aspirations."]
> ["We can discover dreams in manga."]

dreams

Since manga can make fantasies accessible, they are enjoyable:

> ["The fantastic, outside of one's daily life, is possible in manga."]
> ["Although fantastic, I had wanted to do the same."]

What are these dreams and pleasures that readers speak of when they read manga? To begin with, manga have a story and characters that readers can relate to, as these high school and college students wrote on the survey:

Figure 6.1. *Fruits Basket* (Excerpt from *Fruits Basket* by Takaya Natsuki. © 1999 by *Hana to Yume Comics*. Reprinted with permission of Hakusensha.)

["Manga stories are enjoyable."]
["I can relate to the content and characters in manga."]

For instance, the attraction of the story was the main reason a high school student had for reading her favorite manga, the *shōjo Fruits Basket*:[1]

[It (the manga) has a strong message. The manga writer writes exactly what we think in the manga. Therefore when I read her manga, I feel her warm message. This is that kind of manga. That's the only manga that I've been collecting until today.]

Fruits Basket is the story of Honda Tohru, an orphaned high school student. Needing money and a place to stay, she goes to work for the mysterious Sohma family. The manga describes Tohru's life with the family and relations with different family members, some of whom are also high school students like herself. Despite all her difficulties, Tohru is always cheerful and able to solve problems. As the reader pointed out, she likes this manga because it has a positive message.

In addition to an interesting story, readers can gain access to a range of characters and emotions with which they can empathize, as explained by this high school reader: ["I like *DRAGON BALL*. I think it is the best, best manga in the world. The main character Goku is pure and he wants, wants to be strong"]. *DRAGON BALL*, a *shōnen* manga mentioned in chapter 4, is the story of Goku Son, a boy from outer space searching for magic dragon balls. The manga has been serialized and readers can see how he matures. Similar opinions were expressed by another reader when

Figure 6.2. *HUNTER X HUNTER* (Excerpt from © *HUNTER X HUNTER* by POT (Yoshihiro Togashi) All rights reserved/SHUEISHA Inc.)

describing her favorite manga, *HUNTER X HUNTER*,[2] which is also a *shōnen* manga: "[Why do I like it?] Story is so interesting, complicated. Characters, [the characters' emotions.] It is different from other manga." Like *DRAGON BALL*, the hero of *HUNTER X HUNTER* is a young boy on a quest. He is searching for his father, a hunter with special magical powers. His journey includes passing the examination to become a hunter himself, the difficulties that this entails, and forming friendships. These *shōnen* manga have typical *Bildungsroman* narrative structures and readers can be inspired by the characters' struggles and eventual success, as illustrated by a junior high school boy: ["It's the personal growth part. In other words, if you do it, you can achieve"].

By identifying with the characters, readers often learn something new and that can add to the reading pleasure. One senior high school student not only enjoyed the main character in her favorite manga, the "lady's" manga *Nodame Cantabile*,[3] but also the relationships in the story and what she learned from this:

> [Firstly, a man who is a central character is really stunning. *Cantabile* is a musical term and the story is about music. The man can play the piano and violin wonderfully, but he wants to be a conductor. And he gets to know an eccentric woman who is a next-door neighbor. Her name is Nodame. She is bad at doing everything except playing the piano. Her piano playing is very good. It is very interesting to read about the process of helping each other.]

Nodame, or Noda Megumi, does not clean her apartment nor is she a good cook. The lack of domestic skills is contrasted with her outstanding musical ability.

Figure 6.3. *Nodame Cantabile* (Excerpt from *Nodame Cantabile 1* by Ninomiya Tomoko. © 2002 by Kodansha Comics Kiss. Reprinted with permission of Kodansha.)

Her neighbor, Shinichi Chiaki, continually rescues her by cleaning up her room and cooking for her, but it is her passion for music that "saves" him.

Another high school student, in describing her favorite manga, *TENSHI NAN-KAJANAI* (I'm not an angel),[4] emphasized the importance of what she learned from the characters as she identified with them:

> [I can feel empathy for it (her favorite manga) because the characters' feelings are written clearly. They (the characters) are so honest that I want to back them up. This manga is encouraging for me. I feel empathy for the characters' feelings. When I read it, I often think, "Oh, I know exactly how the characters are feeling" or "This case happens a lot." I'm strengthened.]

The story of *TENSHI NANKAJANAI* centers round high school student Sae-jima Midori and her romantic relationships with Sudo Akira and Nakagawa Ken. She eventually finds her true love and despite all the difficulties, she is a cheerful and popular student (see figure 6.4).

Most of the frequently mentioned titles on the surveys focus on school life and thus describe a world familiar to the readers such as classes, relationships, sports clubs, bullying, and examinations. These are issues students have to learn to deal with. Martin Barker points out that if a comic is not relevant to the lives of the readers, they will not read it.[5] In her study of Canadian teenagers reading teenzines, Dawn Currie maintains that these magazines are popular not only because they are enjoyable but also because they provide "meaning about life and the social roles

Figure 6.4.   *TENSHI NANKAJANAI* (Excerpt from *TENSHI NANKAJANAI* © 1991 by Ai Yazawa/ SHUEISHA Inc.)

of women."[6] Dianne Cooper found similar results in her study of readers of teen romances in Australia.[7]

Emphasizing the lessons that readers learn from manga, Natsume Fusanosuke has written a book entitled *Manga ni Jinsei wo Manande Nani ga Warui?* (What's wrong with learning about life from manga?).[8] Through their reading of manga, readers also find ways to deal with personal issues, especially as relationships with friends, classmates, and teachers are common themes in manga: ["I can learn to understand the psychology of people"]. When reading their favorite stories, readers can distance themselves from actual problems and learn about possible solutions through a pleasurable, comfortable medium. While a number of high school and college readers maintained that learning about relationships was important, there were only a handful of students who explicitly wrote on the surveys that manga could help them with romantic relationships. For instance, a male and several female senior high school students stated that they read manga because ["there is romance in manga"] and ["I can learn about falling in love"]. In the interviews, the students did not talk to us about romance directly, preferring to use the more general description of relationships. Yet, as shown by the various readers' comments, many of their favorite manga are about school and deal with romantic relationships. We did, however, interview one college student who had read *yaoi* manga in high school. She liked these manga because she thought they described high school romances more realistically, such as by including bedroom scenes. At the time of the interview, her favorite manga in college was a "lady's" *komikku*, and although she named the title, she was reluctant to tell us about it as she felt it was too erotic. She did say that the author was new and that she had even written to her and become a pen pal.

Being able to empathize with characters in team-playing situations is sometimes viewed positively by adults, so much so that parents and teachers may encourage

Figure 6.5. *Slam Dunk* (Excerpt from *Slam Dunk 3* by Inoue Takehiko. © 1991 by Jump Comics. Reprinted with permission of I.T. Planning, Inc.)

children to read a particular manga. This is often true of the sports manga, which focus on the importance of being a team player and overcoming difficulties. One high school student described how the members of her basketball club would take on the identity of the characters in the manga *Slam Dunk*, based on a high school basketball club.[9] This was one of the most popular manga in the 1990s and was also made into an anime, which was internationally very successful.

> [And we role-played. For example, we decided who would role-play some of the characters. If there was a good three-point shooter in the manga, someone said that she wanted to play Mitsui's role. Yes, we sometimes role-played like that for pleasure. Everyone knew it (*Slam Dunk*).]

Role-playing manga stories is a practice several informants have described. We were unable to find out at what age this practice ended or merged with the practices of *cosplay*.

Another reader, who was member of the softball tennis club, talked about how her club members all read the tennis manga *THE PRINCE OF TENNIS*.[10] Although this was about hardball tennis and thus a different kind of game, the club members copied techniques from the manga.

> [Well, it (*Teni-Puri* [THE PRINCE OF TENNIS]) was about hardball tennis. I played softball tennis. But the numbers of the tennis club members increased as a result of *Teni-Puri*. Although techniques of hardball and softball are completely different, everyone copied from the manga.]

Figure 6.6. *THE PRINCE OF TENNIS* (Excerpt from *THE PRINCE OF TENNIS* © 1999 by Takeshi Ko-nomi/SHUEISHA Inc.)

In addition to learning sports techniques, several high school and college students stated in interviews that they also valued learning new vocabulary and *kanji*:

> ["Manga help me learn vocabulary and *kanji*. They make difficult concepts understandable through stories. They teach me."]
> ["I can learn vocabulary I don't know."]

One junior high school student told us that his grandmother sent him manga so that he could learn *kanji*: ["She said she would be happy to let me read manga as I can learn new vocabulary with manga"]. This was also supported by a number of parents, as explained by one mother describing how her son learned *kanji* from manga and its video game version:

> [He learned *kanji* from manga. He also learned from games because he couldn't play the game if he didn't read *kanji*. It's the same thing. He played the game when he didn't know the *kanji* when he was in grade one. So he studied *kanji* from manga.]

On the surveys, some students wrote about what they learned from the techniques of manga, such as typefaces:

> ["I learn the function of different typefaces."]
> ["Manga helps my drawing."]
> ["When I read manga, my knowledge expands."]

Knowledge about vocabulary or format is more commonly associated with reading in school. Since the surveys were anonymous and we did not know the respondents, there would have been no need for the students to justify their choices to us in ways that they thought would be more acceptable to teachers.

It is widely recognized that kinds of learning can take place by engaging with the popular media. Indeed the blended word "edutainment" represents the range of products available that try to maximize the learning experience through the enjoyment of popular media. Yet manga are not created for "edutainment." Moreover, readers do not turn to manga to learn. In their case study of a manga reader, Donna Alvermann and Alison Heron argue that the learning aspects of reading manga are all a part of the experience of play.[11]

At the same time, there is a great deal of information in manga. Hirokane Kenshi, the creator of the *Shima Kōsaku* series about a successful company executive, contends that the information contained in manga provides the attraction to readers.[12] For example, in his work, he describes the conditions, process, and effects of a hostile company acquisition all in the context of a story. He also describes how such acquisitions can be avoided. Similar kinds of information are provided in the niche titles we introduced in chapters 1 and 2. In spite of the wealth of information, we have no evidence of readers "consulting" manga for a specific purpose. Manga are not reference books. The learning that comes from reading manga is unintentional and often unexpected. The pleasures of reading manga include the pleasure of learning something new.

Reading Manga for Relaxation

Reading manga is often seen as a form of escapism and a way to relieve the tedium of the classroom.[13] High school students, particularly in the final years of junior and senior high school, are under much pressure both in and out of school. In addition to homework, a lot of students attend a *juku* (cram school) after school several days a week in order to prepare for examinations. Reading manga is a welcome relief to the pressures of school, as was pointed out by many readers, including these senior high school and college students:

> ["Reading manga gets rid of stress and is good when I am tired."]
> ["To read manga is refreshing and a change of pace."]
> ["To blow off stress."]
> ["Reading manga is a break from other activities."]
> ["Manga provides an oasis for my mind."]

However, this kind of reading is not necessarily undisciplined, as shown by a senior high school student. In her interview, she explained that as much as she enjoyed the diversion provided by manga, she was able to restrict her reading.

> [And I read it as a break when I study for the entrance examination. Even though I get tired and want to join my club activity, it takes time to come to school. However, reading manga doesn't take time and I can forget about studying while I read them. In order to feel refreshed, I do read like that. But it is sometimes dangerous to read for a long time because I can immerse myself in reading. That's why I preferably read a short story. It has to be complete. If I read a serial, I get curious to read the next episode.]

One of the reasons why manga can be relaxing is because it is amusing. An elementary school boy liked his favorite manga not only because of the interesting story but also for the jokes and puns. He shared them with his sister and often reread the manga ["because it is fun. I read one hundred times over and over when I have free time"]. In the interview, he and his sister enjoyed pointing out and explaining the puns. Here is one example he shared with us, much to the discomfort of his mother:

> [Here are the words "the end," but another place has "bum" (*ushiro*)! "End" and "bum" have the same meaning. There are so many jokes. I read many times here in the current issue.]

A high school student explained how she also enjoyed the humor of her favorite manga *Coji-Coji*[14] and that it helped her, even though she sometimes read it illicitly in school.

> [The imaginary main character is *Coji-Coji* and he is foolish and funny. I like him because he says what he thinks directly and each remark is funny. For example, though he answered perfectly on a test, he made a mistake in writing his name and so his mark was 95. When I read *Coji-Coji* during class, I can't help bursting into laughter. I'm afraid my teacher might notice it. This is really funny. This is the funniest manga I have ever read. So this is a good book to change your mood when you are depressed. Manga is big entertainment, isn't it? So I read it when I want to laugh. It is also good to cry by reading it, but I like to laugh. That's why I prefer funny manga.]

Despite regulations against reading manga in many schools, they are often ignored, as described by a junior high school boy: ["They (teachers) tell us not to read manga in school. . . . But some people brought them secretly. Most of the students brought them secretly"]. When we visited our college students on teaching practice, we observed girls and boys secretly reading manga at the back of the class during the lessons. For many young people, part of the pleasure of this kind of literacy is knowing that it is frowned on in school, hence the enjoyment of secretly reading forbidden texts during class.[15] This was how one student described the pleasure of such kind of reading:

> [Some students hide manga in their desks and read them during their classes. I did it too when I was in the first grade (senior one) in this school. It is more fun to read manga in a thrilling situation. It makes me want to read more. Of course, teachers scold me for doing it. They order me to put it away. They take the manga away from me, but if I go to their office after class, they give it back to me.]

Teachers are often uncomfortable with students reading manga in school. When students do so, this is seen as a sign of boredom or defiance. As Allan Luke points out, having rules on what can and cannot be read in school emphasizes that reading is not a neutral practice.[16]

Aside from the stories and the characters, a number of readers stated that they enjoyed reading manga because of the visual appeal. For example, a college student particularly enjoyed one manga "because the pictures are so cute," while a high school student wrote ["I like the graphics"]. The visual appeal was one of the main reasons a high school student gave for why she liked *ONE PIECE*: ["It is the manga I like. I have read and collected all the books in the series. I think the pictures are very elaborate"]. Another college reader explained that she valued manga because of the graphics. She had recently begun to read *yaoi* in which there is minimal plot and text accompanied by detailed, even colored graphics. In fact, when she bought this type of manga, she focused on the pictures rather than the plot, and the more abstract the graphics were, the more she was attracted to them. The importance of the visual appeal of manga was emphasized time and again in the interviews by readers of all ages telling us that they did not write manga because they were poor at drawing.

Some high school students were attracted by the graphics, not so much by the style but more because they facilitated an understanding of the story:

["Manga are easy to understand because of the graphics."]
["Pictures make it easy to understand the story and feelings."]

Yet it was precisely because of the graphics a college reader disliked *ONE PIECE*, which he claimed appealed only to younger readers: ["This illustration attracts younger people. Something like this, (with) lots of young people, strange people"]. Manga graphics are central to the text, not only because of their function in conveying the meaning of the text, but also because of their aesthetic or visual appeal. Interesting artwork can attract readers even at an early age, as we found when we interviewed an elementary school girl, who began to read *Nausicaä of the Valley of the Wind* because she wanted to copy Miyazaki's style of drawing.[17]

Other reasons for enjoying manga relate to accessibility and cost:

["Because manga are there."]
["Manga are cheap."]

Part of the accessibility of manga is that readers consider them easier to read than books because of the textual and visual clues.

["I can confirm whether my images of a story are accurate or not by looking at manga graphics."]
["Unlike books, manga can be read whenever I like and in a short time."]
["Manga are easy to read."]

However, the ease of understanding was not straightforward, as the responses were often contradictory. Some readers claimed that ["I don't have to use my head as much as when reading books"], while others wrote ["When I read manga, I have to use my head"].

Shifting Preferences of Manga Readers

We present our findings on how preferences shift first because many of our informants were older and their reflections provide a historical context for understanding manga preferences. The changes that our informants reported are due to a number of factors, such as increased literacy skills, in addition to wider access to different types of manga through friends and increased purchasing power. Changes in the kinds of manga being read are not new, as we found when we interviewed adults who grew up reading their own purchased manga.

One such person who grew up reading manga was a woman who began reading manga in elementary school and continues to read and collect manga. She described, in English, how manga gradually developed in response to changes in the readers such as herself:

> My generation, cartoon generation. Cartoon generation of elementary school or before elementary school, I was a kindergartner and I read manga. Our generation, all cartoon generation, so precious target. And so of course, story, heroine and hero according to the generation. The story is, of course, it's each manga generation's real life or real problem.

The changes she described relate not only to content but also to the artwork, such as the importance of using screen tone for shading and panel order. She explained that the order of panels in modern manga is more complex compared with manga of her mother's generation. As a result, her mother was unable to read contemporary manga. To be a successful manga reader, you needed the experience of regular reading:

> My mother cannot read manga. In her age, just very simple. And so the number, they put the number, one, two, three. So the reader just read, look at the picture according to the number. But recently, there are no numbers so my mother cannot read. Some of my friends, they have so little experience to read manga. They cannot read the first time. But I have lots of experience.

The same reader also commented on differences in the story content:

> But when I was an elementary kid, no scene like this. Just very sad story. And mom and children separated. So miserable. A beautiful girl bullied by a stepmother. Cinderella, just like Cinderella. Or success story. And sometimes ballerina stories and sportsmen. Sports stories. That's volleyball. It depends on the trend. But now mostly love stories. And of course characters' face have become different.

This reader had read the monthly *shōjo* manga magazine *Ribon* in elementary school.[18] First published in 1955 by Shueisha, the magazine continues to be published. Many of the successful serialized stories are then published as *komikku* and even made into anime. She remembers being shocked discovering later that one of her favorite writers from that time had begun to write more adult stories in "lady's" comics. Although she realized that this change was in response to the increasing adult market, she found it hard to accept.

> I was very disappointed, my favorite cartooner when I was an elementary kid. My favorite one. She wrote so cute story. But someday I notice that she wrote so adult, so very sexual story. And I was so shocked because the publishing company asked her to write much more adult, serious story.

When she entered junior high school, a new *shōjo* manga magazine, *Margaret*, appeared in 1963.[19] As we pointed out in chapter 2, not only did she enjoy the content, but, more importantly, it became a biweekly manga instead of a monthly one, and this had an impact because she did not have to wait so long for the next episode in a serial.

Another woman and part of this same generation who could afford to purchase manga described the kinds of manga she read as a young girl. What is interesting is the influence of current events on story themes—in this case, the 1964 Tokyo Olympics:

> [And I remember one story of the girl who is a ballet dancer. I liked it. And the second one is the story of volleyball. I read it when I was in junior high. It came out after the Tokyo Olympics. There were so many manga then like *Atakku No. 1* or *Sign V* and so on. At that time, baseball manga were for boys. When I was a child, sports or special occupation stories were popular. For example, *Garasu no Kamen* is the story of a girl who longs to be a ballet dancer.* Also there was a story of a girl who wanted to be an actress. In addition, a kind of animal story was popular too. The warmhearted story between a dog and a girl was popular. There were a lot of these kinds of stories at that time. . . . I liked manga and reading books because I liked stories.]
>
> (**Garasu no Kamen is about actors. The reader has confused it with *Swan*, a ballet manga published in *Margaret* at the same time in 1976.)

These readers' comments indicate some of the changes that have appeared over the years in *shōjo* manga, that is, from Cinderella type stories to *yaoi* love stories. Kazuko Suzuki maintains that these developments also reflect the influence of feminist ideas and women's changing status, as illustrated by the heroine in *Atakku No. 1*.[20]

Our data showed that many girls read both *shōnen* and *shōjo* manga. This pattern was also pointed out by one of the adult readers. She stated that when she was growing up, a number of her girl friends read *shōnen* manga, so this practice of cross-reading is not new. However, most girls she knew preferred *shōjo* manga for both the content and artwork.

Interviewer: [So at the very beginning you have *shōjo* and *shōnen* manga?]

Reader: [Of course. Quite a few my friends said they preferred *shōnen* manga, *shōnen* manga like that *Sunday Magazine*. But most girls preferred *shōjo* manga. The story is quite different and the characters and details are easy to compare. I preferred *shōjo* manga because of the characters of course, and the details.]

The reading practices of a high school reader we interviewed illustrate how these practices can be influenced by types of manga, as well as generational differences. The reader stated that her favorite manga was a *shōnen* manga, *HUNTER X HUNTER*, which she began reading in grade 4, elementary school. However, she encountered much opposition from her mother, who wanted her daughter to spend the time studying rather than reading manga. Yet once she actually looked at a copy of her daughter's manga, she changed her mind. The mother found that manga today are more engaging compared with those of her childhood, so much so that she began reading her daughter's manga:

> But now my mother read my manga. [I feel like saying, "You see, Mom. That's what I told you." The story has become complicated compared with the old manga, which my mother read. That's why she can read it right now. The stories she used to read were so simple that she thought manga were trivial. She insisted that I should study instead of reading them.]

Gendered Preferences of Manga Readers

We found that the range of titles chosen by readers increases with age. Obviously, interests diversify. Yet female readers report a broader range of titles than male readers. The female junior high school readers prefer many of the same manga that male readers like and actively cross-read. However, in high school and university, a preference among female readers for *shōjo* manga increases, indicating shifts in interests and increasing capabilities to read works describing subtle human relationships. In spite of the many titles that our respondents reported, our interviews with individual readers lead us to believe that our respondents have more varied preferences than they were willing to report.

Preferences of Junior High School Readers

In the surveys to junior and high school students, we asked the respondents to list the titles of their favorite manga, together with the number of times they read it and other titles if this had changed over the years. Some provided one title while others provided multiple titles. By becoming more proficient readers, there is a greater variety of manga available.

One of the main reasons for reading new titles is increasing literacy skills, especially *kanji* proficiency, as pointed out by this grade 6 boy when talking about his first manga: ["When we were in first or second grade, we might not have talked about manga so much. I could read *kanji*, but I read just simple manga when I was a child"]. In addition to increased reading proficiency, moving to junior high school can mean access to a wider variety of clubs and friends. This change is illustrated by a reader, who described how he started reading manga in the first year of junior high school: ["Well, other students brought manga to school and talked about them. Then I thought maybe I should read too. I didn't read (manga) until junior high school"]. A high school student similarly explained how she began to read the *shōnen* manga *Slam Dunk* in junior high school.

[Maybe I saw the anime first. And I saw it when I was an elementary school student. Then after starting to play basketball, I began to read it because it became popular again. Then I was moved again from the different point of view compared with my childhood.]

Asked if the other members of her junior high school club also read *Slam Dunk*, she replied: ["Yes, not everyone, but a lot of them read it at the time. And we role-played"].

When we looked at the number of manga being read by junior high school students, we found that for both boys and girls, there is an increase in the number of titles, as the readers grow older (see table 6.1). It should be noted that since the students had to remember what they read before and during elementary school, their memories might not be accurate. Yet they wrote down actual titles. We have only counted single instances of a title and that if, for example, *Doraemon* was cited for preschool, grades 1–3, and grades 4–6, it was only counted once, at the first level it was referred to.[21]

Even though there are fewer female respondents, table 6.1 shows that the number of titles is greater for girls than for boys. One major reason is that girls are reading more widely than boys. As described in earlier chapters, there are two basic genres of manga for children: *shōnen* manga (for boys) and *shōjo* manga (for girls). These preferences are generally delineated along gender lines. However, from the very beginning of their reading, girls read both kinds of manga. Except for four boys who reported reading *shōjo* manga in junior high school, boys prefer to read *shōnen* manga and do not read *shōjo* manga. On the other hand, girls are more open to reading across the genres. In fact, by junior high school, the three most popular titles for second-year girls were *shōnen* manga, as described in table 6.2. The most popular *shōjo* manga, *Peach Girl*, was a distant sixth in popularity.[22]

Table 6.1:   Number of Preferred Manga Titles Among Junior High School Readers

	Preschool	Grades 1–3	Grades 4–6	Junior High
Girls n=218	46 (38)*	42 (35)	66 (52)	171 (140)
Boys n=228	63	53	76	163+

*The number of *shōnen* titles that are also being read by the girls is in parenthesis.
+This includes four boys who read three different *shōjo* manga.

Table 6.2:   Second Year Female Junior High School Students' Favorite Manga

Title (n=109)	Type	Setting/Theme
(1) *ONE PIECE*	*Shōnen*	Fantasy/Adventure
(2) *THE PRINCE OF TENNIS*	*Shōnen*	School/Sports
(3) *Hikaru no Go* (Hikaru's go)	*Shōnen*	School/Board game/Fantasy

n=94

Table 6.3: Second Year Male Junior High School Students' Favorite Manga

Title (n=82)	Type	Setting/Theme
(1) *ONE PIECE*	*Shōnen*	Fantasy/Adventure
(2) *THE PRINCE OF TENNIS*	*Shōnen*	School/Sports
(3) *Slam Dunk*	*Shōnen*	School/Sports

n=130

The finding that girls read across manga genres is similar to reading patterns in the United States, where it has been found that girls also read books aimed at boys. North American publishers are aware of this and so have published more boys' titles, as they know the girls will read them, whereas boys will not read girls' titles.[23] In Japan, *shōnen* manga dominates the market so the greater number of titles could be a reason for girls reading across the genres. Another reason could be that reading *shōnen* manga would enable girls to cross gender boundaries and thus have the possibility of exploring different identities. This pattern of cross-reading by the female readers was found in all age groups, though it did become less pronounced among the senior high school and college students in our study.

In the table above, we have listed the three most popular titles among second year junior high school boys. The first two titles are the same as the girls (see table 6.2). The most popular manga, *ONE PIECE*, is a fantasy adventure about a group of pirates searching for the treasure, one piece. There is also plenty of humor, with both TV anime and movie anime versions. The second most popular manga for both the boys and girls is *THE PRINCE OF TENNIS*. It focuses on sports teams and relationships among the team members. The boys' third choice, *Slam Dunk*, is about a school basketball team. On the other hand, the girls' third choice is *Hikaru no Go* (Hikaru's go).[24] It is about a sixth-grade elementary school boy who becomes a champion go player with the help of his reincarnated medieval personal coach. Similar to sports manga, there are rivalries, struggles, and relationships with other students and the coach.

At the junior high school level, there is a convergence of preferences among both boys and girls. For many students, reading manga is a way of being part of a community. There is a shared knowledge because everyone knows what the others are reading and how tastes change, as explained by this junior high school boy:

> Everybody knew what was the one everyone was reading, what ones everybody didn't like and that stuff. Because like this one, this is *Jump*. Like there's ones that come out every week. There's *Jump* and *Conan* and *Sunday*, and there's one called *Magazine*. So like when I was in elementary school, I used to read one that's called *COROCORO*. It comes out every month. When I became junior high school, everybody's reading *Jump* or *Sunday*, so everybody reads that one.

In addition to the influence of friends, many of the interviewees spoke of how after they gained more experience reading manga and understanding the layout, they moved onto new titles. This tended to take place in junior high school, as explained by a reader: ["In junior high school . . . I started reading serious manga"]. He offered *Burakku Jakku* (Black Jack) as an example of this kind of manga.[25] Whether or not *shōjo* manga are easier to read than *shōnen* manga, some of the girls did believe that *shōjo* manga were easier. For instance, the *shōnen* magazine *SHŪKAN SHONEN JUMP* with its action stories was considered to have more complex and interesting stories, so many girls read *shōnen* manga because they enjoyed the stories, action, and graphics. These observations may change as the girls grow older.

In comparison with manga read by elementary students, such as the individual stories of *Doraemon* or monthly magazines like *COROCORO*, the ones read in junior high school are longer, serialized, and have more complex plots. The page layouts are also more demanding, as the rectangular panel layout, such as that found in *Doraemon*, is generally not used. This increasing complexity, both visual and textual, is part of the attraction of the manga read by older students. As one of the college students referred to earlier pointed out, the illustrations were more important to her than the story. She looked for manga that had what she considered good quality artwork and the more abstract the graphics were the better, as this allowed her to use her imagination.

Preferences of Senior High School Readers

In a survey of senior high school students, the students were asked to name their current favorite manga. Among the female students, ninety-six titles were given.

As shown in table 6.4, the three most popular manga for these high school students deal with a number of themes. However, in the top two choices, romance is the common theme. The most popular manga, *NANA*, is based on the story of two women with the same name and their relationships.[26] One of the women is a singer in a punk band and the manga describes her struggle for success as a musician. With the other Nana, the emphasis is on her romantic relationships. Separately, they move to Tokyo and end up sharing an apartment. The manga has been made into anime, two movies, and a light novel, emphasizing the appeal of this manga. It was also one that was singled out on the surveys as being read by the few boys who indicated that they read *shōjo* manga. The second most popular manga, *Fruits Basket*, is the story of an orphaned high school girl. A number of students spoke in the interviews about the heroine's optimism and that they were encouraged by her positive approach. The manga has been made into an anime as well as translated into a number of languages. Just like the junior high students, the *shōnen* manga *ONE PIECE* was also a top favorite.

Table 6.4: Female Students' Favorite Manga in Senior High School

Title (n=96)	Type	Setting/Theme
(1) *NANA*	*Shōjo*	Romance
(2) *Fruits Basket*	*Shōjo*	School/Fantasy/Romance
(3) *ONE PIECE*	*Shōnen*	Fantasy/Adventure

n=167

Figure 6.7:   *NANA* (Excerpt from *NANA* © 1999 by Yazawa Manga Seisakusho/SHUEISHA Inc.)

Similar to young girls in Britain and North America, the senior high school girls in our surveys and interviews preferred to read romantic *shōjo* manga, unlike the girls in junior high school. A number of studies have shown that girls read romance novels to learn about relationships.[27] A few of the senior high girls wrote in the surveys that they read manga because ["I can learn about falling in love"]. They also stressed that manga can teach them about relationships and people. Critics have argued that through reading romances, women (and girls) learn about gendered practices and thus how to conform.[28] Linda Christian-Smith also points out that in her study, the skilled readers or more proficient students did not read romances.[29] These were popular with the less academic students, suggesting that reading romances is influenced by intellect and social class. The reading patterns for female manga readers in our study only partly seem to fit this trend. To begin with, the high school students we interviewed were all in the top classes in one of the most prestigious high schools in the prefecture. (The other readers we interviewed reflected a broader range of schools and educational backgrounds.) A more interesting difference is that the girls in the interviews, as well as those in the junior high school surveys, also enjoyed reading *shōnen* manga. This was much stronger among the junior high girls than those in senior high. There seems to be a shift in reading preferences as the girls move from junior to senior high school.

Martin Barker highlights a similar shift in reading preferences among British girls in that they prefer reading romances rather than comics by early adolescence.[30] He suggests that their interest in romantic fiction is related to their emotional and social development.

In a study of readers' comprehension of manga, Nakazawa Jun found that junior high school students had difficulty understanding visual clues that signaled the mood of the story.[31] When presented with different pictures, students had varying success trying to identify the psychological states, especially worry and loneliness. However, in contrast to the junior high readers, those in senior high school were more successful. There are some serious questions about Nakazawa's test, as the students had to describe pictures in isolation. This ignores the basic nature of manga, which combines text and graphics to narrate a story. Despite this major limitation, Nakazawa's finding might be one way of interpreting readers' development and the shift to *shōjo* manga. By senior high school, girls would have become more skillful in understanding and appreciating the more subtle and complex emotions of *shōjo* manga, and so they would be more attracted to this kind of manga at this stage. Except for changes in readers' preferences, we do not have direct evidence for such an interpretation, but it could be one reason for the greater popularity of *shōjo* manga among girls in senior high school. At the same time, there were some readers who still felt that *shōnen* manga are more interesting and more difficult than *shōjo* manga.

Another reason for the change in readers' preferences might be the characters in the stories. The two most popular manga for the senior high girls, *NANA* and *Fruits Basket*, have strong leading female characters. A number of readers described to us how they were encouraged by the optimism of Honda Tohru in *Fruits Basket*. Two of the favorite *shōnen* manga for junior high girls, *THE PRINCE OF TENNIS* and *Hikaru no Go* (Hikaru's go), focus on school relationships and so describe a familiar world. However, the female characters in these manga have minor roles and romantic themes are not as prominent as, for example, in *NANA*.

Among the male senior high students, a list of seventy-five titles was given for their current favorite manga. As shown in table 6.5, the three most popular manga share a common theme of fantasy adventure. *HUNTER X HUNTER* is story of a young boy's search for his father (see figure 6.2). *DEATH NOTE* focuses on a high school student who has a mysterious power that can kill anyone whose name he writes down in a special notebook.[32] He justifies this by killing only criminals. As

Table 6.5: Male Students' Favorite Manga in Senior High School

Title (n=75)	Type	Setting/Theme
(1) *HUNTER X HUNTER*	*Shōnen*	Fantasy/Adventure
(2) *DEATH NOTE*	*Shōnen*	Psychological thriller
(3) *ONE PIECE*	*Shōnen*	Fantasy/Adventure

n=137

Figure 6.8: *DEATH NOTE* (Cover from *DEATH NOTE* © 2003 by Tsugumi Ohba, Takeshi Obata/ SHUEISHA Inc.)

Figure 6.9: *ONE PIECE* (Excerpt from *ONE PIECE* © 1997 by Eiichiro Oda/SHUEISHA Inc.)

he begins using his power to kill criminals and the body count mounts, a detective then investigates him, leading to a battle of wits between the two. The third favorite manga with the male students is the popular *ONE PIECE*.

Preferences of College Readers

When we conducted our initial survey of college students, we asked them to name the favorite manga they were reading in college, and one hundred women responded with a list of fifty-five titles. Compared with when they were in high school, fewer college women claimed to be reading manga, preferring magazines instead. This was also reflected in comments on the surveys or in the interviews, such as:

["I don't like manga because I like music magazines, fashion magazines, and books better than manga."]

["Now I don't read manga."]

However, among those who did read, some of the manga they were reading were the same as those read at high school. As shown in table 6.6, two of the manga are clearly about school. Similar to girls in senior high school, romance manga seem to be especially popular. *HANA-YORI DANGO* (Boys over flowers) is set in an elite high school.[33] The heroine, Tsukushi Makino, is from a family that has financial difficulties and so she feels out of place in school as she is surrounded by rich students. This, together with her relationships with Domyōji Tsukasa, the wealthiest student in the school, and Hanazawa Rui, another wealthy student, becomes the basis of the plot (see figure 6.10).

Similar to *HANA-YORI DANGO*, *Peach Girl* is also about a high school romance (see figure 6.11). The heroine, Adachi Momo, is looked down on because of her tan and light-colored hair. In fact, she is thought to be promiscuous. Momo's best friend, Kashiwagi Sae, is the cause of all her problems. Sae spreads gossip about Momo and continually tries to undermine the latter's romantic relationships. In both *shōjo* manga, the heroines have to deal with being social outcasts as they try to succeed in their romantic endeavors. These manga are very popular and have been translated into a number of different languages as well as been made into anime. In the case of *HANA-YORI DANGO*, there has also been a movie and television drama.

In a 2007 survey of college students ranging from first to fourth year, we asked respondents to name their current favorite titles. Table 6.7 shows the women's choices. Similar to the students in table 6.6, the readers read a wide range of titles. The most popular manga, *NANA*, was also the favorite for the senior high school readers (see table 6.4). Despite its long run, *ONE PIECE* is still one of the most popular choices for both sets of the college students, as well as the high school students. On the other

Table 6.6: **Female College Students' Favorite Manga**

Title (n=55)	Type	Setting/Theme
(1) *HANA-YORI DANGO* (Boys over flowers)	*Shōjo*	School/Romance
(2) *ONE PIECE*	*Shōnen*	Fantasy/Adventure
(3) *Peach Girl*	*Shōjo*	School/Romance

n=100

Figure 6.10:   *HANA-YORI DANGO* (Cover from *HANA-YORI DANGO* © 1992 by Kamio Yoko/ SHUEISHA Inc.)

Figure 6.11:   *Peach Girl* (Cover from *Peach Girl* 1 by Ueda Miwa. © 1998 by Kodansha Comics. Reprinted with permission of Kodansha.)

hand, *shōnen* manga seem to be more popular with the 2007 college students in that two of the three choices are in that genre. When asked if they read other titles, the students listed, in order of popularity, *NANA*, *ONE PIECE*, and *DEATH NOTE*, thus confirming the broad appeal of *shōnen* titles. These college students also listed their favorite titles at senior high school. The results were very similar to their current choices, in that *NANA* and *ONE PIECE* were the top two choices. The third choice at high school was a tie between the *shōjo HANA-YORI DANGO* and the *shōnen DEATH NOTE*. *HANA-YORI DANGO* was also the most popular manga for the earlier group of college students in table 6.6. It is still a popular manga, but it now seems to appeal more to younger readers. The results suggest that for the 2007 survey students, there is not much of a change in their reading preferences as they moved from high school to college. The results also show the continuing appeal of a number of titles and that female readers are comfortable reading across genres.

In the first survey given to college students, the male readers' tastes paralleled those of the senior high boys in that they enjoy *shōnen* manga with plenty of action and adventure. Seventy-five men gave forty-eight different titles for their favorite manga at college. As shown in table 6.8, of the three most popular manga read at college, the favorite is a period story about sword fighters. *Vagabond* is loosely based on the sixteenth-century *samurai* Miyamoto Musashi.[34] As he travels through Japan, he is continually challenged to fight and defend his reputation (see figure 6.12). The manga has been widely translated. The second choice is the ever-popular *ONE PIECE*. The third choice, *Baki* (Baki the grappler), is about martial arts.[35] Baki struggles against his father to become the strongest fighter in the world. There is a lot of action and different styles of martial arts are displayed. The male college students seemed to prefer the more violent action stories that are typical of *shōnen* manga. However, among these men, there is a similar pattern to the women in that there was a slight drop in the number of manga readers at college, but, at the same time, they were reading a wider range of titles.

Table 6.7:   2007 List of Female College Students' Favorite Manga

Title (n=67)	Type	Setting/Theme
(1) *NANA*	*Shōjo*	Romance
(2) *ONE PIECE*	*Shōnen*	Fantasy/Adventure
(3) *Slam Dunk*	*Shōnen*	School/Sports

n=267

Table 6.8:   Male College Students' Favorite Manga

Title (n=48)	Type	Setting/Theme
(1) *Vagabond*	"Adult"	Period/Adventure
(2) *ONE PIECE*	*Shōnen*	Fantasy/Adventure
(3) *Baki* (Baki the grappler)	*Shōnen*	Martial arts/Action

n=75

Figure 6.12:   *Vagabond* (Excerpt from *Vagabond* 21 by Inoue Takehiko. © 1998–2009 by I. T. Planning, Inc. Reprinted with permissions of I. T. Planning, Inc.)

When we compared the results of the 2007 survey with the above students, we found that there were some differences, as shown in table 6.9. Both groups of college students had chosen the same two favorite manga, though these differed in ranking. Despite the years separating the two surveys, it would seem that tastes have not changed greatly among the male college students.

In the 2007 survey, fifty-two college students (thirty-four women and eighteen men) indicated that they read manga but did not give any title. It should be noted that the survey was anonymous and that there was no possibility of identifying the students. Despite this, these students preferred not to state their reading preferences. One possible interpretation is that they may have been reading more sexually explicit titles of "lady's" manga and "young" manga, as well as *yaoi*/BL, and they did not want to write this down explicitly. However, these kinds of manga do sell.

We have presented the communities of readers in a positive light. We find that they are supportive in dealing with reading difficulties; moreover, the communities of readers use manga as a kind of mediated discourse in maintaining and strengthening relationships. This includes not only talking about story content, but in the practices of borrowing and lending. At the same time, there may be sides to the communities that may not be so positive. These communities might also perpetuate entrenched views regarding the kinds of manga titles that are to be read. The

Table 6.9:   2007 List of Male College Students' Favorite Manga

Title (n=51)	Type	Setting/Theme
(1) *ONE PIECE*	*Shōnen*	Fantasy/Adventure
Slam Dunk	*Shōnen*	School/Sports
(2) *DRAGON BALL*	*Shōnen*	Fantasy/Martial arts
(3) *Vagabond*	*Adult*	Period/Adventure

n=129

silence of many readers regarding their preferences may be symptomatic of attitudes learned in their communities of practice. These readers may have acquired the street wisdom of not revealing all of one's literacy preferences.

Summary

Our respondents reported that the main reasons for reading manga are for pleasure and to relax. While seemingly overlapping reasons, each one has a complex set of subreasons. The pleasurable reasons include fantasy, engaging stories, attractive characters, a message that encourages, and something to learn. The learning aspects include learning how to deal with interpersonal situations, involving appropriate expressions and even script and vocabulary training. Other learning aspects include learning lessons in life and acquiring information of general interest. Manga helps readers relax, because in many titles there is something funny. For some readers, reading manga is a useful contrast to other tasks such as doing homework. Many manga readers find the graphics easy to understand, thus contributing to manga's relaxing qualities. Other readers find it exciting to read manga in school, where manga are forbidden.

In spite of the decline in manga sales, reading manga is still popular among the high school readers. Many readers go on to other reading material while others continue with reading manga. Older manga readers reported how changing social norms are reflected in manga. Some adults who read manga in their youth, but did not continue, find manga today more challenging and engaging.

The range of titles preferred by readers increases with age and diversifying interests. Yet female readers report a broader range of titles than male readers. The female junior high school readers prefer many of the same manga that male readers select. However, in high school and university, a preference among female readers for *shōjo* manga increases, indicating shifts in interests and increasing capabilities to read works describing subtle human relationships. In spite of the many titles that our respondents reported, our interviews with individual readers lead us to believe that our respondents have more varied preferences than they were willing to report.

Notes

1. Takaya Natsuki, *Fruits Basket* (Tokyo: Hakusensha, 1999).
2. *HUNTER X HUNTER* © by POT (Yoshihiro Togashi), all rights reserved/ SHUEISHA Inc.

3. Ninomiya Tomoko, *Nodame Cantabile* (Tokyo: Kodansha, 2001).

4. *TENSHI NANKAJANAI* © 1991 by Ai Yazawa/SHUEISHA Inc.

5. Martin Barker, *Comics: Ideology, Power and Critics* (Manchester, UK: Manchester University Press, 1989), 261.

6. Dawn H. Currie, *Girl Talk: Adolescent Magazines and Their Readers* (Toronto: University of Toronto Press, 1997), 141.

7. Dianne Cooper, "Retailing Gender: Adolescent Book Clubs in Australian Schools," in *Texts of Desire: Essays on Fiction, Femininity and Schooling*, ed. Linda K. Christian-Smith (London: The Falmer Press, 1993), 9–27.

8. Natsume Fusanosuke, *Manga ni Jinsei wo Manande Nani ga Warui?* (What's wrong with learning life's lessons from manga?) (Tokyo: Random House-Kodansha, 2006); see also Yokomori Rika, *Ren'ai wa Shōjo Manga de Osowatta* (I learned how to fall in love from *shōjo* manga) (Tokyo: Shueisha, 1999).

9. Inoue Takehiko, *Slam Dunk* (Tokyo: Shueisha, 1990).

10. *THE PRINCE OF TENNIS* © 1999 by Takeshi Konomi/SHUEISHA Inc.

11. Donna E. Alvermann and Alison H. Heron, "Literacy Identity Work: Playing to Learn with Popular Media," *Journal of Adolescent & Adult Literacy* 45, no. 2 (2001): 118–22.

12. Aso Tarō and Hirokane Kenshi, "Orijinaru Kakuryō Kaigi" (Original cabinet meeting), *Big Comic Original* 34, no. 26 (Tokyo: Shogakukan, 2007), 2.

13. Takeuchi Osamu, *Sengo Manga 50 Nen Shi* (Postwar 50 years of *manga* history) (Tokyo: Chikuma Shobo, 1995); Kate Allen and John E. Ingulsrud, "*Manga* Literacy: Popular Culture and the Reading Habits of Japanese College Students," *Journal of Adolescent & Adult Literacy* 46, no. 8 (2003): 676.

14. Sakura Momoko, *Coji-Coji* (Tokyo: Gentōsha, 1997).

15. David G. O'Brien, "Multiple Literacies in a High-School Program for 'At-Risk' Adolescents," in *Reconceptualizing the Literacies in Adolescents Lives*, ed. Donna E. Alvermann, Kathleen A. Hinchman, David W. Moore, Stephen F. Phelps, and Diane R. Waff (Mahwah, NJ: Lawrence Erlbaum Associates, 1998), 27–50; Martin Barker, *Comics: Ideology, Power and Critics* (Manchester: Manchester University Press, 1989), 240; Angela McRobbie, "Just Like a Jackie Story," in *Feminism for Girls: An Adventure Story*, ed. Angela McRobbie and Trisha McCabe (London: Routledge & Kegan Paul, 1981), 113–28.

16. Allan Luke, "Series Editor's Introduction," in *Texts of Desire: Essays on Fiction, Femininity and Schooling*, ed. Linda K. Christian-Smith (London: The Falmer Press, 1993), vii–xiv.

17. Miyazaki Hayao, *Nausicaä of the Valley of the Wind* (Tokyo: Takuma Shoten, 1982).

18. *Ribon* (Tokyo: Shueisha, 1955).

19. *Margaret* (Tokyo: Shueisha, 1963).

20. Kazuko Suzuki, "Pornography or Therapy? Japanese Girls Creating the Yaoi Phenonenon," in *Millennium Girls: Today's Girls Around the World*, ed. Sherrie A. Inness (Lanham, MD: Rowman & Littlefield, 1998), 243–67; Urano Chikako, *Atakku No. 1* (Tokyo: Shueisha, 1968).

21. Fujio Fujiko, *Doraemon* (Tokyo: Shogakukan, 1969).

22. Ueda Miwa, *Peach Girl* (Tokyo: Kodansha, 1998).

23. Alleen P. Nilsen, "Sexism in Children's Books and Elementary Classroom Materials," in *Sexism and Language*, ed. Alleen P. Nilsen, Haig Bosmajian, H. Lee Gershuny, and Julia P. Stanley (Urbana, IL: National Council of Teachers of English, 1977), 161–71; Elizabeth Dutro, "But That's a Girl Book! Exploring Gender Boundaries in Children's Reading Practices," *The Reading Teacher* 55, no. 4 (2001): 534–61.

24. Hotta Yumi, *Hikaru no Go* (Hikaru's go), illustrated by Obara Takeshi (Tokyo: SHUEISHA Inc., 1998).

25. Tezuka Osamu, *Burakku Jakku* (Black Jack) (Tokyo: Akita Shoten, 1973).

26. *NANA* © 1999 by Yazawa Manga Seisakusho/SHUEISHA Inc.

27. Linda K. Christian-Smith, "Sweet Dreams: Gender and Desire in Teen Romance Novels," in *Texts of Desire: Essays on Fiction, Femininity and Schooling*, ed. Linda K. Christian-Smith (London: The Falmer Press, 1993): 45–68; Linda K. Christian-Smith, "Popular Texts and Young Women," in *Difference, Silence, and Textual Practice: Studies in Critical Literacy*, ed. Peter Freebody, Sandy Muspratt, and Bronywn Dwyer (Cresskill, NJ: Hapaton Press, 2001): 189–207; and McRobbie, "Just Like a Jackie Story," 113–28.

28. See Janice A. Radway, *Reading the Romance: Women, Patriarchy and Popular Literature* (Chapel Hill: University of North Carolina Press, 1984).

29. Christian-Smith, "Sweet Dreams," 58–65.

30. Barker, *Comics: Ideology*, 140.

31. Nakazawa Jun, "Manga no Koma no Yomi Riterashī no Hattatsu" (The development of manga panel reading literacy), *Manga Studies* 7 (2005): 6–21.

32. *DEATH NOTE* © 2003 by Tsugumi Ohba, Takeshi Obata/SHUEISHA Inc.

33. *HANA-YORI DANGO* © 1992 by Kamio Yoko/SHUEISHA Inc.

34. *Vagabond* © 1998–2009 by Inoue Takehiko/I. T. Planning, Inc.

35. Itagaki Keisuke, *Baki* (Baki the grappler) (Tokyo: Akita Shoten, 1991).

The Effects of Literacy

7

The efforts of acquiring literacy skills and engaging in literacy practices are neither neutral nor benign. They carry with them the goals and values of a nation, a society, and institutions, as well as the personal interests and desires of individuals. Yet once engaged in literacy, what are the effects? Curiously, the issue does not emerge when literacy is operating in a balanced manner, that is, when there is no particular awareness of problems. Literacy skills and practices are such an integral part of modern life, they are simply assumed to exist. It is only when they are seen to be operating in an unbalanced manner that they are brought to our attention.

In this chapter, we consider the effects of literacy. By effects, we mean the nature of skills and the knowledge acquired through literacy, and the representation of the choices people make when engaging in literacy practices. In traditional China and later in traditional Japan, it was assumed and expected that the text had an effect on the reader. Because only the literate could access the texts on philosophy and morals, it was a requisite that readers adopt identities consonant with the content and act accordingly. Yet today, when most people engage in literacy, we observe conflicting expectations of what people should achieve. On the one hand, there is the complaint that young people do not read enough, implying that, as a result, their knowledge is deficient. On the other hand, there is a fear that they can acquire too much. In particular, acquiring knowledge through popular culture media products, and that knowledge, without articulating specifically what it is, is seen as possessing little value, while at the same time it is seen as potentially threatening. It is the kinds of knowledge not associated with popular culture that are prized, as parents and others project their imagined communities on to young people.

The intention of our three-part discussion on the effects of literacy is to bring together the patterns of manga literacy and discourse that we have presented. Instead of summarizing the patterns in terms of the categories we have employed in earlier chapters, we have chosen two positions with a view to emphasize the open nature of our findings. We do so by casting the patterns in light of the "literacy crisis" discourse on the one hand and, on the other, the alarmists' urge to censor. Although the effects of literacy are perhaps considered, as we mentioned above, only when there is a sense of unbalance, these two parts, the "literacy crisis" and the urge to censor, are not really poles on the same axis. They could be better understood in terms of M. A. K. Halliday's explanation of language's three aspects, a scheme widely used as a basis for the analysis of genre. The three parts consist of the textual (media features or structure), the ideational (content), and the interpersonal.[1] The textual aspect corresponds to the "literacy crisis" discourse, the ideational aspect corresponds to the urge to censor, and the interpersonal aspect corresponds to the communities of practice—that is, the communities of readers, who, as agents, serve to mitigate the negative effects of the former parts.

Too Little Effect—The Discourse of Literacy Crisis

At the beginning of chapter 1, we began with a litany of newspaper quotations lamenting the decline of reading books in Japan. The assumption behind these complaints is that so much of value to society and the national culture is contained in the book medium, and that with the smaller readership there would be less of this valuable content transmitted to the next generation. There is also the assumption that books, unlike other media, contain the most valuable content. In fact, books cover perhaps the widest range of content of any medium, including content that these alarmists would surely object to. Yet because books continue to be the medium of choice for scholarly, literary, legal, and technical discourse, these preferences contribute to the maintenance of the book as the medium of prestige.

The next set of complaints is the decline of literacy skills. Without adequate literacy skills, books cannot be accessed. Although literacy skills in school are measured through reading tests, there are more fundamental notions that go with possessing literacy skills. For example, literacy skills provide the learner with the identity of being a reader. This identity goes beyond being able to read books to access what Marshall McLuhan calls the print medium, a superordinate category for all media containing non-handwritten writing.[2] We have discussed this notion of the literate identity in our book *Learning to Read in China*, where we observed Chinese six-year-olds, who were on the threshold of learning the roman alphabet, proclaim to their teacher that they had in their grasp the whole world. This notion is important when considering declining literacy skills because anyone who has acquired them, even partially, is able to think that as readers, they can access any book or print medium whenever they need. But can they?

The metaphors of literacy and illiteracy in Japanese tend to refer to the process of decoding. Decoding involves the identification of the phonological (sound) value for the visual symbol. For written Japanese, however, the four scripts themselves carry different linguistic structures and cultural representations. *Hiragana* and *katakana* are syllabaries and, unlike *rōmaji*, they stand for syllables, not individual sounds. Historically they represented gender, being used primarily by women.

While *hiragana* can still evoke femininity, it is normally used for function words or more precisely, function morphemes. Both *katakana* and *rōmaji* are used to represent foreign words or names. Because *katakana* is a script used to represent difference, it is also the script to provide emphasis when needed. In the case of *kanji*, there can be multiple phonological values, but usually there is only one semantic value.

Being able to link symbol to sound is basic, but, as the eight-year-old manga reader in chapter 5 demonstrated, she was able to decode yet she was not able to comprehend—to understand the vocabulary and thus the text as a whole. Indeed, most manga these days have *hiragana* and *katakana* rubies as well as *rōmaji* ones on the side of *kanji*, so that all readers can decode. We do not want to belittle decoding because being able to do so provides readers with a level of confidence that would otherwise discourage them from reading. Still, the goal of learning literacy skills is the comprehension of the texts. Then what exactly is comprehension?

Instinctively, many educators would say high scores on reading tests. Others would say that comprehension is the ability to follow directions in order to operate something like a machine. Yet others working with literary or legal texts would argue that comprehension is not so straightforward, that the texts require interpretations resulting in plural ways to comprehend. Comprehension becomes even murkier when we focus on texts of popular culture, where the correct way to comprehend is hardly ever considered. This is because readers of manga, for example, read out of their own volition. Although we have documented a few accounts of readers reporting they felt the pressure to read by their peers or their parents, in most cases readers are motivated by their own desire to read.

Motivation in foreign-language education is an issue that receives continual attention. Having to learn English, for example, is a reluctant task for many. In their extensive study of French-language learners in Canada, Robert Gardner and Wallace Lambert analyzed motivation into two types—instrumental and integrative.[3] The former is driven by grades, employment prospects, and other tangible rewards. The latter is driven by personal interest in the target culture, a desire to know the speakers as people, a disposition to make friends, and so on. More recent researchers like Zoltan Dornyei have fine-tuned this dichotomy, demonstrating the existence of more kinds of motivation, but for our purposes, we would like to utilize the two types, instrumental and integrative motivation.[4]

Instrumental motivation to read includes performing well on a test or in a course while including reading in order to do something. It would also include reading in order to learn because learning transports the learner to something better. In these cases, "comprehension" makes sense. One informant in chapter 5 stated he read the manga *Zettai Zetsumei Dangerous Jīsan* in order to understand the video game by the same name. This is instrumental motivation. However, we have documented numerous respondents who say they learned from reading manga valuable lessons about life or learned appropriate expressions for sensitive interpersonal situations. As mentioned in chapter 6, Natsume Fusanosuke has written an entire book about life's lessons learned from manga. His topics include "the logic of adulthood," "the possibilities of youth," "dealing with fate," "the meaning of life," and so on.[5] Yet neither our respondents nor Natsume would admit that learning life's lessons provided the motivation to read manga. These lessons came as byproducts of reading, as unintentional discoveries. Because these discoveries are unexpected, the lessons can be profound. Perhaps it is difficult to simulate such profundity when manga or other forms of popular culture are appropriated for various purposes, as in education.

At the same time, educational philosophers like Philip Phenix argue that learning such lessons in life is essential in a curriculum. This kind of learning, he explains, is the growth in personal knowledge. The problem is there is no one discipline that would lend itself to facilitating this kind of knowledge. Phenix suggests that knowledge from areas such as psychotherapy (human relations) and existentialism (human agency and the nature of responsibility) are useful, but he contends that it is literature, in its many manifestations, that provides the most numerous and profound insights leading to growth in personal knowledge.[6] People are taught that literature can deliver this kind of knowledge. It is more unexpected when it happens while reading texts like manga.

In contrast to the motivation to study subjects in school, the motivation to read manga and engage in other popular media is almost always integrative. Kimiko Manes describes the changes in the types of Japanese language students she teaches in a community college near Philadelphia. She used to have many mature students, mostly professionals preparing for commercial opportunities with Japan. Recently, she has many younger students whose interest in learning Japanese comes from watching anime, reading manga, and engaging in other aspects of Japanese popular culture. She says that the younger students have a better grasp of Japanese culture, particularly in the realm of human relations.[7] These students' integrative motivation is evident in that as they view both their interests and language learning as part of their expanding identities. The efforts by the young students stand in contrast to those of the older professionals who studied hard, but kept things Japanese at a distance.

Integrative motivation can also be seen in readers who participate in book clubs. These readers are attracted to genres of literature and even include readers who are people of faith focusing on scriptures. For these readers, "comprehension" is also somehow dissonant. Terms like "enjoyment," "fun," "discovery," and "inspiration" collocate better to describe the readers' literacy preferences. Despite the sharing of integrative motivation by both popular culture reader-consumers, and readers of poetry, novels, and scriptures, critics are quick to point out that on the one hand poetry, novels, and scriptures are worthwhile, whereas popular culture is not. Reading manga has often been characterized as escapist. Indeed, many of our respondents have reported that they read manga to relax and take their mind off the worries at hand. Certainly readers of poetry, novels, and scripture could say the same thing. Still critics maintain these are edifying practices while reading manga is mindless. One such critic, Matsuzawa Mitsuo, went so far as to say that manga makes readers stupid.[8]

The sight of people flipping through manga, sitting dazed in front of the television, or glued to the computer screen, as well as *otaku* obsessed with characters or niche genres incapable of or uninterested in personal relationships, has led to critics making a range of judgments, not only about popular media, but also of the people who engage in them. Many manga commentators have spoken out against these judgments. The arguments of the manga apologists have focused on aesthetics, social adjustment, communication skills, and exposure to the liberal arts. Commentator Okada Toshio has argued in his promotion of *otaku* culture that reading manga and engaging with the kindred media can make you smart.

Although not dealing with comics directly, there have been some researchers in media and literacy who assert that we should not fear popular culture. Steven Johnson argues in his book *Everything Bad is Good for You* that popular culture is actually beneficial. He has examined television programs, video games, and the Internet longitudinally and has found that they have increased in complexity, thus demanding more cognitive involvement from those who engage in them. He calls this increase in complexity "the sleeper curve."[9] James Paul Gee, who has written extensively on literacy and discourse analysis, has turned his attention to media use. In his book *What Video Games Have to Teach Us about Learning and Literacy*, Gee introduces thirty-six learning principles involved in learning video games. He describes the cycles of repetitions that come, each time, with a new challenge. Many games allow for the player to reflect on their structure and so enable players to understand systems. Moreover, some games allow players to assume a virtual identity, as well as an additional identity that involves an ongoing negotiation between one's real identity and the virtual identity.[10]

Johnson and Gee describe people who are very much focused on their media products and they consider this focus as beneficial for a person's development, especially cognitive development. Our respondents who read manga speak of linguistic benefits, which, taken in a wider sense, are also cognitive. Furthermore, what our respondents and the people Johnson and Gee studied share is the integrative motivation to access the media and the focus with which they engage in them. While critics complain that print media like books have had too little effect, some critics find the focus with which young people engage in popular culture media as threatening, that the media have too much of an effect.

Too Much Effect—The Discourse of Media Control

What alarmed Fredric Wertham—the psychiatrist in the 1940s and 1950s we referred to in chapter 2, who criticized comics as a hazard to young people—was the image of boys and girls reading comics with "extreme avidity."[11] The focus of criticism is on the reader when literacy skills are seen as lacking. In cases where literacy skills of young people are seemingly operating well, the media products and their creators are criticized, rather than the reader-consumers themselves. Instead of suggesting strategies for self-control or group control on the part of the reader-consumer, the criticism often results in calls for censorship.

We have briefly described the censorship of manga in chapter 2. There we explain that censorship by the authorities has been occasional, without relentless national campaigns. Censorship activities at the civic level have been the result of local efforts. A lack of centralized censorship regarding manga does not mean that there is no deliberation over the issue. A high school girl whom we interviewed expressed her ideas of whether or not to censor:

> [I know that violent stories are happening in real life. I don't care about them even when they are in manga. I think writers of novels use their violent descriptions to criticize these actions. But some people don't agree with manga artists drawing violence because they believe manga is just entertainment. They are afraid that violent depictions are harmful for children because they will enjoy reading them. Of course, everyone wants to read interesting manga. But I don't completely agree with people who try to censor violence. I don't like violence either, but in my opinion I suspect that the inhumane scenes may be harmful for children who don't have any background information.]

For this girl, reading about violence in novels is acceptable because, as a medium, novels are seen to contain an edifying function. The edifying function does not exist *a priori* for manga. As explained above, manga can be edifying, but edification is rarely the reason for reading. The danger of violent scenes to children is that they are unable to put the violence in a meaningful context. Still, this tendency is not seen to be harmful enough to censor manga. In this section, we consider censorship of comics in the United States. We examine how comics were criticized and subjected to censorship, while reflecting on manga's very different development. Some of Wertham's criticisms, such as toward superheroes and racist depictions of characters, are compelling and still resonate with us today. However, the results of the anti-comics campaign as a whole were destructive. In his book *The Ten-Cent Plague: The Great Comic-Book Scare and How it Changed America*, David Hajdu provides a "Comics Code Memorial" in the appendix, a somber two-column list of nearly nine hundred names of creators who, since the mid-1950s, never created comics again.[12] The list is a powerful reminder of the gaping hole left in the production of popular American culture. Moreover, seen through the lens of manga's development, the hole is an even wider cavity.

In 1945, comics publishing in the United States was much larger and more varied than the manga industry in Japan. Similar to manga readers today, there was an adult readership. The reading material of choice among GIs was comic books.[13] Yet American comics suffered criticism and censorship, subsequently becoming a much more limited industry in terms of numbers of readers and range of content. This is why reading comics became associated with juvenile reading practices, as comics safe for children were the main ones to survive. According to Bradford Wright, criticism of comics came in two waves: one in the late 1940s and another in the mid-1950s. The champion of the censorship movement was Fredric Wertham. His efforts in the 1940s met with limited success. However, in 1954, he published a book called the *Seduction of the Innocent: The Influence of Comic Books on Today's Youth* that summarized his research findings and clinical experience, as well as the criticisms of comics that had been already made.[14] Wertham spent his career counseling adolescents and, based on his sessions with delinquent adolescents, he found a common background: they all read comics. He resisted saying there was a causal link between reading comics and committing criminal acts, but he insisted it was one of the factors, a factor that was possible to target and one that was subsequently largely eliminated, demonstrating the possibility of vanquishing a modern social menace. He analyzed comics, especially crime and horror comics, since they provided the ideas and the moral laxity that would lead to delinquent acts.

We are attracted to Wertham's work because he attempted to provide a comprehensive social critique of comics, based on their discourse features and the literacy practices of their readers. His work resembles studies that have employed critical discourse analysis (CDA). These studies, based on an analysis of genres, syntactic patterns and vocabulary use, provide interpretations of the assumptions and ideological positions, as well as positions of power, used to legitimate actions. The purpose of CDA is described by Norman Fairclough in the following way: "The aim of critical social research is better understanding of how societies work and produce both beneficial and detrimental effects, and of how the detrimental effects can be mitigated if not eliminated."[15] Wertham felt comics were detrimental to society and should be eliminated. Despite his training, some of his claims were weakly substantiated and he frequently employed sensational arguments. Yet his arguments had far-reaching effects. His book interests us also because it is an example of a critical analysis that actually worked—comic books were eventually censored. Moreover, the campaigns against comics virtually erased from memory the literacy practices engaged in by both genders and various age groups. This loss of memory is evident in the curious surprise expressed by Americans at seeing Japanese people reading manga in public. Below we have inventoried Wertham's main arguments. His polemics are contrasted with the situation and practices of reading manga.

Negative Effect on Readers

Wertham made a sweeping assumption immediately in his title, *Seduction of the Innocent*, that young people are innocent. He skillfully used the "garden to be tended," "tabula rasa," and "noble savage" tropes to appeal to our instincts about the nature of a child. He did not attempt to place his argument of innocence in any philosophical or theological tradition. The force of his arguments lay in his counseling sessions with delinquents, where they often mentioned comics as providing some of the ideas for the crimes they committed. However, he did not provide material from non-delinquents who make up the majority of the comic readership.

When young people in Japan commit crimes, their reading and other media preferences are often exposed, sparking debate about the popular media and their effects. This has led to some local acts of censorship, but, as pointed out earlier, juvenile crime is statistically still low in comparison with, for instance, the United

States. At the same time, the phenomenon of bullying is widespread in Japanese schools, from elementary through to high school. Wertham asserted that reading comics encouraged bullying in school, as young people were eager to apply the sadistic knowledge they had learned.[16] In spite of the soul-searching nature of the discourse on bullying in Japanese schools,[17] reading manga is rarely, if at all, identified as fostering acts of bullying. What we often find in manga stories, particularly in both *shōnen* and *shōjo* manga, are main characters suffering from bullying and discovering ways to deal with it.

It is the main character in a *Bildungsroman* narrative that most often appears in manga, a character who, assertively or patiently, takes on challenges and, in the process, transforms himself or herself. What is more threatening to society's future than being influenced by sex and violence is the prospect of young people doing nothing at all. Many passive, introverted young people are joining the ranks of the *freeters* and NEETs. *Freeters* フリーター (furītā), whether by choice or otherwise, work part-time in low-paying jobs. Although *freeters* at least make an effort to provide for their livelihoods, NEETs (ニート) do not. Referring to "Not currently engaged in Employment, Education or Training," NEETs live at home with few prospects of gainful employment and even less desire to seek out options for their lives. There are differing estimates as to how many NEETs exist, but, for our purposes here, a 2004 survey conducted by the Nomura Institute found that among one thousand respondents, 92 percent of them felt a sense of crisis about the NEET issue because they felt it will negatively affect society.[18]

Wertham was right in pointing out there was no causal evidence for comics prompting a young person to commit a crime. Today in the United States, video games are in the spotlight for social scrutiny. Games are well known for their violence and many products contain sexual content as well. Researchers Lawrence Kutner and Cheryl Olson have conducted a study with thirteen hundred children. They found that children who played violent games regularly did not exhibit extra violent behavior. It was rather the children who did not play at all that seemed to be at risk because they were outside of the networks of children who played the games.[19] As we have described in chapter 4, reading manga is not only an individual practice but also a communal one. The multifunctional nature of these communities of practice cannot be underestimated in their value.

Ideology and Character Representation

Like critical analysts of discourse, Wertham engaged in identifying ideologies in comics that were either assumed or projected. His most well-known criticism was that of superhero characters. Superheroes who triumph over evil would seem on the surface to be simply innocuous. Writers who have examined Wertham's work have drawn attention to his comments that superheroes promoted fascism and therefore comics were seen as detrimental to the promotion of democracy.[20] For Wertham, superheroes were troublesome because society's problems were solved through strong-arm tactics, with hardly a pause to consider competing positions.

Furthermore, superheroes offered young people a panacea to disputes and challenges, without encouraging them in the more difficult and humane processes of negotiation and compromise.[21] The panacea that the superheroes offered was almost always violent. This can be seen, for instance, when children demand a parent to intervene in their disputes, sometimes with corporal punishment. Children often expect the parent to act as the superhero.

Racism was another ideology he detected in comics. The bad people were almost always depicted as people of color or foreign-looking. The good people were almost always white. He found the jungle comics particularly disturbing, as white beefy thugs kept order, while people of color were subservient, stupid, or crafty—thus untrustworthy.[22] An immigrant himself, he was sensitive to people who were different and was sympathetic to the plight of African Americans. He befriended prominent African American writers.[23] In Harlem, he regularly volunteered his counseling services. Through these activities, he found that many troubled young African Americans read comics.

Another point that Wertham found problematic was the depiction of over-developed characters of both men and women since they provided unrealistic expectations of what people should look like. However, he found large-breasted women with curved hips more questionable than muscle-bound men. He reported that some of his female clients claimed they experienced a loss of self-confidence, thinking that such shapeliness was the norm.[24] Wertham's feminism had in its scope the unrealistic expectations aroused by overdeveloped characters and the depiction of violence against women; however, he found the image of Wonder Woman to be highly threatening with her assertiveness, strength, and violent acts. He also was uncomfortable with her closeness to her female comrades. He also found Batman and Robin to be uncomfortably close.[25] He described in detail, over a course of six pages, examples where he and others had construed the relationship between Batman and Robin as homosexual. Wertham's mindset here is very much like the *fukei* (the male counterpart to *fujoshi*), who find pleasure in imagining sexual relationships where they are not necessarily apparent. At the same time, he was in a privileged position to engage in such analysis. He was a psychiatrist and, in the 1950s, homosexuality was still categorized as pathologic. Because of his expert position, it was accepted that he could engage in this kind of speculation.

Manga also has its superheroes. Tezuka Osamu created the most famous superhero, *Tetsuwan Atomu* (Mighty Atom) (*Astro Boy* in English-language anime versions). There are also *Kamen Raidā*, *Urutoraman*, and so on.[26] Frederik Schodt has written a book entirely on *Astro Boy*, including biographical details about his creator. Schodt introduces the character from multiple perspectives and describes his development.[27] The impression is a complex character unlike the one-dimensional personalities that Wertham describes. However, fans of well-known American superheroes would no doubt argue that their characters also play complex roles.

Yet in manga for boys, that is, *shōnen* manga, superhero stories are not the mainstay. The most common kind of story is the *Bildungsroman*. The ideology in manga often lies in its narrative structure, not so much in its superheroes. These narratives describe boys or groups of boys going through difficulties to attain a goal or simply to better themselves. Many of these stories revolve around sports. On the train to work, we overheard a group of junior high school girls exclaiming how inspiring it was to read *Slam Dunk*, the story of a high school basketball team. Other young people report that they are encouraged by reading these kinds of manga. At the same time, some manga stories combine elements of *Bildungsroman* with superhero attributes. In both the *Naruto* and *YU-GI-OH!* series, a young man goes through multiple "challenges," but he also possesses some supernatural strength.[28] Both boys do not know how to use this strength; therefore, learning to use the strength and the frequent mistakes provide further material for the narrative.

Regarding the depiction of overdeveloped characters, certainly Wertham would be repulsed by female characters drawn in the *moe* style. They also tend to be over-developed. In his history of *shōjo* representation, Yoshida Masutaka complains that the *moe* trend has homogenized the newer characters and he longs for the strong combative *shōjo* characters of the 1990s.[29] Many of the strong *shōjo* characters, Sharalyn Orbaugh contends, play at being *shōnen* manga characters, taking on the same roles as boys and young men.[30] At the same time, strong heroes such as Tezuka Osamu's *Ribon no Kishi* (Princess knight), Ikeda Riyoko's Oscar in *Berusaiyu no Bara* (Rose of Versailles), or Takahashi Rumiko's *Ranma ½* might be more acceptable to Wertham than American women superheroes because they cross-dress as men or, as in *Ranma ½*, they are transgendered as a woman.[31] This trope occasionally appears in what Wertham considered "proper" literature, such as in Shakespeare's *Twelfth Night*. However, these kinds of characters transmit the message that, given the right circumstances, they would be nice ladies or nice boys. Wonder Woman is threatening because she is, unmistakably, a woman, not a woman playing at being a man.

Indeed, manga today—through *shōjo*, *yaoi*/BL, as well as "lady's" and "young," manga—provide the reader with multiple gender vantage points, multiple kinds of character dyads, and a range of sexual encounters. By reading these various genres of manga, one might gain the impression that Japanese society must be a wildly promiscuous world. In real life, it is more subdued. Our data indicate that young people, particularly boys, are conservative or, shall we say, reticent, reporting that they prefer works with *shōnen* manga values of male perseverance and camaraderie. No respondent in the surveys, male or female, described reading *yaoi*/BL manga. A few stated they read *ero manga* エロマンガ (pornographic manga), although they did not specify what type it was. One female interviewee claimed she read "lady's" manga and another female interviewee showed us her favorite *yaoi* manga. Our male interviewees and students, even those whom we have gotten to know well, seem to be reluctant to appear to be deviating from the macho preference for *shōnen* manga. Yet these alternative varieties of manga do sell, which means there are readers. These readers simply have not identified themselves to us, even on anonymous surveys. One seminar student showed John Ingulsrud a *yaoi*/BL manga he was reading. John responded by encouraging him to analyze it. The student answered by saying, "No, this is for me."

Perhaps it is unrealistic to expect that people would impart all or most of their literacy preferences to researchers. We both are white and are perceived to represent Western norms and sensibilities. Consequently we would be seen to make judgments based on this background. It is widely known among Japanese that adults reading manga are considered by foreigners to be strange and juvenile. Why provide more evidence that would confirm or enhance this perception? Sociologist Kaneda Junko suggests that the readers, by their preferences to read and create certain manga, bear a "stigmatized identity."[32] For this reason, they are reluctant to speak of their practices; moreover, they prefer to be left alone. The tabloid *Spa!* carried an article describing adult men afraid to talk about their *otaku* practices to not only their workplace colleagues and superiors but also to friends and lovers.[33] We do not have a full understanding of the readers' reluctance to speak. Our description of manga literacy includes practices that are both communal and individual. Because in most cases readers themselves choose to read manga, we have also called manga literacy a personal literacy. No doubt there are levels of personal literacies, including ones that are not easily disclosed.

Detrimental to Literacy

The content in comics, Wertham argued, contributed to the tendency of children to become delinquent. He also claimed that comics harmed the development of the reading process. This was because the comic format itself was a sign of illiteracy. Moreover, he asserted that comics readers were "not really readers," that they only "picture read."[34] He further pointed out that reading disability correlated highly with juvenile delinquency.

In spite of this low evaluation of comics because they did not require normal literacy skills and had little relation to other kinds of reading, Wertham admitted that reading comics was a challenge:

> Reading the comic-book text is often difficult. For example, the reading material in the huge present crop of horror comics is hard to make out even for the average adult reading. But all the emotional emphasis of comics is on the pictures, and that is where they do the most harm to reading. The discrepancy between the easy appeal of the pictures and the difficulty of reading the text is too great to encourage anyone to try to follow what the characters are supposed to be saying.[35]

We can sympathize with Wertham's feelings about the difficulty of reading comics, as we also experienced such obstacles when we started to read manga. Yet he was mistaken to criticize comics because adults had difficulty reading them. However, Wertham's remarks here are important since he did recognize that comics required special literacy skills. The problem was that he did not value these skills, since he did not see them as serving the transition to real literacy, which was the reading of "proper" literature.

A parallel could be drawn with the view of Basil Bernstein that skills and content of popular culture literacies do not transfer, particularly to school literacies.[36]

This is because popular culture literacies are context-based. The content quickly becomes obsolete and thus the skills needed to access them are then discarded. When considering "transferability," it is important to recognize the assumed purposes of the literacies in question. School literacy must provide transferable skills and content, whereas popular culture literacy does not have this mandate. The value of manga literacy is not its transitional functions to other literacies, but the ability to read manga. Because manga include a wide range of topics and are written for all age groups, we can safely say that manga literacy is an end in itself, despite reports from readers that they learned skills that have transferred to school literacy.

Let us present another way to explain transferability. School literacy and popular culture literacy are at different levels in the general curriculum. Traditionally, school literacy begins with decoding, that is, the area of the symbolics. Together with mathematics, reading skills become the basis for processing the entire curriculum. There are also symbolic aspects to various media, but school literacy implies language and print. Literature, on the other hand, together with history, philosophy, and religion, possesses facts and relationships between facts and thus differs.[37] What is transferable are the symbolics. The problem is that once readers have learned how to decode words, specific context-based texts are needed to develop literacy skills and knowledge. Consequently, choices have to be made. In school, texts from disciplines, such as literature and history, that provide "synopses" of the culture, are chosen. In addition, it is assumed that an acquaintance with these texts would lead to an appropriation of prestige codes that could be used in speech, and especially in writing. It is perhaps safe to say that the selected disciplines and texts by definition carry high cultural capital. Proponents of "cultural literacy" argue that a shared body of knowledge is desirable in order to identify and comprehend the intertextualities drawn from canonical sources, so that a common frame of reference can be maintained.[38]

Because of their canonical status, certain works of literature are, by definition, ends in themselves. We do not see them serving as a transition to something else. Their value is self-evident by virtue of social and cultural approval. Indeed, their high cultural capital enables them to be regarded as "terminal" cultural products. Based on this assumption, Wertham accepted folklore in Shakespeare and Goethe, but did not accept it in comics.[39] Works of "proper" literature are consumed in their own right, in contrast to lower products that must be assessed for their transferability. This notion of "terminality" might serve as an additional tool to separate the canonical from the non-canonical. Yet it might also open a Pandora's box of incipient prejudices, hierarchies, and perceptions of taste. Take, for example, the place of Charles Dickens's novel *A Tale of Two Cities* in the tenth-grade curriculum. Is this an easier work? Does it serve as a transition? If so, then to what? Does our familiarity with the warhorses of classical music such as Johann Pachelbel's *Canon* or Gioachino Rossini's overtures serve as a transition to, say, Arnold Schoenberg's atonal pieces? If "terminality" is relative on a scale, then should we value the ever more esoteric? Perhaps most consumers of high culture would reject this notion with an argument for diversity. If diversity is to be argued, why can we not consider works of popular culture as "terminal," possessing cultural value in their own right, works that we might also want to revisit? What, then, is the status of popular culture knowledge, such as manga, in the maintenance of a common frame of reference?

Some large publishers have begun to offer titles containing numerous parodies and other intertextualities of earlier manga. This is a business decision, with the expectation that readers would be interested in purchasing the reissued versions of the older manga. Using manga content in anime, light novels, video games, and television dramas is also a business decision. "Capital" for popular culture is not only conceived in terms of Bourdieu's metaphors, it is inherently connected with economic capital. Popular culture products must sell, just as school literacy must transfer to other contexts, that is, be relevant. Schools, however, will receive governmental support and the content can receive additional support from sources keen to preserve their heritage; consequently, less relevant aspects can be maintained. In contrast, popular culture has only commercial sources and the products must attract purchasers.[40]

The attraction of people to popular culture content is looked on with envy among many educators who wish their students would engage in school content with the same level of interest and focus. It is widely assumed that appropriating popular culture products into the classroom is a good thing. Indeed, a teacher who uses popular culture for teaching is seen as innovative. Moreover, by doing so, it is seen as affirming the students' literacy practices. In spite of these trends, we find ourselves hesitating to do so. Gemma Moss and others suggest that when teachers use popular culture to reach out to young people, they in fact encroach on the student's sense of space. Using what one enjoys freely in personal time for a task that was chosen by the teacher, an agent of power, might not be so attractive.[41] Furthermore, Donna Alvermann and Alison Heron make the following point: "When teachers attempt to situate popular media texts alongside the more traditional texts of classrooms, they run the risk of burying youth's pleasures by exposing them to adult critique." They provide examples where teachers have instinctively reacted to the media examples of students with their own prejudices without providing students with the tools by which they could examine the works.[42] We too have found that students are very well aware of the social value of popular culture products like manga, and some students resent taking school time to study with it. When selecting products of popular culture for classroom use, great care is needed.

There seem to be no ready templates for popular culture products to be smoothly integrated into classroom activity. What reading researchers agree on is that educators need to have an awareness of the literacy skills which children can acquire through popular media engagement. Already Adam Schwartz and Elaine Rubinstein-Avila call on North American educators to be aware of students' manga literacy skills.[43] Such an awareness, hopefully, will lead to a sensitivity whereby teachers—and students—can recognize a skill, piece of information, or interactive strategy when it is transferred to the school context. The recognition provides an opportunity to affirm the student and that affirmation can lead to multiple possibilities for growth.

One of the greatest forms of affirmation is recognition by a group of people that one values. It is well known that the literacy practices of manga and its kindred media, like anime and video games, are accessed individually. The personal literacy spaces that readers value are usually individual. In contrast, we have also found that there are many communal aspects. For example, when first learning to read manga, readers are introduced to manga by other readers. In the same way, readers choose titles that other people are reading and therefore create a common frame of reference, a kind of cultural literacy that can be shared with peers and family members. This often involves the practice of lending and borrowing manga. While we have described these practices as positive, Wertham found this practice of borrowing and lending highly problematic. He quoted an eight-year-old girl saying, "I have lots of friends and we buy about one comic book a week and then we exchange. I can read about ten a day."[44] Wertham saw these social networks as disseminating harmful content, that is, content that might influence acts of delinquency in an exponential manner. He viewed the communities as conduits of antisocial behavior, without recognizing the many affirmative social behaviors that such practices could spawn or the role of such communities in mitigating the negative effects that Wertham identified.

Wertham also complained that children read comics selectively, that they "picture read," looking for the interesting parts, ones usually depicting sex and violence.[45] His complaint carried the assumption that comics should be read sequentially from beginning to end. In our observation of manga readers, we have documented a variety of strategies. Certainly, some readers did read sequentially, looking carefully at every panel. Others read sequentially, but left out information that they thought was irrelevant. Through the eye movement tracing task that we asked interviewees to perform, we were able to construct a hierarchy of salient features that readers choose when reading manga: the most salient feature was reading the text in the speech balloons. The next salient feature was reading the faces of the characters. The third was paying attention to the sound effects and expressions describing texture. The final feature, the least salient, was the graphic background and the commentary text—if there was any at all.

Like Wertham's clients, some of our interviewees also skimmed through the manga looking for interesting parts. Our interviewees, however, have described these parts as gags or the funny bits. Yet looking for these parts was not the sum of their reading. The readers went back and read carefully the sections they were interested in. Perhaps Wertham's assumptions of reading sequentially lay in his association of comics with short stories and novels, for which they should serve as a transition. Since "graphic novels," and in this instance manga, are written as narratives, they would bear the creator's intention for the work to be read sequentially. Still, the reading strategies of Wertham's clients and our interviewees should not surprise us. For instance, in our own instruction of reading, even of academic articles, we train our students to read in a manner that is not sequential. We ask them first to read the abstract and the introduction. Then we suggest they read all the section headings, the figures, and the illustrations (i.e., the interesting bits). Then we direct them to the conclusion where there is usually a summary of findings. Finally, we ask them to decide what points are relevant and then go back to those sections and read carefully. Unlike manga, academic articles are usually expository texts and not narratives. Nonetheless, academic writers also compose in such a way that their texts would be read sequentially.

Reading a text sequentially is one assumption. Another assumption is that readers only have a single encounter with the text. For both readers of academic text and manga readers, the single sitting with the text may not be the only one. If the article is relevant, the reader may download it or make a photocopy to have on hand to read later. If it is only marginally relevant, at least the reader will note the bibliographical information so that the text could be accessed again. If the manga reader likes the story, the reader will usually purchase the bound *komikku* version of the series to have on hand to read again. The results of our surveys indicate that nearly 90 percent of manga readers read their favorite work more than once and over 35 percent read the work more than ten times. According to our interviewees, there is something new discovered in each encounter. Unfortunately, the survey did not probe deeper for reasons. Is it the graphics? Is it the story? Is it the encouraging message? Furthermore, we do not know how these manga rereading practices compare with other rereading/reengaging practices (with other media). What we can conclude is that manga stories are capable of sustaining the interest of the majority of its readers through multiple rereadings.

Comics and Other Media

Stories in comics, Wertham asserted, were of lower value than stories in folklore and in "proper" literature because they were formulaic. Side-stepping the notion that stories in literature might also conform to certain formulas, he complained that movie directors and directors of the then-emergent television programs selected aspects from comics that were harmful to children.[46]

Today manga stories and characters are found in anime, light novels, video games, television dramas, and toys. In fact, manga itself is not limited to the newsprint magazine and bound *komikku*. The more successful the series, the more they move across different media. Based on the successful "lady's" manga title *Nodame Cantabile*, Fuji TV began broadcasting the dramatization in 2006. To coincide with the commencing of the broadcast, a restaurant in the Harajuku area of Tokyo opened a café to replicate the pianist heroine's messy apartment and serve her badly cooked food. A stringed ensemble serenades the diners with classical music pieces mentioned in the manga.[47]

Manga also moves technologically beyond print. It can be found on the Internet not only accessible on PC screens but also available on mobile phones. To gain access requires a fee for a single "comic" volume in a series. This fee provides access for one month. What is interesting about the Kodansha site is that older, well-known titles have a higher fee than newer, less known titles.[48]

Both Yonezawa Yoshihiro and Frederik Schodt have expressed reservations in newspaper interviews about the future of manga on mobile phones.[49] Both have explained that manga is rooted in the print medium and thus offers readers freedom in employing various reading strategies. With the small screen, the reader is locked into a strict sequential reading of the work. Yet while these differences have been raised, perhaps we should not be too quick to dismiss this format. Already there are six times as many readers of manga on mobile phones than on personal computers. New software is developed that allows for zooming and multiple ways of scrolling, as well as features that send out tactile vibrations to coincide with the visual sound effects. The single panel-to-panel scrolling is called *kamishibai*, referring to the cardboard paper plays that were popular in the first half of the twentieth century.[50] Moreover, if well-known titles are more popular, as mentioned above, this consumer pattern may reflect the preference of readers to reread on their mobile phones rather than to read new titles. That way, they can focus on the panels of the more memorable scenes. In addition, there is simply the attraction to see a favorite work rendered in another format.

Yet the readers of manga on mobile phones do not represent the full spectrum of manga readers. It is rather those readers who read the newer forms of manga like *yaoi*/BL who access manga on mobile phones. Yoshiba Osamu and Niina Shin of the respective publishers Kodansha and Kadokawashoten say that most readers of manga and light novels on mobile phones are women in their twenties. The content includes mostly teen love and boys love, the latter being the more popular. Therefore, the stories are not serialized. While it may be assumed that these women would read the manga on their mobile phones while commuting, in fact the publishers have found that women prefer to read them in bed, just before going to sleep.[51] One of Wertham's girl clients reported a similar literacy practice: "I like to read the comic books about love because when I go to sleep at night I love to dream about love."[52]

Another format where manga has found a venue is the plasma screens on certain JR East commuter trains in the Tokyo area. These screens, only about forty centimeters square, provide riders with news clips, weather reports, and commercials. They offer the only diversion for riders when the trains are overcrowded. Because they are soundless, manga stories have been shown in the *kamishibai* form: one panel at a time. The speech balloons have been enlarged so that viewers several meters away can also read them. The balloons appear sequentially as in power points and anime-esque movements are occasionally given to the characters.

This process of stories moving across different media and formats is called intermedia ("media mix" in Japanese). It seems that in intermedia activity, stories and characters are moving back and forth across media in a relatively equal manner, affected only by economic factors fueled by popular demand. Yet we find that this is not the case. Intermedia movement does not flow equally, the direction of the flow is imbalanced. In Japan, stories and characters move out of manga, but tend not to move into manga.

While finding it compelling to see the new adaptations, people like to complain when a story moves into another medium, that somehow their imaginations have been disturbed. We have documented readers who have reported disappointment when their favorite manga has been rendered into an anime. Usually the complaints are over the quality of voices. For years, people have expressed dismay over their favorite novels and other pieces of literature rendered in the cinema. After a while, the disappointment can disappear and sometimes the receiving medium can supersede the urtext. For example, the film *Gone with the Wind* is as famous or even more so than the novel.

The situation of stories rendered in comics and manga has some disadvantages. Wertham complained not only of superhero, jungle, romance, and horror comics, but of the "classics" comics as well.[53] These kinds of comics provided many works of "proper" literature in the comic format. *Classics Illustrated* together with *Treasure Chest of Fun and Fact* were seen as useful in supplying a great deal of school-related knowledge.[54] *Classics Illustrated*, in particular, provided readers with the gist of literary works that were otherwise daunting for many to read. More importantly, they gave readers the confidence to read the literary work when the occasion arose. Still, Wertham ignored these assets and claimed that these comics degraded the literary classics. On the other hand, maybe Wertham had a point. Let us explain.

Due to the arrangement of panels and gutters, much of the story, dialogue, and action would have to be left out. As Scott McCloud insists, the meaning is in the gutter.[55] Readers of comics and manga learn to infer information with the gutter. Readers familiar with a story can find where the gutter has been placed and may find it disconcerting, perhaps more so than the cuts made by the movie director. Furthermore, because there is less dialogue, a choice has been made and the reader familiar with the story may not agree with the particular dialogues that were chosen. Yamato Waki made such choices when she created the thirteen-volume manga rendition of the eleventh-century novel-like classic *Tale of Genji*.[56] These structural conditions appear to make manga renditions difficult to compete with the other media versions. Well-known works of manga that are beginning to be hailed as classics are almost all original manga works.

Comics and manga provide easy, if not convenient, drafts for novel writers and animators, as well as television, movie, and stage directors. We have given several examples of how manga stories and characters have been appropriated by other media. In a further example, the television dramatization in 2005 of the manga *Doragon Zakura* increased the number of characters, highlighting the relative difficulty for manga creators to draw a large number of distinguishable characters in contrast to the ease of adding characters for dramatization.[57] Obtaining stories from comics is also occurring in the United States. Movie producers are looking for stories from graphic novels and they are looking among the smaller publishers. Sales of the graphic novel go up once the movie production is announced. Moreover, producers frequently consult reactions from comics fans at gatherings such as Comic-con.[58] In the other direction, the effect of works rendered in manga is that of reduction, in spite of the cinematic techniques that are capable of providing details.

A more successful intermedia movement to manga is not identifying directly with the urtext. In August 2007, a book by Mizuguchi Fumino was published called *Chiran Kara no Tegami* (Letters from Chiran), about the true story of the fiancé of a kamikaze pilot and the letters he sent her. Several months earlier, Seo Kōji published a short, two-part manga series in the weekly *Shōnen Magazine*. For several years, the story of this romance was known through television documentaries. Using the story, Seo created the manga with fictitious characters. It was an instant success and the *komikku* version was released roughly the same time as the book.[59] Still, efforts are continually made to render literature into manga. In 2008, a new manga magazine called *Pianissimo* was launched to carry manga versions of popular novels.[60]

We have made the argument that manga and comics are primarily originators, thus transmitters, of stories and function less well as receptors. In spite of these patterns, there are exceptions. Inoue Takehiko is currently working on a series called *Vagabond*. Although twenty-eight volumes of *komikkusu* have already been published, Inoue is publishing an episode in the weekly magazine *Morning* about once a month. The series is based on the life of the great sixteenth-century swordsman Miyamoto Musashi. Numerous novels, films, and television series have been made out of the swordsman's own chronicle. Inoue's handsome characters, lines drawn with a range of pens and brushes, and his creative use of panels describe an artist keen to stretch the boundaries of the medium. In figure 7.1, notice, from top to bottom, the range of pen and brush strokes, as well as the charcoal water content. Could *Vagabond* become the definitive Musashi story of our generation?

In 2008, Inoue put on an exhibition based on *Vagabond*.[61] This was not the usual manga exhibition with enlarged panels and original galleys on display. Instead, these were special renderings of panels, characters, and landscapes in *sumie* 墨絵 (traditional charcoal painting) on a variety of materials including *washi* 和紙 (traditional paper), enormous canvases, and wall surfaces all with distinctive lighting effects. In many of the works, the linguistic elements were retained. Toward the end of the exhibition, many of the viewers were in tears. These were manga readers, men and women in their twenties, thirties, and forties, who on a weekday stood in line for over two hours to see a favorite work transposed deliberately into the modes of fine art.

Comics Going Abroad

One of Wertham's most effective arguments against comics was that they misrepresented America. Using the same arguments against superheroes, Wertham asserted that comics depicted a fascist society where people of color were depicted as evil or stupid. Comics did not promote democratic values. These assertions were seriously considered in the Cold War context as they suggested that comics content could be used as counter-propaganda.[62] Wertham was successful in his critique of comics to construct American racism as a risk to national security.

Figure 7.1:   *Vagabond* (Cover from *Morning* by Inoue Takehiko. © 2007 by *Morning*. Reprinted with permission of Kodansha.)

Yet the censorship of American comics came more swiftly in other countries. Both France and Canada banned American comics in 1949. Wright explains that the French ban was part of a larger campaign to resist American cultural imperialism. The Canadians, however, were concerned about crime comics due to many of the reasons that Wertham had raised.[63] It was American horror comics that prompted the British authorities to ban comics through the Children and Young Persons (Harmful Publications) Act of 1955.[64] George H. Pumphrey published a widely disseminated booklet called *Comics and Your Children* emphasizing the moral dangers.[65] Later on, Richard Hoggart argued that comics were inferior reading material.[66]

According to Martin Barker, these objectionable comics from the United States were initially brought to Britain by the GIs after World War II.[67] Similarly in Japan, the GIs also brought comics with the occupation, although a range of comics types were introduced earlier. The difference was the soldiers' comics were not rejected in Japan. Perhaps the full impact of American comics on the development of manga has yet to be studied. Kure Tomofusa says the impact was great.[68] Takeuchi Osamu, in his history of postwar manga, writes of deep cultural influences.[69] In contrast, others like Natsume describe how manga became distinctive from structural norms of American comics. Manga creators began to draw speech balloons in a variety of ways, making them part of the message.[70] However, while these sources and others speak of the American occupation as providing new ideas and attitudes, we are not aware of any studies that detail these influences.

Manga today is seen as so thoroughly Japanese that it would seem reckless to suggest otherwise. The construction of Japan Cool is founded on perceptions that its contents and practices are unique to Japan. Yet the notion of reading manga as an adult literacy practice in Japan may not have been well established in 1945. Although we have been unable to independently verify Wright's sources on GI reading preferences in the early 1950s, they indicate that comics were the number one choice of reading material.[71] In that case, many soldiers were reading comics and their comics would be left around. These GIs, coming from a cross-section of American society, may have suggested to observers that comics can be interesting for adults. The practice of adults reading comics—ones that are written for adults—is considered now to be a practice that is quintessentially Japanese. However, it may have had its origin in the American occupation. For now, this issue remains a question. More archival research is needed. Indeed, manga's appeal, according to Natsume, is its diversity in content and diversity in age-group targets.[72]

The influence of manga has been longest in East Asia where creators in Taiwan, Hong Kong, and South Korea have emulated manga. Eventually creators began to develop their own styles, although manga was not the only influence.[73] Yet the transfer of manga works and manga styles to Asia has not been a smooth one. They were not allowed, officially, into South Korea until the late 1990s. At the same time, manga has been widely pirated.[74] Moreover, there have been accusations of plagiarism, such as the Chinese anime *Dou Dou the Big Mouth* and the well-known manga and anime series *Crayon Shin-chan*.[75] This situation has colored the discourse on manga in Asia, together with its kindred media, as the focus tends to be on protecting copyrights. Yet, as Aita Kaoruko points out, the interest in anime and manga in Asia was not promoted by the publishers. Instead, because of the demand, the publishers contracted local publishers to make titles legally available.

Regarding the spread to the United States, Roland Kelts reports that manga publishers and anime producers were very slow to act on the popularity.[76] There has been neither a coordinated effort nor any marketing strategy to spread manga or its kindred media abroad. Instead, one of the ways manga has spread is via scanlation, that is, groups of readers who scan, translate, and then share the manga through the Internet.[77] Similar to communities of readers described in chapter 4, these readers are determined to share their resources quickly rather than wait for publishers to translate works. The lack of planned marketing makes the appeal of manga abroad a compelling phenomenon.

However, while it was not coordinated, there were individuals and companies, such as TOKYOPOP and Viz MEDIA, LLC, who in their own way, promoted manga abroad. CEO Horibuchi Seiji of Viz MEDIA, LLC, chronicled his three decades in the United States and describes how he linked with Japanese publishers and established Viz Communications, then Viz MEDIA, LLC. His book is called *Moeru Amerika: Beikokujin wa Ikanishite Manga wo Yomuyōninatta* (The *moe*-ization of America: How Americans began to read manga).[78] It is interesting that he has chosen the word *moe* to describe the manga movement, since only a fraction of the titles that he publishes would be described as *moe*. However, his choice indicates a shift in describing the reading/consumption of manga and its kindred media. *Moe* not only refers to a set of esthetic sensibilities but also to the intense interest of a reader-consumer in a character. *Moe* refers to obsessions, as does *otaku*. Yet, unlike *otaku*, *moe* has a more positive sense and a more feminine nuance. For Horibuchi, since the majority of his readers in North America are female, *moe* is appropriate. Still, *moe* cannot be used to label anyone in the way *otaku* can.

We have already mentioned in earlier chapters the South African magazine *Otaku*. Kate Allen comes from Zimbabwe and travels regularly to southern Africa to see her family. On one of her trips, she picked up *Otaku* at Johannesburg's Oliver Tambo International Airport. This magazine, as described earlier, presents manga concepts, stories, and kindred media products in a readable and accessible format.[79] Subsequently, she subscribed to the magazine and then received a telephone call from the editor congratulating her on being the first subscriber from Japan. Through the conversation, she found that the magazine is written, edited, and published entirely by South Africans without any financial or consultative input from Japan. The magazine engages the reader first around anime, with a number of reviews. This is because anime products are most widely known through television broadcasts. There are game, music, and movie reviews, followed by manga reviews. There are also articles about manga creators and their work. Japanese-language concepts are presented together with articles about Japanese society and culture. The reviews and articles stress themes like love, relationships, style, moods, and combat. The magazine meets the reader with the familiar and then takes the reader further into products that demand an ever-sophisticated knowledge of things Japanese; yet the pull is not simply into the esoteric, as the reader is reminded of more universal themes in order to make contact with the material at another level. Because there are multiple points to connect with the content, readers need not be intimidated by a lack of knowledge of the Japanese world.

Wertham frequently wrote of a conspiracy among comic publishers.[80] In contrast, manga has spread abroad through the dedication of fans and the resourcefulness of individuals. The spread of manga and its kindred media has occurred without large-scale strategic marketing. The situation may be changing as the number of stakeholders increase with government sponsorship and corporate interest. These stakeholders may be directed more strategically with the spread of Japan Cool. Indeed, the Japanese foreign ministry has launched the International Manga Award for manga creators overseas. The first award was granted to Hong Kong creator Lee Chi Ching; in the second year, the prize again went to a Hong Kong creator, Lau Wan Kit.[81]

The increase of fans, particularly in North America, has affected, in reverse, Japanese society in some of the most conservative sectors. Several universities are scrambling to offer courses in popular culture. As a result, manga commentators are being hired for full-time academic positions. Will the new identities of these writers shape their discourse and the direction of the study of manga?

Comics as Inferior: Too Many Pictures

We have already described how Wertham viewed comics as inferior to "proper" literature, and that in spite of his admission of the difficulty of reading comics, he saw them as having no connection to other types of reading and, moreover, detrimental to literacy. His main criticism, the harmful content, also played into his polemic on the inferiority of comics. Wertham, however, provided additional reasons why comics were so inferior.

First of all, he felt the quality of the paper matched the quality of the content. If the content were of more lofty subjects, comics should be printed on better paper.[82] Indeed, his complaint of comics being difficult to read was exacerbated by the quality of the paper. Yet the quality of the paper enabled publishers to charge less, thereby giving children and young people access to comics on their own. The same economic patterns exist for manga. The range of stories in the manga magazines is only possible with the printing on cheap paper. Moreover, Japanese readers continue to be content with monochrome, while comics by the 1940s had shifted to color, a more expensive process. Nonetheless, it is the financial independence of children and young people that is vital in comics and manga publishing and reading practices. In the case of manga, it was the rise in allowances around 1960 that fueled the manga magazine market, taking customers away from the book rental shops.[83] Children's manga lags behind in sales because the readers are dependent on parents. The industry still depends on children's financial independence. At the same time, children may choose to buy used *komikku* of their favorite titles at used bookshops or simply borrow from friends, thus contributing to the decline of manga sales.

The inferiority of paper quality together with the inferiority of content led Wertham to speculate that no one would want to collect comics:

> I have never come across any adult nor adolescent who had outgrown comicbook reading who would ever dream of keeping these "books" for any sentimental or other reason.[84]

Here again he was mistaken, as there were and still are many adult comics collectors in the United States. In Japan, we have met readers with extensive collections. This kind of practice may be unsustainable in large urban areas, but as long as people keep books, manga would be among them.

Related to the low quality of paper, just because comics were mass-produced meant that they were inferior. Mass production for Wertham indicated mediocrity, especially when creativity was stifled by industry prescriptions. He claimed the following:

> It is in an artistic sense that these artists are victims. I know that quite a number of them are highly gifted; but they have to turn out an inartistic assembly-line product. That is what is essentially wrong with comic books: There are too many pictures.[85]

Too many pictures; in manga's case, there are even more. The cinematic techniques of drawing panels increased the number of panels. The reflective scenes in
shōjo manga have also produced a similar result. Yet Wertham's concern here was the
invariability that came with mass production. Manga stories are also mass-produced,
in even greater volume, with seeming invariability in types of stories.

There are manga commentators and researchers concerned about the pressures
in the industry to create quantities of manga in a short time. They feel that these
pressures foster mediocrity and entrenched attitudes. As regular manga readers, we
also see monotony in many works, and as a result we notice the publishers endlessly
repeating a story line that has sold, thereby intimating that they are playing safe.
At the same time, there are works that have compelled us to take note, hooked us
into the story, and have offered us wonderment with the drawings. Do these "better" works result from less pressured work conditions? If one could reflect on the
work situation of say, Anthony Trollope, Charles Dickens, or even J. S. Bach and W.
A. Mozart, a leisured work environment does not necessarily guarantee quality—or
what would be later seen as quality.

To improve the perception of a cultural product's quality is to establish a relationship with previous products in history. Pierre Bourdieu describes how linking
with the past can increase a person's or a product's cultural capital.[86] This is how
manga's status improves when connections are made to the *Chōjū Giga* drawings of
the twelfth century. Further cultural capital is acquired by linking manga to *kibyōshi*,
ukiyoe, and other woodblock print products of early modern Japan. The same link-
age is attempted by some between *yaoi* manga with the traditional homosexual
cultural practices and products known as *nanshoku*. Largely due to the tremendous
interest in manga and its kindred media overseas, these earlier connections such
as to the *Chōjū Giga* and *ukiyoe* are enthusiastically embraced as manga in general is being reconstructed as a national cultural asset. In contrast, *nanshoku* is not
embraced. When the culture wars in the West die down and homosexual practices
receive wide social and legal acceptance, perhaps the *nanshoku* cultural products will
be reclaimed as heritage.

Not all researchers accept the connection of manga to traditional drawing and
publishing. Many insist that the rise of manga publishing is primarily a post–World
War II phenomenon in which economic conditions, stimulus from American comics, and gifted creators all came together. As we examined the promoters of the
historical roots and the critics of this position, we found that among the promoters
were many people who have had at least some experience in drawing and creating
manga. As practitioners of critical linguistics, we would be sympathetic to the position that would deconstruct the connection to the earlier roots. At the same time,
we realize we carry a bias toward language and we lack training in and experience
with the graphic arts. It is more difficult for us to perceive the historical connections
in graphic representation.

Both positions on manga's origins agree that the works of key creators after
1945 were important for manga's development. However, several manga researchers

are genuinely concerned that new stories are not being created. There are the economic constraints of publishers sticking to patterns that have sold. There is also what appears to be a heavy burden of the post–World War II legacy of the master creators. Many creators are reluctant to deviate from forms that are fast evolving into what are seen to be high culture forms. These concerned researchers point to the mostly amateur participants of *Comiket* as the source of new manga. The participants create parodies in their *dōjinshi* and experiment with stories on their own. It is through these activities of mainly girls and young women that the newer narrative forms like *yaoi* and new sensibilities like *moe* have developed.

Indeed, the *Bildungsroman* narrative that pervades much of *shōnen*, "young," and "adult" manga, as well as many *shōjo* manga stories, may have begun to run out of steam. People find that the expectations that these stories raise somehow do not ring true. Hard work and perseverance do not necessarily bring rewards. The human body does not indefinitely go from strength to strength. *Bildungsroman* provides one of the "grand" narratives that form the basis of ethos, be it national, institutional, or personal. It is also the narrative of the social sciences, particularly education. *Bildungsroman* was the narrative of Japan's economic miracle. It was also the narrative of those who identified with the economic success. Now most of its participants are old, witnessing the decline of their bodies with few accolades for their efforts. Do these kinds of narratives continue to offer meaning to these people? Are the achievements and material successes that the narratives foster really sustainable, even in the environmental sense?

Some of the newer manga narratives show that without *Bildungsroman*, the result is not necessarily nihilism. Nor is the focus on the present, as in a *yaoi* narrative, necessarily hedonistic. It is in this zone, of not quite nihilism and not quite hedonism, that unlikely characters come together and produce a relationship. Does the relationship made out the friction of the characters' otherness inspire hope? Characters drawn in the *moe* style are said to evoke a sense of arousal, but also sympathy for the character. Does this emotion bear any relationship to what we value as compassion?

More stories are told in an atmosphere of pastiche. These *yaoi* stories disturb because they contain a lesser degree of temporal sequence and thus cause and effect. These are the building blocks of what we construct as "responsibility." Responsibility can only be conceived within a temporal cause and effect sequence. Therefore responsibility is most often placed in the context of a narrative. The stories with different senses of narrative, subtly present a challenge to some of society's basic values. At the same time, they might send a gleam across some circumstances where we are not sure how to cope. Faced with the gloom of our environmental predicament, for example, it is difficult to locate any kind of dynamism as we find ourselves boxed in with ever more rules of conformity to conserve and recycle. Can new stories help us reimagine our roles in the ecosystem?

Young Japanese people are creating thousands of new manga stories through their clubs at school or by themselves. Ethnographic studies are needed to understand the cultural literacy resourced in the creating process and the nature of the creator's agency to produce these stories. At the same time, the number of young people engaged in creating manga is small compared with the numbers of readers. Moreover, the number of readers who read these "new" genres is also small compared with those who read manga commercially published. Their methods are, however, not without influence. We have pointed out how large publishers, presumably with the permission of the creators, publish works with parodies. These parodies, in turn, spark interest in the urtexts and sales of the *komikku* versions.

Much of the popular media in Japan owes a debt to manga creators for their stories. Some estimate nearly 70 percent of media production draws on material originating in manga.[87] This indicates how manga is still very much a part of the cultural literacy and literacy practices of many Japanese. Should a book like Steven Johnson's *Everything Bad for You is Good for You* be written in Japan, reading manga would surely be a part of it. The fact that Johnson completely ignores comics is one indication of how irrelevant they are in the United States. On the surface, it would seem that Hollywood, network television, and other American media providers have had ample material and stories to draw on. Certainly it would seem that these providers were and are not lacking. However, just imagine that if comics were not subjected to Wertham's polemics and the campaigns that led them to be censored, and that they were allowed to freely develop with a vibrant adult readership, it is likely that there would be many more stories. Like a language with no more speakers and with its passing all the nuances lost, the stunting of a popular medium has left us with many stories untold. This loss is even more acutely felt when beholding the rich manga tradition and its varied literacy practices.

Mitigating the Effects: The Communities of Practice

We have described manga literacy as being sustained by the literacy practices of other readers. We have called reading in the context of other readers as engaging in a community of practice. Some of these communities may possess a great deal of cohesion while others have less. The communities are evident in the developmental stage when readers first learn to read manga. The communities are also evident when reading manga, knowing about manga, and owning manga become an integral part of social interaction among peers. The communities continue into adulthood, especially among those who engage in manga creation and seek venues to share their work. Among the larger group that does not create, opportunities exist for communicating with creators and thereby participating in a work's creation. More common is engaging as fans, seeking out commentaries on favorite works, participating in events, and exchanging views on Internet sites.

How do the communities mitigate the perceived lack of literacy skills? Communities of family members including parents, siblings, and others participate as readers themselves or providers of manga. Most readers begin to read manga at the same time they begin elementary school. Their school literacy and manga literacy develop together in a complementary way. When readers have difficulties reading manga, the communities of readers among family members are a more secure place to ask for help. As readers engage in communities of readers among peers, it is more difficult to admit to difficulties and readers learn strategies to solicit help indirectly. Moreover, having to engage in these strategies allows readers to pay attention to the dialogue in manga and thus learn appropriate expressions for situations while expanding their vocabulary.

How then do the communities mitigate the perceived harmful effects of manga content? In short, by talking about the content. Ōnishi Jun asked upper elementary and junior high school boys and girls what were their favorite topics of conversation. The first was their friends, the second was television, and the third was manga.[88] Most likely the content in the second and third topic would overlap. In our surveys to high school students, we asked respondents to rank their preferences from a list of seven choices: books, magazines, manga, anime, television, video games, and the Internet. The most popular was television for girls and magazines for boys. Yet manga was the second most popular for both groups. Although the boys did rank television, they tended not to give it their first choice. We then adjusted the rankings, by giving the value of seven to all the instances of the first choice, six to the second choice and so on. With this method, manga became the most popular choice, followed by television and magazines.

Lawrence Kutner and Cheryl Olson have documented examples of video game players playing with other players. They point out that through gaming, players have something to talk about. They provide evidence that these practices mitigate the violence contained in the games.[89] Another attraction to gaming is its competition. There is less overt competition among manga readers, but it does exist regarding knowledge of works and access to works. Many readers have expressed a desire to talk about their favorite works, so that others could share in the pleasure. Others enjoy exhibiting their expert status. By talking about the work, readers have the opportunity to acquire a sense of values, a ranking of taste, as well as limits on behavior.

Our assessment of the roles of the communities of practice in developing and maintaining manga literacy has been positive. At the same time, there are sides to these communities that may not be so positive. We were alerted to this possibility from our survey data on preferences where we found whole genres ignored. We suspect that the sensibility not to reveal certain preferences was acquired in the communities of practice. We have been unable to have access to the conversations over manga titles to understand what they are like. Are they really as supportive as we say they are? In the paragraph above, we list some positive attributes that could be acquired, but these could also be interpreted negatively. For example, we do have evidence from readers that they felt pressured to read manga to stay a part of their group. We also know that readers like to be experts. What kinds of discourse strategies do they use to demonstrate their expert status? Do they dominate?

Ōnishi's results on what children talk about have a sobering side. The most frequent topic is about friends. We cannot imagine that all the talk is about affirmation. There are members who are more central and others who are more peripheral. The communities of practice regarding the reading of manga serve readers' needs, whether they are skill-based or needs for self-actualization. However, the needs are served but they might not necessarily be met or fulfilled. For those whose needs are not fulfilled, they can go back to their personal literacy practices and continue to read their favorite titles or genres, or reread their favorite works. Like readers of novels, poetry, or scriptures, and even viewers of movies and videos, manga readers can revisit a favorite work and be encouraged by the story and characters. Yet, more importantly, as readers have reported, they can appropriate for themselves the language of and the strategies for dealing with sensitive interpersonal situations. Thus empowered, they can reengage in the communities of practice.

Notes

1. M. A. K. Halliday, "The Linguistic Study of Literary Texts," in *Linguistic Studies of Text and Discourse*, ed. Jonathan Webster (London: Continuum, 1964/2002), 26–29. In systemic-functional linguistics, the ideational, interpersonal, and textual relate to field, tenor, and mode, respectively. These three make up registers, which are then used as analytical categories for genres.

2. Marshall McLuhan, *Understanding Media: The Extensions of Man* (New York: McGraw-Hill, 1964), 170–78.

3. Robert C. Gardner and Wallace E. Lambert, *Attitudes and Motivation in Second Language Learning* (Rowley, MA: Newbury House, 1972).

4. Zoltan Dornyei, *Motivational Strategies in the Classroom* (Cambridge: Cambridge University Press, 2001), 5–30.

5. Natsume Fusanosuke, *Manga ni Jinsei wo Manande Nani ga Warui?* (What's wrong with learning life's lessons from manga?) (Tokyo: Random House-Kodansha, 2006).

6. Philip H. Phenix, *Realms of Meaning: A Philosophy of the Curriculum for General Education* (New York: McGraw Hill, 1964), 191–211. Phenix calls the study of personal knowledge "synoetics."

7. Kimiko Manes, "Anime Gives U.S. Students Window on Japan," *Daily Yomiuri*, April 26, 2005, 17.

8. Matsuzawa Mitsuo, *Nihonjin no Atama wo Dame Nishita Manga Gekiga* (Manga graphic novels have damaged Japanese people's minds) (Tokyo: Yamate Shobo, 1979).

9. Steven Johnson, *Everything Bad is Good for You—How Today's Popular Culture is Actually Making Us Smarter* (New York: Riverhead, 2005).

10. James Paul Gee, *What Video Games Have to Teach Us about Learning and Literacy* (New York: Palgrave Macmillan, 2003).

11. Fredric Wertham, *Seduction of the Innocent: The Influence of Comic Books on Today's Youth* (New York: Rinehart, 1954), 50.

12. David Hajdu, *The Ten-Cent Plague: The Great Comic-Book Scare and How it Changed America* (New York: Farrar, Straus and Giroux, 2008), 337–51.

13. Bradford W. Wright, *Comic Book Nation: The Transformation of Youth Culture in America* (Baltimore: Johns Hopkins University Press, 2003), 155.

14. Wright, *Comic Book Nation*, 86–108, 154–79.

15. Norman Fairclough, *Analyzing Discourse: Textual Analysis for Social Research* (London: Routledge, 2003), 202–3.

16. Wertham, *Seduction of the Innocent*, 59.

17. For example, Shoko Yoneyama, *The Japanese High School: Silence and Resistance* (London: Routledge, 1999), 157–85.

18. "Over 90% of People Have a Sense of Crisis Regarding the NEET Issue," *2004-11-01, Nomura Research Institute, Ltd.*, www.nri.co.jp/english/news/2004/041101.html (accessed May 6, 2008).

19. Lawrence Kutner and Cheryl Olson, *Grand Theft Childhood: The Surprising Truth about Violent Video Games and What Parents Can Do* (New York: Simon and Schuster, 2008).

20. Martin Barker, *A Haunt of Fears: The Strange History of the British Horror Comics Campaign* (Jackson: University Press of Mississippi, 1984), 56–70; Martin Barker, "Fredric Wertham: The Sad Case of the Unhappy Humanist," in *Pulp Demons: International Dimensions of the Postwar Anti-Comics Campaign*, ed. John A. Lent (Madison, NJ/London: Fairleigh Dickinson University Press and Associated University Presses, 1999), 215–33; and Wright, *Comic Book Nation*, 154–72. The connection between superheroes and fascism was made already by church groups in the early 1940s; see David Hadju, *The Ten-Cent Plague*, 75–82.

21. Wertham, *Seduction of the Innocent*, 85–99.

22. Wertham, *Seduction of the Innocent*, 101–7.

23. David Hajdu, *The Ten-Cent Plague*, 99–100.

24. Wertham, *Seduction of the Innocent*, 196–208.

25. Wertham, *Seduction of the Innocent*, 187–93; William M. Marston, *Wonder Woman* (New York: DC Comics, 1944); and Bob Kane, *Batman* (New York: Detective Comics, 1939).

26. Tezuka Osamu, *Tetsuwan Atomu* (Mighty Atom) (Tokyo: Kobunsha, 1952); Ishinomori Shōtarō, *Kamen Raidā* (Masked rider) (Tokyo: Shonen Magazine (Kodansha), 1972); and Uchiyama Mamoru, *Urutoraman* (Ultraman) (Tokyo: Shogaku Ninensei (Shogakukan), 1971).

27. Frederik L. Schodt, *The Astro Boy Essays: Osamu Tezuka, Mighty Atom and the Manga/Anime Revolution* (Berkeley, CA: Stone Bridge Press, 2007).

28. Inoue Takehiko, *Slam Dunk* (Tokyo: Shueisha, 1990); Takahashi Kazuki, *YU-GI-OH!* (Tokyo: SHUEISHA Inc., 1996); and Kishimoto Masashi, *Naruto* (Tokyo: SHUEISHA Inc., 1999).

29. Yoshida Masataka, *Nijigen Bishōjoron: Otaku no Megami Sōzōshi* (The theory of the two-dimensional *bishōjo*: The history of *otakus*' goddess creation) (Tokyo: Nimi Shobo, 2004), 253–54.

30. Sharalyn Orbaugh, "Busty Battlin' Babes: The Evolution of the *Shōjo* in 1990s Visual Culture," in *Gender and Power in the Japanese Visual Field*, ed. Joshua S. Mostow, Norman Bryson, and Maribeth Graybill (Honolulu: University of Hawai'i Press, 2003), 209–15.

31. Tezuka Osamu, *Ribon no Kishi* (Princess knight) (Tokyo: Kodansha, 1953); Ikeda Riyoko, *Berusaiyu no Bara* (Rose of Versailles) (Tokyo: Shueisha, 1972); and Takahashi Rumiko, *Ranma ½* (Tokyo: Shonen Sunday (Shogakukan), 1987).

32. Kaneda Junko, "Manga Dōjinshi: Kaishaku Kyōdotai no Poritikusu" (Manga dōjinshi: The interpretive community's politics)," in *Bunka no Shakaigaku* (The sociology of culture), ed. Sato Kenji and Yoshimi Shunya (Tokyo: Yuhikaku Arma, 2007), 185–86.

33. "'Hontō no Jibun' wo Sarakedashita Hitobito no Meian" (The mixed results of people confessing about "The real me"), *Spa!* May 28, 2008, 41.

34. Wertham, *Seduction of the Innocent*, 122.

35. Wertham, *Seduction of the Innocent*, 139.

36. Basil Bernstein, *Pedagogy, Symbolic Control and Identity: Theory, Research, Critique* (London: Taylor & Francis, 1996), 169–81.

37. Phenix, *Realms of Meaning*, 26–29. Although Phenix puts literature in the aesthetic realm with art, literature is clearly synoptic in its integrative capabilities similar to history and philosophy. It is also in the "synoetic" realm of personal knowledge. This flexibility of literature can be explained by employing Halliday's three-part definition of language: a) textual—literature in the aesthetic realm provides sources of pleasure and models to be emulated for textual production; b) ideational—literature in the synoptic realm provides information that is organized, thus aiding memory; and c) interpersonal—literature in the "synoetic" realm informs thought and action.

38. For example, E. D. Hirsch, Joseph F. Kett, and James Trefil, *Dictionary of Cultural Literacy: What Every American Needs to Know* (New York: Houghton Mifflin, 2002).

39. Wertham, *Seduction of the Innocent*, 232–33.

40. This point is also made by Roger Fowler, "The Referential Code and Narrative Authority," in *Critical Discourse Analysis: Critical Concepts in Linguistics*, vol. 1, ed. Michael Toolan (London: Routledge, 2002/1977), 203.

41. Gemma Moss, "Children Talk Horror Videos: Reading as a Social Performance," *Australian Journal of Education* 37, no. 2 (1993): 169–81.

42. Donna E. Alvermann and Alison H. Heron, "Literacy Identity Work: Playing to Learn with Popular Media," *Journal of Adolescent & Adult Literacy* 45, no. 2 (2001): 121.

43. Adam Schwartz and Elaine Rubinstein-Avila, "Understanding the Manga Hype: Uncovering the Multi-Modality of Comic-Book Literacies," *Journal of Adolescent & Adult Literacy* 50, no. 2 (2006): 40–49.

44. Wertham, *Seduction of the Innocent*, 39.

45. Wertham, *Seduction of the Innocent*, 140.

46. Wertham, *Seduction of the Innocent*, 353–84.

47. Ninomiya Tomoko, *Nodame Cantabile* (Tokyo: Kodansha, 2001); Ichihara Shoji, "Nodame: From Manga to TV to Café," *Daily Yomiuri*, November 11, 2006, 21.

48. "Kodansha Mobile Contents," www.kt.kodansha.co.jp/pc/index.html (accessed September 1, 2007).

49. Sato Kenichi, "Manga Migrating to New Medium: Will Pixels Pummel Paper?" *Daily Yomiuri*, May 20, 2006, 26; John Jerney, "Tezuka's Manga Faces Tough Transition to New Media," *Daily Yomiuri*, August 21, 2007, 18.

50. Yoshiba Osamu and Niina Shin, "Shuppansha Kara Mita Dejitaru Jijyō" (The digital situation from the perspective of publishers), presentation at *Akihabara Enta Matsuri!* Tokyo, October 20–28, 2007.

51. Yoshiba and Niina, "Shuppansha Kara Mita Dejitaru Jijyō."

52. Wertham, *Seduction of the Innocent*, 39.

53. Wertham, *Seduction of the Innocent*, 36–38.

54. Albert L. Kanter, *Classics Illustrated* (New York: Elliot Publications, 1947); *Treasure Chest of Fun and Fact* (Dayton, OH: George A. Pflaum, 1946–1972).

55. Scott McCloud, *Understanding Comics: The Invisible Art* (New York: HarperPerennial, 1994), 60–93.

56. Ihara Hiroko, "Manga Boosts Tale's Popularity," *Daily Yomiuri*, July 7, 2007, 3.

57. Mita Norifusa, *Doragon Zakura* (Dragon Zakura) (Tokyo: Kodansha, 2003).

58. Heidi MacDonald, "Movies Still Woo Graphic Novels," www.publishersweekly.com/index.asp?/layout=articlePrint&articleID=CA6469935 (accessed September 4, 2007); Jeremy Kay, "Comic-con or Bust: The Geek Fest that Can Break a Movie," www.guardian.co.uk/film/2008/aug/01/sciencefictionandfantasy (accessed August 2, 2008).

59. Mizuguchi Fumino, *Chiran Kara no Tegami* (Letters from Chiran) (Tokyo: Shinshōsha, 2007); Seo Kōji, *Rabu Retā* (Love letters) (Tokyo: Shōnen Magazine Comics (Kodansha), 2007).

60. Sato Kenichi, "Manga Retell Novels in Pictures," *Daily Yomiuri*, March 7, 2008, 13.

61. *Inoue Takehiko: The LAST Exhibition* (Tokyo: Ueno Royal Museum, May 24–July 6, 2008).

62. Wertham, *Seduction of the Innocent*, 273–94.

63. Wright, *Comic Book Nation*, 100–101.

64. Barker, *A Haunt of Fears*, 9.

65. George H. Pumphrey, *Comics and Your Children* (London: Comics Campaign Council, 1952).

66. Richard Hoggart, *The Uses of Literacy: Changing Patterns in English Mass Culture* (Fair Lawn, NJ: Essential Books, 1957).

67. Barker, *A Haunt of Fears,* 8.

68. Kure Tomofusa, *Gendai Manga no Zentaizō* (The portrait of modern manga) (Tokyo: Futaba Bunkō, 1997), 126.

69. Takeuchi Osamu, *Sengo Manga 50 Nen Shi* (Postwar 50 years of *manga* history) (Tokyo: Chikuma Shobo, 1995), 11–12.

70. Natsume Fusanosuke, *Manga no Fuka-Yomi, Otona-Yomi* (Deep reading and adult reading of manga) (Tokyo: Īsuto Puresu, 2004b), 101–4.

71. Wright, *Comic Book Nation*, 155.

72. Natsume Fusanosuke, *Manga Sekai Senryaku* (Manga world strategy) (Tokyo: Shogakukan, 2001), 210–16.

73. Wendy Suiyi Wong, *Hong Kong Comics: A History of Manhua* (New York: Princeton Architectural Press, 2002), 20.

74. Aita Kaoruko, "'Manga' Making Asian Cultural Inroads," *Daily Yomiuri*, October 8, 1995, 1; Wendy Suiyi Wong, *Hong Kong Comics*, 19.

75. Yoshida, K., "H. K. Fans Say CCTV Show Rips off Creyon Shin-chan," *Daily Yomiuri*, July 30, 2007, 3.

76. Roland Kelts, *Japanamerica: How Japanese Pop Culture has Invaded the U.S.* (New York: Palgrave Macmillan, 2006), 69–80.

77. Anne Allison has a general description of how fans download work from the Internet, "The Japan Fad in Global Youth Culture and Millennial Capitalism," in *Mechademia: Emerging Worlds of Anime and Manga*, vol. 1, ed. Frenchy Lunning (Minneapolis: University of Minnesota Press, 2006), 11–21; a more detailed description of scanlation can be found in Dirk Deppey, "Scanlation Nation: Amateur Manga Tranlators Tell Their Stories," *The Comics Journal*, no. 269, www.tcj.com/269/n_scan.html (accessed August 31, 2008).

78. Seiji Horibuchi, *Moeru Amerika: Beikokujin wa Ikanishite Manga wo Yomuyōninatta* (The Moe-ization of America: How Americans became readers of manga) (Tokyo: Nikkei BP Sha, 2006).

79. *Otaku* (Johannesburg: Xvolve, 2005).

80. Wertham, *Seduction of the Innocent*, 11, 252–72, 295–52.

81. "H. K. Artist Bags 1st Manga Award for Non-Japanese," *Daily Yomiuri*, July 1, 2007, 3; "Hong Kong Artist Lau Wins International Manga Award," *Daily Yomiuri*, August 29, 2008, 13.

82. Wertham, *Seduction of the Innocent*, 139.

83. Nakano Haruyuki, *Manga Sangyōron* (Theory of manga industry) (Tokyo: Chikuma Shobō, 2004), 32–39.

84. Wertham, *Seduction of the Innocent*, 89–90.

85. Wertham, *Seduction of the Innocent*, 267.

86. Pierre Bourdieu, *Distinction: A Social Critique of the Judgement of Taste*, trans. Richard Nice (Cambridge, MA: Harvard University Press, 1984), 70–71.

87. Aso Tarō and Hirokane Kenshi, "Orijinaru Kakuryō Kaigi" (Original cabinet meeting), *Big Comic Original* 34, no. 26 (Tokyo: Shogakukan, 2007), 1.

88. Ōnishi Jun, "Kodomo to Manga: Kodomo Eno Ankēto Chōsa Kara" (Children and manga: From a survey to children), in *Kodomo to Manga: Manga Dokkairyoku wa Dō Hattatsu Suruka* (Children and manga: How manga comprehension develops), ed. Akashi Yōichi and Nakazawa Jun (Tokyo: Gendaijidōbunka Kenkyūkai, 1993), 11–54.

89. Kutner and Olson, *Grand Theft Childhood*, 129–33.

Appendix

マンガ・リテラシーについてのアンケート

学年＿＿＿＿＿＿＿＿＿＿＿女・男
マンガを読んだことがありますか？　はい・いいえ　もし「はい」と答えたら、
つぎの項目にお答えください。よろしくお願いします。

(1)　　a. マンガを始めて読んだのはなん才でしたか。
　　　　　4才＿＿＿　5才＿＿＿　6才＿＿＿　7才＿＿＿　8才＿＿＿その他＿＿＿
　　　　b. どなたがマンガを紹介してくれましたか。
　　　　　父＿＿＿　母＿＿＿　兄弟＿＿＿　姉妹＿＿＿　友だち＿＿＿　その他＿＿＿
　　　　c. 最初に読んだマンガのタイトルはなんですか。＿＿＿＿＿＿＿＿＿
　　　　d. そのアニメ版はマンガを読む（前　・　後　・　同時）に見た。
　　　　e. そのマンガを何回ぐらい読み返しましたか。
　　　　　1回だけ＿＿＿　3回ぐらい＿＿＿　5回ぐらい＿＿＿　7回ぐらい＿＿＿
　　　　　10回以上＿＿＿
　　　　f. マンガを読みながら分からないことがありましたか。はい・いいえ・
　　　　　わからない
　　　　g. もし「はい」と答えたらどう対処したのですか。
　　　　　＿＿＿＿＿＿＿に聞く　また読み返す＿＿＿その他＿＿＿＿＿＿

(2)　　a. 小学校1年と3年の間、一番好きなマンガはなんでしたか。　＿＿＿＿
　　　　　＿＿＿＿＿＿＿＿＿＿＿
　　　　b. そのマンガを何回ぐらい読み返しましたか。
　　　　　1回だけ＿＿＿　3回ぐらい＿＿＿　5回ぐらい＿＿＿　7回ぐらい＿＿＿
　　　　　10回以上＿＿＿
　　　　c. そのアニメ版はマンガを読む（前　・　後　・　同時）に見た。
　　　　d. 友だちもマンガを読んでいましたか。はい・いいえ・わからない
　　　　e. 友だちとマンガを貸したり借りたりしましたか。はい・いいえ・わか
　　　　　らない

　　　　f. マンガを読みながら分からないことがありましたか。はい・いいえ・
　　　　　わからない
　　　　g. もし「はい」と答えたらどう対処したのですか。

　　　　　＿＿＿＿＿＿＿＿に聞く　また読み返す＿＿＿　　　その他＿＿＿＿＿＿

(3)　　a. 小学校4年と6年の間、一番好きなマンガはなんでした
　　　　　か。＿＿＿＿＿＿＿
　　　　b. そのマンガを何回ぐらい読み返しましたか。
　　　　　1回だけ＿＿　3回ぐらい＿＿　5回ぐらい＿＿　7回ぐらい＿＿
　　　　　10回以上＿＿
　　　　c. そのアニメ版はマンガを読む（前　・　後　・　同時）に見た。
　　　　d. 友だちもマンガを読んでいましたか。はい・いいえ・わからない
　　　　e. 友だちとマンガを貸したり借りたりしましたか。はい・いいえ・わか
　　　　　らない
　　　　f. マンガを読みながら分からないことがありましたか。はい・いいえ・
　　　　　わからない
　　　　g. もし「はい」と答えたらどう対処したのですか。
　　　　　＿＿＿＿＿＿＿＿に聞く　また読み返す＿＿＿その他＿＿＿＿＿＿

(4)　　a. 中学校の時、一番好きなマンガはなんでしたか。　＿＿＿＿＿＿＿＿＿
　　　　　＿＿＿＿＿
　　　　b. そのマンガを何回ぐらい読み返しましたか。
　　　　　1回だけ＿＿　3回ぐらい＿＿　5回ぐらい＿＿　7回ぐらい＿＿
　　　　　10回以上＿＿
　　　　c. そのアニメ版はマンガを読む（前　・　後　・　同時）に見た。
　　　　d. 友だちもマンガを読んでいましたか。はい・いいえ・わからない
　　　　e. 友だちとマンガを貸したり借りたりしましたか。はい・いいえ・わか
　　　　　らない
　　　　f. マンガを読みながら分からないことがありましたか。はい・いいえ・
　　　　　わからない
　　　　g. もし「はい」と答えたらどう対処したのですか。
　　　　　＿＿＿＿＿＿＿＿に聞く　また読み返す＿＿＿＿＿その他＿＿＿＿＿＿

(5)　　a. 現在、どれが好きですか（優先順位で番号をふってください）。
　　　　　本を読む＿＿　雑誌を読む＿＿　マンガを読む＿＿　アニメを見る＿＿
　　　　　他のテレビ番組を見る＿＿　コンピューターゲームをする＿＿　イン
　　　　　ターネットを検索する＿＿
　　　　b. 現在、マンガは好きですか。はい・いいえ・わからない
　　　　c. もし「はい」とこたえたら、一番好きなマンガはなんですか。＿＿＿＿
　　　　d. そのマンガをなん回ぐらい読み返しましたか。
　　　　　1回だけ＿＿　　3回ぐらい＿＿　　5回ぐらい＿＿　　7回ぐらい＿＿
　　　　　10回以上＿＿

e. 他のマンガも読んでいますか？　はい・いいえ・わからない

f. もし「はい」と答えたらタイトルを書いてください。＿＿＿＿＿＿＿
＿＿＿＿＿＿＿＿＿＿＿＿＿＿＿

g. マンガをどのぐらい読んでいますか。

毎日＿＿＿　　週一回＿＿＿　　二週間一回＿＿＿　月一回＿＿＿　　たまに＿＿＿

h. マンガはどこで読むのですか（優先順位で番号をふってください）。

家＿＿＿　電車の中＿＿＿　店で立ち読み＿＿＿　学校＿＿＿　友だちの家＿＿＿
その他(例)＿＿＿＿＿＿＿

i. 友だちもマンガを読んでいますか。はい・いいえ・わからない

j. 友だちとマンガを貸したり借りたりしますか。はい・いいえ・わからない

k. マンガを読みながら分からないことがありますか。はい・いいえ・わからない

　　l. もし「はい」と答えたらどう対処するのですか。
　　＿＿＿＿＿＿＿＿＿に聞く　また読み返す＿＿＿　　その他＿＿＿＿＿＿＿

(6)　　a. なぜマンガを読むのですか。＿＿＿＿＿＿＿＿＿＿＿＿＿＿＿＿＿＿＿
＿＿＿＿＿＿＿

b. マンガを集めていますか。はい・いいえ・以前したことある

c. 自分のマンガを画いたことありますか。はい・いいえ・わからない
ありがとうございました！

Glossary

anime—television and video cartoons produced in Japan

Bildungsroman—a narrative genre based on the maturing process of a person, usually a young person

Chōjū Giga—twelfth-century drawings on scrolls depicting personified animals, such as frogs and rabbits, in satirical scenes

Comiket—the biannual comic market held in Tokyo for amateur creators to display and sell their work

cosplay—the practice of dressing up as manga characters and engage in role play

dōjinshi—amateur manga publications including fanzines or parodies of well-known works

Edo—the former name of Tokyo and the seat of power for the Tokugawa Shogunate (1603–1868)

fujoshi—women who enjoy imagining romantic relationships of unlikely pairs of people and are creators and consumers of *yaoi*/BL manga

fukei—the male counterpart to *fujoshi*

furigana—glosses (also called rubies) printed in small font to the side of *kanji* to indicate pronunciation

gekiga—graphic novels, but specifically the narrative works written for the book rental market of the 1950s

gutter—the borders between panels in comics

hiragana—a syllabary used to indicate function words and common items, as well as increasingly for proper nouns and is the usual script for *furigana*

interdiscursivity—mixing of genres, such as the mixing of content types, rhetorical structures, and levels of formality

intertextuality—the presence of other texts either through quotation or appropriation

kamishibai—theater with illustrated cardboard sheets

kanbun—traditional Chinese text (*wenyan*) with diacritics indicating Japanese syntax

kanji—Chinese characters and the usual script to indicate content words *katakana*—a syllabary used to indicate foreign words and emphasis, increasingly for proper nouns

komikku/komikkusu—bound volumes of single-title manga (singular and plural forms)

lexico-grammar—vocabulary and syntax as well as function words for textual cohesion

Meiji—the reign of the Emperor Meiji (1868–1912) when Japan modernized and became a world power

moe—the esthetic sense of cuteness, seductiveness, and vulnerability while evoking both pity and arousal

morpheme—a word unit including prefixes, suffixes, and stems

multimodal discourse—texts that contain more than print such as illustrations

otaku—a person obsessed with a certain kind of media or hobby

pragmatics—the study of meaning in context, especially the intentional aspect of speech

rōmaji—roman script used in Japanese as an additional resource

scanlation—the practice of readers who scan, translate, and then share the manga through the Internet

shōjo—girls

shōnen—boys

systemic-functional linguistics—regards language as operating simultaneously in several systems and emphasizes the social and semantic aspects of language over the psychological. The movement began in Britain, centered on the work of M. A. K. Halliday, and today it is the theoretical framework of choice among applied linguists around the world.

tachiyomi—the practice of standing and reading books and magazines in shops

Tokugawa Period—analogous to the Edo Period (1603–1868)

urtext—the original version of a story or the story in its original medium

Bibliography

Abel, Jessica, and Matt Madden. *Drawing Words and Writing Pictures: Making Comics: Manga, Graphic Novels, and Beyond*. New York: First Second, 2008.

Adams, Marilyn J., and Allan Collins. "A Schema-Theoretic View of Reading." In *Theoretical Models and Processes of Reading*, third ed., edited by Harry Singer and Robert B. Ruddell, 404–25. Newark, DE: International Reading Association, 1985.

Aihara, Kōji, and Kentarō Takekuma. *Even a Monkey Can Draw Manga*. San Francisco: Viz MEDIA LLC, 2002.

Akashi, Yōichi. "Hajimeni: Kenkyū no Izu" (Introduction: Research intent). In *Kodomo to Manga: Manga Dokkairyoku wa Dō Hattatsu Suruka* (Children and manga: How manga comprehension develops), edited by Akashi Yōichi and Nakazawa Jun, 1. Tokyo: Gendaijidōbunka Kenkyūkai, 1993.

Alexander, Patricia A., and Tamara L. Jetton. "Learning from Text: A Multidimensional and Developmental Perspective." In *Handbook of Reading Research*, vol. 3, edited by Michael L. Kamil, Peter B. Mosenthal, P. David Pearson, and Rebecca Barr, 285–310. Mahwah, NJ: Lawrence Erlbaum Associates, 2000.

Allen, Kate, and John E. Ingulsrud. "*Manga* Literacy: Popular Culture and the Reading Habits of Japanese College Students." *Journal of Adolescent & Adult Literacy* 46, no. 8 (2003): 674–83.

———. "Reading *Manga*: Patterns of Personal Literacies among Adolescents." *Language and Education* 19, no. 4 (2005): 265–80.

Allison, Anne. *Permitted and Prohibited Desires: Mothers, Comics, and Censorship in Japan*. Berkeley: University of California Press, 2000.

———. "The Japan Fad in Global Youth Culture and Millennial Capitalism." In *Mechademia: Emerging Worlds of Anime and Manga*, vol. 1, edited by Frenchy Lunning, 11–21. Minneapolis: University of Minnesota Press, 2006.

Alt, Matt, and Hiroko Yoda. *Hello, Please! Very Helpful Super Kawaii Characters from Japan*. San Francisco: Chronicle Books LLC, 2007.

Alvermann, Donna E., and Alison H. Heron. "Literacy Identity Work: Playing to Learn with Popular Media." *Journal of Adolescent & Adult Literacy* 45, no. 2 (2001): 118–22.

Alvermann, Donna E., Kathleen A. Hinchman, David W. Moore, Stephen F. Phelps, and

Diane R. Waff, eds. *Reconceptualizing the Literacies in Adolescents Lives*. Mahwah, NJ: Lawrence Erlbaum Associates, 1998.

Alvermann, Donna E., Jennifer S. Moon, and Margaret C. Hagood. *Popular Culture in the Classroom: Teaching and Researching Critical Media Literacy*. Newark, DE: International Reading Association, 1999.

Anderson, Richard C., and P. David Pearson. "A Schema-Theoretic View of Basic Processes in Reading Comprehension." In *Interactive Approaches to Second Language Reading*, edited by Patricia L. Carrell, Joanne Devine, and David E. Eskey, 37–55. Cambridge: Cambridge University Press, 1988.

Aso, Tarō, and Hirokane Kenshi. "Orijinaru Kakuryō Kaigi (Original cabinet meeting)." *Big Comic Original* 34, no. 26 (2007): 1–3. Tokyo: Shogakkan.

Azuma, Hiroki. *Dobutsu-ka Suru Posuto Modān: Otaku Kara Mita Nihon Shakai* (Postmodernism with animal instincts: Japanese society as seen by *otakus*). Tokyo: Kodansha, 2001.

Barker, Martin. *A Haunt of Fears: The Strange History of the British Horror Comics Campaign*. Jackson: University Press of Mississippi, 1984.

———. *Comics: Ideology, Power and Critics*. Manchester, UK: Manchester University Press, 1989.

———. "Fredric Wertham: The Sad Case of the Unhappy Humanist." In *Pulp Demons: International Dimensions of the Postwar Anti-Comics Campaign*, edited by John A. Lent, 215–33. Madison, NJ/London: Fairleigh Dickinson University Press and Associated University Presses, 1999.

Barton, David. *Literacy: An Introduction to the Ecology of the Written Language*. Oxford: Blackwell, 1994.

Barton, David, and Mary Hamilton, "Literacy Practices." In *Situated Literacies*, edited by David Barton, Mary Hamilton, and Roz Ivanič, 7–15. London: Routledge, 2000.

Bauman, Zygmunt. *Hermeneutics and Social Science: Approaches to Understanding*. Aldershot, UK: Gregg Revivals, 1992.

Baynham, Mike. *Literacy Practices: Investigating Literacy in Social Contexts*. Harlow, UK: Longman, 1995.

Beers, Terry. "Commentary: Schema-Theoretic Models of Reading: Humanizing the Machine." *Reading Research Quarterly* 22, no. 3 (1987): 369–77.

Berger, Arthur. "Comics and Culture." *Journal of Popular Culture* 5, no. 1 (1971): 164–78.

Berndt, Jaqueline. "Considering Manga Discourse: Location, Ambiguity, Historicity." In *Japanese Visual Culture: Explorations in the World of Manga and Anime*, edited by Mark W. MacWilliams, 295–310. Armonk, NY: M. E. Sharpe, 2008.

Bernstein, Basil. *Pedagogy, Symbolic Control and Identity: Theory, Research, Critique*. London: Taylor & Francis, 1996.

Berry, Mary Elizabeth. *Japan in Print: Information and Nation in the Early Modern Period*. Berkeley: University of California Press, 2006.

Bongco, Mila. *Reading Comics: Language, Culture, and the Concept of the Superhero in Comic Books*. New York: Garland Publishing, 2000.

Bourdieu, Pierre. *Distinction: A Social Critique of the Judgement of Taste*, translated by Richard Nice. Cambridge, MA: Harvard University Press, 1984.

Brown, Ann L. "Metacognition: The Development of Selective Attention Strategies for Learning from Texts." In *Theoretical Models and Processes of Reading*, third ed., edited by Harry Singer and Robert B. Ruddell, 501–26. Newark, DE: International Reading Association, 1985.

Chambliss, Marylyn J. "Text Cues and Strategies Successful Readers Use to Construct the Gist of Lengthy Written Arguments." *Reading Research Quarterly* 30, no. 4 (1995): 778–807.

Cherland, Meredith R., and Carole Edelsky. "Girls and Reading: The Desire for Agency and Horror of Helplessness in Fictional Encounters." In *Texts of Desire: Essays on Fiction, Femininity and Schooling*, edited by Linda K. Christian-Smith, 28–44. London: The Falmer Press, 1993.

Ching, Leo T. S. *Becoming "Japanese": Colonial Taiwan and the Politics of Identity Formation.* Berkeley: University of California Press, 2001.

Christian-Smith, Linda. K. "Sweet Dreams: Gender and Desire in Teen Romance Novels." In *Texts of Desire: Essays on Fiction, Femininity and Schooling*, edited by Linda K. Christian-Smith, 45–68. London: The Falmer Press, 1993.

———. "Popular Texts and Young Women." In *Difference, Silence, and Textual Practice: Studies in Critical Literacy*, edited by Peter Freebody, Sandy Muspratt, and Bronywn Dwyer, 189–207. Cresskill, NJ: Hampton Press, 2001.

Coles, Martin, and Christine Hall. "Taking Comics Seriously: Children's Periodical Reading in England in the 1990s." *Reading* (November 1997): 50–54.

Comickers Magazine, ed. *Japanese Comickers: Draw Manga and Anime like Japan's Hottest Artists.* New York: Collins Design, 2003.

———. *Japanese Comickers 2: Draw Manga and Anime like Japan's Hottest Artists.* New York: Collins Design, 2006.

Cook-Gumperz, Jenny. "Introduction: The Social Construction of Literacy." In *The Social Construction of Literacy*, edited by Jenny Cook-Gumperz, 1–15. Cambridge: Cambridge University Press, 1986.

Cooper, Dianne. "Retailing Gender: Adolescent Book Clubs in Australian Schools." In *Texts of Desire: Essays on Fiction, Femininity and Schooling*, edited by Linda K. Christian-Smith, 9–27. London: The Falmer Press, 1993.

Cooper-Chen, Anne, and Miiko Kodama. *Mass Communication in Japan.* Ames: Iowa State University Press, 1997.

Coulmas, Florian. *The Writing Systems of the World.* Oxford: Blackwell Publishers, 1991.

Currie, Dawn H. *Girl Talk: Adolescent Magazines and Their Readers.* Toronto: University of Toronto Press, 1997.

Deshler, Donald D., and Michael F. Hock. "Adolescent Literacy: Where We Are, Where We Need To Go." In *Shaping Literacy Achievement: Research We Have, Research We Need*, edited by Michael Pressley, Alison K. Billman, Kristen H. Perry, Kelly E. Reffitt, and Julia Moorhead Reynolds, 98–128. New York: The Guildford Press, 2007.

Dokusho Yoronchōsa 2008 Nenban (2008 reading survey). Tokyo: Mainichi Shimbun Tokyo Honsha Kōkokukyoku, 2008.

Dore, Ronald P. *Education in Tokugawa Japan.* Berkeley: University of California Press, 1965.

Dornyei, Zoltan. *Motivational Strategies in the Classroom.* Cambridge: Cambridge University Press, 2001.

Downing, John. *Comparative Reading: Cross-national Comparisons of Reading Achievement.* New York: Macmillan, 1973.

Drum, Priscilla A. "Children's Understanding of Passages." In *Promoting Reading Comprehension*, edited by James Flood, 61–78. Newark, DE: International Reading Association, 1984.

Dutro, Elizabeth. "But That's a Girl Book! Exploring Gender Boundaries in Children's Reading Practices." *The Reading Teacher* 55, no. 4 (2001): 534–61.

Dyson, Anne Haas. *Writing Superheroes: Contemporary Childhood, Popular Culture, and Classroom Literacy.* New York: Teachers College Press, 1997.

Eisner, Will. *Comics and Sequential Art: Principles and Practice of the World's Most Popular Art Form.* Tamarac, FL: Poorhouse Press, 1985.

Fairclough, Norman. *Analyzing Discourse: Textual Analysis for Social Research.* London: Routledge, 2003.

Ferdman, Bernado M. "Literacy and Cultural Identity." *Harvard Educational Review* 60, no. 2 (1990): 181–204.

Foljanty-Jost, Gesine. "Heartful Guidance: Strategies of Preventing Deviancy in Japanese Schools." Paper presented at the JSAA 2001, Japan Studies Association of Australia, Biennial Conference, Sydney, Australia, June 27–30, 2001.

Fowler, Roger. "The Referential Code and Narrative Authority." In *Critical Discourse Analysis: Critical Concepts in Linguistics,* vol. 1, edited by Michael Toolan, 202–37. London: Routledge, 2002/1977.

Fujimoto, Junko. "Kankeisei Kara Miru BL no Genzai" (BL today in terms of relationships). *Eureka: Poetry and Criticism* 39, no. 16 (2007): 89–95.

Fujimoto, Yukari. *Watakushi no Ibasho wa Dokoniaruno? Shōjo Manga ga Utsusu Kokorono Katachi* (Where is my place to be? The human psyche through *shōjo* manga). Tokyo: Gakuyōshobō, 1989.

———. *Shōjo Manga Damashii* (The soul of *shōjo* manga). Tokyo: Hakusensha, 2000.

———. *Aijyō Hyōron: "Kazoku" wo Meguru Monogatari* (A critique of love: Narratives about "the family"). Tokyo: Bungei Shunshū, 2004.

———. "Shonen Ai/Yaoi-BL: 2007 Nen Genzai no Shiten Kara (*Shonen* love/*Yaoi*-BL: From the perspective of 2007)." *Eureka: Poetry and Criticism* 39, no. 16 (2007): 36–47.

Fujimoto, Yukari, Murakami Tomohiko, and Yumemakura Baku. *Tatsujin ga Erabu Josei Notameno Manga Bunko 100* (The experts' choice of 100 manga for women). Tokyo: Hakusensha, 2004.

Fukuzawa, Rebecca Erwin, and Gerald K. LeTendre. *Intense Years: How Japanese Adolescents Balance School, Family, and Friends.* New York: RoutledgeFalmer, 2001.

Fuse, Hideto. *Manga wo Kaibo Suru* (Dissecting *manga*). Tokyo: Chikuma Shinsho, 2004.

Gallego, Margaret A., and Sandra Hollingsworth. "Introduction: The Idea of Multiple Literacies." In *What Counts as Literacy: Challenging the School Standard*, edited by Margaret A. Gallego and Sandra Hollingsworth, 1–23. New York: Teachers College Press, 2000.

Gardner, Robert C., and Wallace E. Lambert. *Attitudes and Motivation in Second Language Learning.* Rowley, MA: Newbury House, 1972.

Gee, James Paul. *What Video Games Have to Teach Us about Learning and Literacy.* New York: Palgrave Macmillan, 2003.

Gibson, Mel. "Reading as Rebellion: The Case of the Girls' Comic in Britain." *International Journal of Comic Art* 2, no. 2 (2000): 135–51.

Gluck, Carol. *Japan's Modern Myths: Ideology in the Late Meiji Period.* Princeton, NJ: Princeton University Press, 1985.

Goldman, Susan R., and John A. Rakestraw Jr. "Structural Aspects of Constructing Meaning from Text." In *Handbook of Reading Research*, vol. 3, edited by Michael J. Kamil, Peter B. Mosenthal, P. David Pearson, and Rebecca Barr, 311–35. Mahwah, NJ: Lawrence Erlbaum Associates, 2000.

Goodman, Kenneth S. "Reading: A Psycholinguistic Guessing Game." *Journal of the Reading Specialist* 6 (1967): 126–35.

Gottlieb, Nanette. *Language and Society in Japan.* Cambridge: University of Cambridge Press, 2005.

Gravett, Paul. *Manga: 60 Years of Japanese Comics.* London: Laurence King Publishing, 2004.

Groensteen, Thierry. "Why Comics are Still in Search of Cultural Legitimization." In *Comics Culture: Analytical and Theoretical Approaches to Comics,* edited by Anne Magnussen and Hans-Christian Christiansen, 29–41. Copenhagen: Museum Tusculanum Press, 2000.

Hajdu, David. *The Ten-Cent Plague: The Great Comic-Book Scare and How it Changed America.* New York: Farrar, Straus and Giroux, 2008.

Halliday, M. A. K. "The Linguistic Study of Literary Texts." In *Linguistic Studies of Text and Discourse,* edited by Jonathan Webster, 5–22. London: Continuum, 1964/2002.

Hanamaru Henshūbu. *Boizurabu Shōsetsu no Kakikata* (How to write boys' love novels). Tokyo: Hakusensha, 2004.

Hannas, William C. *Asia's Orthographic Dilemma.* Honolulu: University of Hawai'i Press, 1997.

Hart, Christopher. *Manga Mania: How to Draw Japanese Comics.* New York: Watson-Guptill, 2001.

Hasegawa, Yutaka. *Kashihonya no Boku wa Manga ni Muchūdatta* (Living in a book rental shop, I was obsessed with manga). Tokyo: Sōshisha, 1999.

Hatano, Kanji. "Children's Comics in Japan." In *Japanese Popular Culture,* edited by Hidetoshi Kato, 103–8. Tokyo: Tuttle, 1959.

Heath, Shirley Brice. *Ways With Words: Language, Life, and Work in Communities and Classrooms.* Cambridge: Cambridge University Press, 1983.

Hill, Clifford, and Kate Parry. "The Models of Literacy: The Nature of Reading Tests." In *From Testing to Assessment: English as an International Language,* edited by Clifford Hill and Kate Parry, 7–34. New York: Longman, 1994.

Hirsch, E. D., Joseph F. Kett, and James Trefil. *Dictionary of Cultural Literacy: What Every American Needs to Know.* New York: Houghton Mifflin, 2002.

Hoggart, Richard. *The Uses of Literacy: Changing Patterns in English Mass Culture.* Fair Lawn, NJ: Essential Books, 1957.

Horibuchi, Seiji. *Moeru Amerika: Beikokujin wa Ikanishite Manga wo Yomuyōninatta* (The *Moe*-ization of America: How Americans became readers of manga). Tokyo: Nikkei BP Sha, 2006.

Hosogaya, Atsushi, and Jacqueline Berndt. *A Guide to Books on Japanese Manga.* Yokohama: Asian *Manga* Summit Japan Executive Committee, 2002.

Hotta, Junji. *Moe Moe Japan* (Moe moe of Japan). Tokyo: Kodansha, 2005.

Huisman, Rosemary. "Narrative Concepts." In *Narrative and Media,* edited by Helen Fulton, Rosemary Huisman, Julian Murphet, and Anne Dunn, 11–27. New York: Cambridge University Press, 2005.

Hull, Glynda A., and Katherine Schultz. "Connecting Schools with Out-of-School Worlds: Insights from Recent Research on Literacy in Non-School Settings." In *School's Out: Bridging Out-of-School Literacies with Classroom Practice,* edited by Glynda A. Hull and Katherine Schultz, 32–57. New York: Teachers College Press, 2002.

Ichikawa, Hiroaki, and Ishiyama Hidekazu. *Edo no Manabi* (Learning in Edo). Tokyo: Kawade Shobo Shinsha, 2006.

Ingulsrud, John E., and Kate Allen. *Learning to Read in China: Sociolinguistic Perspectives on the Acquisition of Literacy.* Lewiston, NY: The Edward Mellen Press, 1999.

Ingulsrud, John E., and Kai Kimiko. "A Lexical Analysis of Children's TV Programs in Japan." *Visio* 24 (1997): 157–64.

Inoue, Manabu. *Kono Manga ga Sugoi* (These manga are awesome). Tokyo: Takarajimasha, 1996.

Ishida, Saeko. "Dare no Tame no Manga Shakaigaku: Manga Dokusharon Saikō" (Sociology of manga for whom? Reconsidering the theory of manga readers). In *Manga no Shakaigaku* (The sociology of manga), edited by Miyahara Kōjiro and Ogino Masahiro, 157–87. Kyoto: Shakaishisōsha, 2001.

Ishinomori, Shōtarō. *Ishinomori Shōtarō no Manga-ka Nyūmon* (Ishinomori Shōtarō's manga artist course). Tokyo: Akita Shoten, 1998.

Itō, Gō. *Tezuka izu Deddo: Hirakareta Manga Hyōgenron e* (Tezuka is dead: Postmodernist and modernist approaches to Japanese manga). Tokyo: NTT Shuppan, 2005.

Ito, Kinko. "Manga in Japanese History." In *Japanese Visual Culture: Explorations in the World of Manga and Anime*, edited by Mark W. MacWilliams, 26–47. Armonk, NY: M. E. Sharpe, 2008.

Johnson, Steven. *Everything Bad is Good for You—How Today's Popular Culture is Actually Making Us Smarter*. New York: Riverhead, 2005.

Jones, Gretchen I. "Bad Girls Like to Watch: Writing and Reading Ladies' Comics." In *Bad Girls of Japan*, edited by Laura Miller and Jan Bardsley, 97–109. New York: Palgrave Macmillan, 2005.

Kaneda, Junko. "Yaoi Izu Araibu" (*Yaoi* is alive). *Eureka: Poetry and Criticism* 38, no. 1 (2006): 166–78.

———. "Manga Dōjinshi: Kaishaku Kyōdotai no Poritikusu" (Manga *dōjinshi*: The interpretive community's politics). In *Bunka no Shakaigaku* (The sociology of culture), edited by Sato Kenji and Yoshimi Shunya, 163–90. Tokyo: Yuhikaku Arma, 2007.

———. "Yaoiron, Asuno Tameni Sono 2 (*Yaoi* theory for tomorrow 2)." *Eureka: Poetry and Criticism* 39, no. 16 (2007): 48–54.

Kawamata, Takanori, "The Aftermath of an Accident of a Uranium Processing Plant: A Critical Discourse Analysis of Public Briefing Minutes." *Annual Bulletin of the Graduate School of Humanities and Social Sciences, Meisei University* 4 (2006): 3–28.

Kelts, Roland. *Japanamerica: How Japanese Pop Culture has Invaded the U.S.* New York: Palgrave Macmillan, 2006.

Kern, Adam L. *Manga from the Floating World: Comicbook Culture and the Kibyōshi of Edo Japan.* Cambridge, MA: Harvard University Asia Center, 2006.

Kinoshita, Junji, and Imanishi Yuyuki. *Hirogaru Kotoba: Shogaku Kokugo 1 Jyo* (Increasing vocabulary: Elementary Japanese 1a). Tokyo: Kyoiku Shuppan, 2007.

Kinsella, Sharon. *Adult Manga: Culture and Power in Contemporary Japanese Culture*. Richmond, UK: Curzon, 2000.

Kintsch, Walter. "An Overview of Top-Down and Bottom-Up Effects in Comprehension." *Discourse Processes* 39 (2005): 125–28.

Kintsch, Walter, and Teun A. van Dijk. "Toward a Model of Text Comprehension and Production." *Psychological Review* 85 (1978): 363–94.

Kornicki, Peter F. "Obiya Ihei, a Japanese Provincial Publisher." *British Library Journal* 11 (1985): 131–42.

———. *The Book in Japan: A Cultural History From the Beginnings to the Nineteenth Century.* Leiden, The Netherlands: Koninklijke Brill NV, 1998.

———. "Literacy Revisited: Some Reflections on Richard Rubinger's Findings." *Monumenta Nipponica* 56, no. 3 (2001): 381–94.

Kress, Gunther, and Theo van Leeuwen. *Multimodal Discourse: The Modes and Media of Contemporary Communication*. London: Arnold, 2001.

Kubota, Mitsuyoshi. *Dōjin Yōgo Jiten* (Dictionary of *dōjin* terminology). Tokyo: Hidekazu System, 2004.

Kure, Tomofusa. *Gendai Manga no Zentaizō* (The portrait of modern manga). Tokyo: Futaba Bunkō, 1997.

Kutner, Lawrence, and Cheryl Olson. *Grand Theft Childhood: The Surprising Truth about Violent Video Games and What Parents Can Do*. New York: Simon and Schuster, 2008.

Lent, John A. "Comics Controversies and Codes: Reverberations in Asia." In *Pulp Demons: International Dimensions of the Postwar Anti-Comics Campaign*, edited by John A. Lent, 179–214. Madison, NJ/London: Fairleigh Dickinson University Press and Associated University Presses, 1999.

Luke, Allan. "Series Editor's Introduction." In *Texts of Desire: Essays on Fiction, Femininity and Schooling*, edited by Linda K. Christian-Smith, vii–xiv. London: The Falmer Press, 1993.

Luke, Allan, and Peter Freebody. "Critical Literacy and the Question of Normativity: An Introduction." In *Constructing Critical Literacies: Teaching and Learning Textual Practice*, edited by Sandy Muspratt, Allan Luke, and Peter Freebody, 1–18. Cresskill, NJ: Hampton Press, 1997.

Luke, Carmen. *Pedagogy, Printing, and Protestantism: The Discourse on Childhood*. Albany, NY: State University of New York Press, 1989.

Makino, Keiichi, and Ueshima Yutaka. *Shikaku to Manga Hyōgen: Kagaku to Manga no Nabegēshon* (Perception and manga expression: Navigating science and manga). Kyoto: Rinkawa Shoten, 2007.

Makita, Kiyoshi. "The Rarity of Reading Disability in Japanese Children." *American Journal of Orthopsychiatry* 38, no. 4 (1968): 599–614.

Marsh, Jackie, and Elaine Millard. *Literacy and Popular Culture: Using Children's Culture in the Classroom*. London: Paul Chapman Publishing, 2000.

Marshall, Byron K. *Learning to be Modern: Japanese Political Discourse on Education*. Boulder, CO: Westview Press, 1994.

Masami, Toku. "Cross-cultural Analysis of Artistic Development: Drawing by Japanese and U.S. Children." *Visual Arts Research* 27, no. 1 (2001), www.csuchico.edu/~mtoku/vc/Articles/toku/Toku_Cross-cultural_VAR01.html (accessed June 29, 2008).

Masson, Pierre. *Lire La Bande Dessinée* (Reading comics). Lyon: Presses Universitaires de Lyon, 1985.

Masters, Coco. "America is Drawn to Manga." *Time*, August 10, 2006, A5.

Matthiessen, Christian M. I. M. "The Multimodal Page: A Systemic Functional Exploration." In *New Directions in the Analysis of Multimodal Discourse*, edited by Terry D. Royce and Wendy L. Bowcher, 1–62. Mahwah, NJ: Lawrence Earlbaum Associates, 2007.

Matsuzawa, Mitsuo. *Nihonjin no Atama wo Dame Nishita Manga Gekiga* (Manga have damaged Japanese people's minds). Tokyo: Yamate Shobo, 1979.

Maynard, Senko. *Principles of Japanese Discourse*. Cambridge: Cambridge University Press, 1998.

McCloud, Scott. *Understanding Comics: The Invisible Art*. New York: HarperPerennial, 1994.

———. *Reinventing Comics: How Imagination and Technology Are Revolutionizing an Art Form*. New York: HarperCollins, 2000.

McLelland, Mark. "Local Meanings in Global Space: A Case Study of Women's 'Boy Love' Web Sites in Japanese and English." *Mots Pluriels* 19 (2001): 1–22.

———. *Queer Japan from the Pacific War to the Internet Age*. Lanham, MD: Rowman & Littlefield, 2005.

McLuhan, Marshall. *Understanding Media: The Extensions of Man*. New York: McGraw-Hill, 1964.

McRobbie, Angela. "Just Like a Jackie Story." In *Feminism for Girls: An Adventure Story*, edited by Angela McRobbie and Trisha McCabe, 113–28. London: Routledge & Kegan Paul, 1981.

MEXT (Ministry of Education, Culture, Sports, Science, and Technology). *Shōgakkō Shidō Yōryō Kaisetsu (Kokugohen)* (Elementary school curriculum notes (national language volume)). Tokyo: Tōyōkan, 1999.

Mezynski, Karen. "Issues Concerning the Acquisition of Knowledge: Effects of Vocabulary Training on Reading Comprehension." *Review of Educational Research* 53, no. 2 (1983): 253–79.

Millard, Elaine. *Differently Literate: Boys, Girls and the Schooling of Literacy*. London: The Falmer Press, 1997.

Millard, Elaine, and Jackie Marsh. "Sending Minnie the Minx Home: Comics and Reading Choices. *Cambridge Journal of Education* 31, no. 1 (2001): 25–38.

Miller, Roy A. *Japanese and the Other Altaic Languages*. Chicago: The University of Chicago Press, 1971.

Minagawa, Hiroshi. "Jojo no Kimyō na Bōken: Parodī-Inyō" (Parody and allusion in *Jojo's Bizarre Adventures*). Bachelor's thesis, Meisei University, 2007.

Minami, Masahiko. *Culture-Specific Language Styles: The Development of Oral Narrative and Literacy*. Clevedon, UK: Multilingual Matters, 2002.

Miyahara, Kojiro, and Ogino Masahiro, eds. *Manga no Shakaigaku* (The sociology of manga). Kyoto: Sekaishisōsha, 2001.

Mizuguchi, Fumino. *Chiran Kara no Tegami* (Letters from Chiran). Tokyo: Shinshōsha, 2007.

Morikawa, Keiichiro. "Sūji de Miru Fujoshi" (*Fujoshi* through the numbers). *Eureka: Poetry and Criticism* 39, no. 16 (2007): 122–35.

Morinaga, Takurō. *Moe Keizaigaku* (The economics of *moe*). Tokyo: Kodansha, 2005.

Moss, Gemma. *Un/Popular Fictions*. London: Virago Press, 1989.

———. "Children Talk Horror Videos: Reading as a Social Performance." *Australian Journal of Education* 37, no. 2 (1993): 169–81.

———. "Informal Literacies and Pedagogic Practice." *Linguistics and Education* 11, no. 1 (2000): 47–64.

———. "On Literacy and the Social Organisation of Knowledge Inside and Outside School." *Language and Education* 15, nos. 2 and 3 (2001): 146–61.

Mostow, Joshua. S. "Introduction." In *Gender and Power in the Japanese Visual Field*, edited by Joshua S. Mostow, Norman Bryson, and Maribeth Graybill, 1–15. Honolulu: University of Hawai'i Press, 2003a.

———. "The Gender of *Wakashu* and the Grammar of Desire." In *Gender and Power in the Japanese Visual Field*, edited by Joshua S. Mostow, Norman Bryson, and Maribeth Graybill, 49–70. Honolulu: University of Hawai'i Press, 2003b.

Murakami, Takashi. "Earth in My Window." In *Little Boy: The Arts of Japan's Exploding Subculture*, edited by Takashi Murakami, 98–149. New York: The Japan Society/New Haven, CT: Yale University Press, 2005.

Muspratt, Sandy, Allan Luke, and Peter Freebody, eds. *Constructing Critical Literacies: Teaching and Learning Textual Practice*. Cresskill, NJ: Hampton Press, 1997.

Nagai, Hitoshi. *Manga wa Tetsugaku Suru* (*Manga* can philosophize). Tokyo: Kodansha, 2000.

Nagai, Ryō, "An Essay on Panel Transitions: Panel-to-panel no Kanōsei." Bachelor's thesis, Meisei University, 2007.

Nagy, William. "On the Role of Context in First- and Second-Language Vocabulary Learning." In *Vocabulary: Description, Acquisition and Pedagogy*, edited by Norbert Schmitt and Michael McCarthy, 64–83. Cambridge: Cambridge University Press, 1997.

Naiki, Toshio. "Kashihon Manga no Hakkō Nendo Kakutei no Hōhō Nitsuite" (A method for determining the publication dates for rental manga). *Manga Studies* 4 (2003): 180–89.

Nakano, Haruyuki. *Manga Sangyōron* (Theory of manga industry). Tokyo: Chikuma Shobō, 2004.

Nakazawa, Jun. "Manga no Koma no Yomi Riterashī no Hattatsu (The development of manga panel reading literacy)." *Manga Studies* 7 (2005): 6–21.

Nakazawa, Jun, and Nakazawa Sayuri. "How children understand comics: Analysis of comic reading comprehension." *Annual Research Early Childhood* 15 (1993a): 35–39.

———. "Manga Dokkairyoku no Hattatsu: Manga ga Wakaru Towa Nanika? Manga Dokkairyoku Chōsa Kara" (The development of manga comprehension: What does it mean to understand manga? Results from a manga comprehension instrument). In *Kodomo to Manga: Manga Dokkairyoku wa Dō Hattatsu Suruka* (Children and manga: How manga comprehension develops), edited by Akashi Yōichi and Nakazawa Jun, 85–189. Tokyo: Gendaijidōbunka Kenkyūkai, 1993b.

Napier, Susan J. *Anime from Akira to Princess Mononoke: Experiencing Contemporary Japanese Animation*. New York: Palgrave, 2001.

Natsume, Fusanosuke. "Manga Byōsen Genron" (The theory of drawn lines). In *Manga no Yomikata* (How to read manga), edited by Inoue Manabu, 52–59. Tokyo: Takarajimasha, 1995.

———. "Manga Bumpō Niokeru Koma no Hōsoku" (Rules for frames in manga syntax: Categories and relationships between frame to frame and frame to page). In *Manga no Yomikata* (How to read manga), edited by Inoue Manabu, 196–205. Tokyo: Takarajimasha, 1995.

———. *Manga wa Naze Omoshiroi Noka* (Why manga are so interesting). Tokyo: Nihon Hōsō Shuppan Kyōkai, 1997.

———. *Manga no Chikara: Seijuku Suru Sengo Manga* (The power of manga: The maturing of postwar manga). Tokyo: Shōbunsha, 1999.

———. *Manga Sekai Senryaku* (Manga world strategy). Tokyo: Shogakukan, 2001.

———. *Manga no Ibasho* (The place of manga). Tokyo: NTT, 2003.

———. *Mangagaku Eno Chōsen* (The challenge of manga studies). Tokyo: NTT, 2004a.

———. *Manga no Fuka-Yomi, Otona-Yomi* (Deep reading and adult reading of manga). Tokyo: Īsuto Puresu, 2004b.

———. *Manga ni Jinsei wo Manande Nani ga Warui?* (What's wrong with learning life's lessons from manga?). Tokyo: Random House-Kodansha, 2006.

Natsume, Fusanosuke, and Kure Tomofusa. "Jōdan Kara Koma: Manga Hyo? Manga Ron? Manga Gaku?" (From jokes to panels: Manga discourse, manga criticism, manga studies). *Manga Studies* 1 (2002): 6–39.

Natsume, Fusanosuke, Miyamoto Hirohito, and Itō Gō. "Kyara no Kindai—Manga no Kigen: Tezuka izu Deddo wo Megutte" (The *kyara* of today—the origins of manga: Regarding *Tezuka is Dead*). *Eureka: Poetry and Criticism* 38, no. 1 (2006): 52–67.

New London Group. "A Pedagogy of Multiliteracies: Designing Social Futures." *Harvard Educational Review* 66 (1996): 60–92.

Nilsen, Alleen P. "Sexism in Children's Books and Elementary Classroom Materials." In *Sexism and Language*, edited by Alleen P. Nilsen, Haig Bosmajian, H. Lee Gershuny, and Julia P. Stanley, 161–71. Urbana, IL: National Council of Teachers of English, 1977.

Nippon Otaku Taishō Jikkō Iinkai. *Nippon Otaku Taishō 2003* (Nippon Otaku Award 2003). Tokyo: Fusosha.

———. *Nippon Otaku Taishō 2004* (Nippon Otaku Award 2004). Tokyo: Fusosha.

Noguchi, Mary S. "An American Sabbatical Experience." *Bilingual Japan* 15, no. 3 (2006): 19–24.

Noll, Elizabeth. "Literacy and American Indian Students: Meaning Making through Multiple Sign Systems." In *What Counts as Literacy: Challenging the School Standard*, edited by Margaret A. Gallego and Sandra Hollingsworth, 213–28. New York: Teachers College Press, 2000.

Nyberg, Amy Kiste. "Comic-book Censorship in the United States." In *Pulp Demons: International Dimensions of the Postwar Anti-Comics Campaign*, edited by John A. Lent, 42–68. Madison, NJ/London: Fairleigh Dickinson University Press and Associated University Presses, 1999.

O'Brien, David G. "Multiple Literacies in a High-School Program for 'At-Risk' Adolescents." In *Reconceptualizing the Literacies in Adolescents Lives*, edited by Donna E. Alvermann, Kathleen A. Hinchman, David W. Moore, Stephen F. Phelps, and Diane R. Waff, 27–50. Mahwah, NJ: Lawrence Erlbaum Associates, 1998.

Okada, Toshio. *Otakugaku Nyūmon* (Introduction to otakuology). Tokyo: Shinsho Oh! Bunko, 1996.

———. *Tōdai Otaku Kōza* (University of Tokyo lectures on *otaku* studies). Tokyo: Kodansha, 1997.

———. *Otaku wa Sude ni Shindeiru* (*Otaku* are already dead). Tokyo: Shinshosha, 2008.

Okano, Kaori, and Motonori Tsuchiya. *Education in Contemporary Japan: Inequality and Diversity*. Cambridge: Cambridge University Press, 1999.

Olson, David R. "From Utterance to Text: The Bias of Language in Speech and Writing." *Harvard Educational Review* 47, no. 3 (1977): 257–81.

Ōnishi, Jun. "Kodomo to Manga: Kodomo Eno Ankēto Chōsa Kara" (Children and manga: From a survey to children). In *Kodomo to Manga: Manga Dokkairyoku wa Dō Hattatsu Suruka* (Children and manga: How manga comprehension develops), edited by Akashi Yōichi and Nakazawa Jun, 11–54. Tokyo: Gendaijidōbunka Kenkyūkai, 1993.

Orbaugh, Sharalyn. "Busty Battlin' Babes: The Evolution of the *Shōjo* in 1990s Visual Culture." In *Gender and Power in the Japanese Visual Field*, edited by Joshua S. Mostow, Norman Bryson, and Maribeth Graybill, 201–28. Honolulu: University of Hawai'i Press, 2003.

Ōtsuka, Eiji. *Monogatari Shōmetsuron: Kyarakutāka Suru "Watashi," Ideorogikā Suru "Monogatari"* (The destruction of narrative: "Me" as becoming a character, "the story" as becoming ideology). Tokyo: Kadokawashoten, 2004.

Passin, Herbert. *Society and Education in Japan*. New York: Teachers College Press, 1965.

Peak, Lois. *Learning to Go to School in Japan: The Transition From Home to Preschool Life*. Berkeley: University of California Press, 1991.

Pecora, Norma Odom. "Identity by Design: The Corporate Construction of Teen Romance Novels." In *Growing Up Girls: Popular Culture and the Construction of Identity*, edited by Sharon R. Mazzarella and Norma Odom Pecora, 49–86. New York: Peter Lang, 1999/2001.

Phenix, Philip H. *Realms of Meaning: A Philosophy of the Curriculum for General Education*. New York: McGraw Hill, 1964.

Pollack, David. "Marketing Desire: Advertising and Sexuality in Edo Literature, Drama and Art." In *Gender and Power in the Japanese Visual Field*, edited by Joshua S. Mostow, Norman Bryson, and Maribeth Graybill, 71–88. Honolulu: University of Hawai'i Press, 2003.

Pumphrey, George H. *Comics and Your Children*. London: Comics Campaign Council, 1952.

Pustz, Matthew J. *Comic Book Culture: Fanboys and True Believers*. Jackson: University Press of Mississippi, 1999.

Radway, Janice A. *Reading the Romance: Women, Patriarchy and Popular Literature*. Chapel Hill: The University of North Carolina Press, 1984.

Reitberger, Reinhold, and Wolfgang J. Fuchs. *Comics: Anatomy of a Mass Medium*. Boston: Little, Brown, 1971.

Robertson, Jennifer. *Takarazuka: Sexual Politics and Popular Culture in Modern Japan*. Berkeley: University of California Press, 1998.

Robinson, Muriel. *Children Reading Print and Television*. London: The Falmer Press, 1997.

Rubinger, Richard. *Private Academies of Tokugawa Japan*. Princeton, NJ: Princeton University Press, 1982.

———. "Who Can't Read and Write? Illiteracy in Meiji Japan." *Monumenta Nipponica* 55, no. 2 (2000): 163–98.

———. "Comments." *Monumenta Nipponica* 56, no. 3 (2001): 395.

———. *Popular Literacy in Early Modern Japan*. Honolulu: University of Hawaii'i Press, 2007.

Ruddell, Robert B., and Richard B. Speaker Jr. "The Interactive Reading Process: A Model." In *Theoretical Models and Processes of Reading*, third ed., edited by Harry Singer and Robert B. Ruddell, 751–93. Newark, DE: International Reading Association, 1985.

Rumelhart, David E. "Schemata: The Building Blocks of Cognition." In *Theoretical Issues in Reading Comprehension: Perspectives from Cognitive Psychology, Linguistics, Artificial Intelligence, and Education*, edited by Rand J. Spiro, Bertram C. Bruce, and William F. Brewer, 33–58. Hillsdale, NJ: Lawrence Erlbaum Associates, 1980.

Sabin, Roger. *Comics, Comix, and Graphic Novels: A History of Comic Art*. London: Phaidon Press, 1996.

Saitō, Nobuhiko. "Hajime ni 'Sen' Ariki" (In the beginning there is a "line"). In *Manga no Yomikata* (How to read manga), edited by Inoue Manabu, 26–37. Tokyo: Takarajimasha, 1995.

———. "Manga no Kōzo Moderu" (A model of manga structure). In *Manga no Yomikata* (How to read manga), edited by Inoue Manabu, 220–23. Tokyo: Takarajimasha, 1995.

Schank, Roger C., and Robert P. Abelson. *Scripts, Plans, Goals, and Understanding: An Inquiry into Human Knowledge Structures*. Hillsdale, NJ: Lawrence Earlbaum, 1977.

Schodt, Frederik L. *Manga! Manga! The World of Japanese Comics*. Tokyo: Kodansha International, 1986.

———. *Dreamland Japan: Writings on Modern Manga*. Berkeley, CA: Stone Bridge Press, 1996.

———. *The Astro Boy Essays: Osamu Tezuka, Mighty Atom and the Manga/Anime Revolution*. Berkeley, CA: Stone Bridge Press, 2007.

Schwartz, Adam, and Elaine Rubinstein-Avila. "Understanding the Manga Hype: Uncovering the Multi-Modality of Comic-Book Literacies." *Journal of Adolescent & Adult Literacy* 50, no. 2 (2006): 40–49.

Scribner, Sylvia, and Michael Cole. *The Psychology of Literacy*. Cambridge, MA: Harvard University Press, 1981.

Seeley, Christopher. *A History of Writing in Japan*. Honolulu: University of Hawai'i Press, 2000.

Shigematsu, Setsu. "Dimensions of Desire: Sex, Fantasy, and Fetish in Japanese Comics." In *Themes and Issues in Asian Cartooning: Cute, Cheap, Mad, and Sexy*, edited by John A. Lent, 127–63. Bowling Green, OH: Bowling Green University Popular Press, 1999.

Shimizu, Isao. *Zusetsu Manga no Rekishi* (The illustrated history of manga). Tokyo: Kawade Shobo Shinsha, 1999.

———. *Nempyō Nihon Mangashi* (Chronological history of Japanese manga). Kyoto: Rinkawa Shoten, 2007.

Shimizu, Masashi. *Miyazaki Hayao wo Yomu* (Reading Miyazaki Hayao). Tokyo: Tokeisha, 2001.

Simpson, Anne. "Fictions and Facts: An Investigation of the Reading Practices of Girls and Boys." *English Education* 28, no. 4 (1996): 268–79.

Street, Brian V. *Literacy in Theory and Practice*. Cambridge: Cambridge University Press, 1984.

———. "Introduction: The New Literacy Studies." In *Cross-Cultural Approaches to Literacy*, edited by Brian V. Street, 1–22. Cambridge: Cambridge University Press, 1993.

Stubbs, Michael. *Language and Literacy: The Sociolinguistics of Reading and Writing*. London: Routledge & Kegan Paul, 1980.

Stuckey, J. Elspeth. *The Violence of Literacy*. Portsmouth, NH: Boynton/Cook Publishers, 1991.

Sugiyama, Akashi. "Komiketto 30 Shūnen Kinen Chōsa Kekka Hōkoku" (*Comiket* Thirtieth Anniversary Survey Results). In *Komikku Māketto 30's Fuairu* (Files from the Thirtieth Comic Market), edited by Yonezawa Yasuhiro, 290–305. Tokyo: Comiket, 2005.

Suzuki, Kazuko. "Pornography or Therapy? Japanese Girls Creating the Yaoi Phenonenon." In *Millennium Girls: Today's Girls Around the World*, edited by Sherrie A. Inness, 243–67. Lanham, MD: Rowman & Littlefield, 1998.

Takano, Ryōko. "Hahaoya to Manga: Hahaoya Eno Ankēto Chōsa Kara (Mothers and manga: A survey to mothers)." In *Kodomo to Manga: Manga Dokkairyoku wa Dō Hattatsu Suruka* (Children and manga: How manga comprehension develops), edited by Akashi Yōichi and Nakazawa Jun, 55–84. Tokyo: Gendaijidōbunka Kenkyūkai, 1993.

Takekuma, Kentarō. "Dōgu to Tacchi no Hyōgen Hensen Shi" (The history of changes in expression in terms of drawing tools and techniques). In *Manga no Yomikata* (How to read manga), edited by Inoue Manabu, 38–51. Tokyo: Takarajimasha, 1995.

———. "Hitome de Wakaru 'Keiyu' Zukan" (Easy guide to "graphic symbols"). In *Manga no Yomikata* (How to read manga), edited by Inoue Manabu, 78–105. Tokyo: Takarajimasha, 1995.

Takeuchi, Osamu. *Sengo Manga 50 Nen Shi* (Postwar 50 years of *manga* history). Tokyo: Chikuma Shobo, 1995.

Taylor, Insup, and M. Martin Taylor. *Writing and Literacy in Chinese, Korean and Japanese*. Amsterdam: John Benjamins Publishing Company, 1995.

Tezuka, Osamu. *Manga no Kokoro: Hassō to Tekunikku* (The mind of manga: The inspiration and techniques). Tokyo: Kobunsha, 1994.

Townsend, Susan C. *Yanaihara Tadao and Japanese Colonial Policy: Redeeming Empire*. Richmond, UK: Curzon, 2000.

Unger, J. Marshall. *Literacy and Script Reform in Occupation Japan: Reading Between the Lines*. New York: Oxford University Press, 1996.

van Dijk, Teun A., and Walter Kintsch. *Strategies of Discourse Comprehension*. New York: Academic Press, 1983.

van Leeuwen, Theo. "Multimodality, Genre and Design." In *Discourse in Action: Introducing Mediated Discourse Analysis*, edited by Sigrid Norris and Rodney H. Jones, 73–93. London: Routledge, 2005.

Varley, Paul H. *Japanese Culture*, fourth ed. Honolulu: University of Hawai'i Press, 2000.

Walker, Mort. *The Lexicon of Comicana*. Port Chester, NY: Museum of Cartoon Art, 1980.

Wenger, Etienne. *Communities of Practice: Learning, Meaning, and Identity*. Cambridge: Cambridge University Press, 1999.

Wertham, Fredric. *Seduction of the Innocent: The Influence of Comic Books on Today's Youth*. New York: Rinehart, 1954.

White, Merry. *The Material Child: Coming of Age in Japan and America*. Berkeley: University of California Press, 1994.

Willinsky, John, and R. Mark Hunniford. "Reading the Romance Novel: The Mirrors and Fears of a Preparatory Literature." In *Texts of Desire: Essays on Fiction, Femininity and Schooling*, edited by Linda K. Christian-Smith, 45–68. London: The Falmer Press, 1993.

Wilson, Brent. "Becoming Japanese: *Manga*, Children's Drawings and the Construction of National Character." In *The Arts in Children's Lives: Context, Culture, and Curriculum*, edited by Liora Bresler and Christine M. Thompson, 43–55. Dordrect, The Netherlands: Kluwer Academic Publishers, 2002.

Wong, Wendy Suiyi. *Hong Kong Comics: A History of Manhua*. New York: Princeton Architectural Press, 2000.

Worth, Jo, Megan Moorman, and Margo Turner. "What Johnny Likes to Read Is Hard to Find in School." *Reading Research Quarterly* 34, no. 1 (1999): 12–27.

Wright, Bradford W. *Comic Book Nation: The Transformation of Youth Culture in America*. Baltimore: Johns Hopkins University Press, 2003.

Yagelski, Robert Y. *Literacy Matters: Writing and Reading the Social Self*. New York: Teachers College Press, 1999.

Yamada, Hiroyuki. *Manga ga Kataru Kyōshi Zō* (The representation of teachers in manga). Kyoto: Showadō, 2004.

Yamada, Tomoko. "Boizu Rabu to Nakanaori: Shitataka ni Ikiru Manga no Naka no Gei Kyarakutātachi" (Reconciling with Boys Love: Tough living gay characters in manga). *Eureka: Poetry and Criticism* 39, no. 16 (2007): 82–88.

Yokomori, Rika. *Ren'ai wa Shōjo Manga de Osowatta* (I learned how to fall in love from *shōjo* manga). Tokyo: Shueisha, 1999.

Yokota-Murakami, Takayuki. "Manga to Manga Hihyō: Riron to Sakuhin no Kankei no Kaitai ni Mukete" (Manga and manga criticism: Toward an understanding of the relationship between theory and the work). In *Manga no Shakaigaku* (The sociology of manga), edited by Miyahara Kōjiro and Ogino Masahiro, 34–67. Kyoto: Sekaishisōsha, 2001.

———. *Manga wa Yokubō Suru* (Manga do desire). Tokyo: Chikuma Shobō, 2006.

Yomota, Inuhiko. *Manga Genron* (The principles of manga). Tokyo: Chikuma Shobo, 1994.

Yoneyama, Shoko. *The Japanese High School: Silence and Resistance*. London: Routledge. 1999.

Yonezawa, Yasuhiro. "Shōjo Manga no Keifu" (The roots of *shōjo* manga). In *Bessau Taiyō: Shōjo manga no sekai*, vol. 1 (*Taiyō* special edition: The world of *shōjo* manga, vol. 1), edited by Yonezawa Yasuhiro, 4–8. Tokyo: Heibonsha, 1991.

————. *Manga to Chosakuken: Parody to Inyō to Dōjinshi to* (Manga and copyright: Parody, citing, and *dōjinshi*). Tokyo: Comiket, 2001.

————. *Komikku Māketto 30's Fuairu* (Files from the thirtieth comic market). Tokyo: Comiket, 2005.

Yoshiba, Osamu, and Niina Shin. "Shuppansha Kara Mita Dejitaru Jijyō" (The digital situation from the perspective of publishers). Presentation, *Akihabara Enta Matsuri!* Tokyo, October 20–28, 2007.

Yoshida, Masataka. *Nijigen Bishōjoron: Otaku no Megami Sōzōshi* (The theory of the two-dimensional *bishōjo*: The history of *otakus'* goddess creation). Tokyo: Nimi Shobo, 2004.

Yoshimoto Fumiko, "Gei Manga to BL Manga no ekkyō" (Crossing the boundaries between gay manga and BL manga). *Eureka: Poetry and Criticism* 39, no. 16, (2007): 247–48.

Index